Contents

List of tables and figures

Tables

Figures

Foreword

This is the last of a series of publications produced by the FEANTSA European Observatory on Homelessness. This book looks at the complex relation between two urgent realities in Europe: homelessness and severe housing exclusion on the one hand, and immigration on the other. In spite of the complexity of the theme and the lack of available data, the authors have managed to present a detailed analysis of the dynamic relationship between immigration and homelessness. As in the other books in the series, the crucial importance of housing for social inclusion emerges as a central issue. The authors also address problems, all too often ignored elsewhere, such as housing exclusion experienced by undocumented immigrants.

In Europe, immigrants make up around 20 million of the Union's population of 380 million. Immigration has been increasing across almost all member states in the last decade and even countries that historically have been net exporters of people are now net importers. Net migration is now the largest component of population change in Europe.

A number of patterns, however, make the issue more significant than this statistic would suggest. Immigrants remain concentrated in particular regions and cities, and some remain excluded even after they have become citizens. Migrants come from a far wider range of countries and bring a greater diversity of cultures than in the past. Migration flows include not only economic immigrants (permanent settlers, contracted labour and temporary migrants) and those seeking family reunion, but also asylum seekers and refugees and, increasingly, undocumented migrants. This range of migration types is reflected in the increasingly varied social and demographic profiles of migrants. Many of the 'new wave' immigrants are less able to compete in the housing and labour markets than previous immigrants, whose arrival was associated with a defined labour market need. Immigrants with an undocumented or indeterminate status, together with other vulnerable immigrant groups, such as women and young people, are particularly at risk of becoming homeless and facing housing exclusion.

One of the factors leading to an increased focus on integration at the EU level is the belated recognition that migration will be a permanent part of Europe's future. Access to decent and affordable housing is a key factor in the integration of immigrants, without which integration into the labour market and the other areas of life is very difficult, if not impossible.

My sincere thanks go to the national research correspondents and the coordinators of the European Observatory on Homelessness of FEANTSA for taking up an issue which is increasingly a central concern for organisations working with homeless people, but one which constitutes a difficult and challenging field of research.

Donal McManus, President of FEANTSA, October 2004

Acknowledgements

This is the fifth and final book in a series that began in 1999. The year before the first publication, *Services for homeless people*, we were appointed the Research Coordinators of the European Observatory on Homelessness. Each year since then, with the exception of 2003, has seen the publication of a further book: *Support and housing in Europe* in 2000, *Women and homelessness in Europe* in 2001 and *Access to housing: Homelessness and vulnerability in Europe* in 2002. The publication of the present book, *Immigration and homelessness in Europe*, marks the end of a challenging and productive schedule which would have been impossible to complete but for the dedication, hard work, patience and good humour of the 15 national correspondents of the Observatory on whose research these publications have been based. Our debt to them over the years has been immense. Feedback suggests that, for the most part, the final product has met with their approval.

We would also like to acknowledge the support, encouragement and, when necessary, cajoling provided by the FEANTSA secretariat. They have been instrumental in organising the Observatory meetings and facilitating the debate and discussion that cultivated and refined the focus of our research.

Henk Meert joined us in the writing of this book as he had for the previous publication. His contribution has been invaluable, not just in sharing the writing burden, but also in terms of bringing his extensive knowledge of European affairs and his incisive critical abilities to bear on the final product.

Finally, we are grateful to The Policy Press in displaying exemplary forbearance in the face of the long delay in getting this typescript to press and in their seemingly magical abilities to produce a first-class product in such a short period of time.

FEANTSA and the European Observatory on Homelessness

FEANTSA (the European Federation of National Organisations Working with the Homeless) is a European non-governmental organisation founded in 1989. FEANTSA currently has about 100 member organisations in 24 of the 25 member states of the European Union and other European countries. FEANTSA is the only major European non-governmental organisation which deals exclusively with homelessness. FEANTSA works to facilitate networking, exchanges of experiences and best practices, research and advocacy in the field of homelessness at the European level. FEANTSA maintains regular dialogue with the institutions of the European Union and with national governments in order to promote effective action in the fight against homelessness. FEANTSA receives financial support from the European Commission for carrying out a comprehensive work programme. FEANTSA has very close relations with the institutions of the European Union, in particular the European Commission and the European Parliament, and has consultative status with the Council of Europe and with the Economic and Social Council (ECOSOC) of the United Nations.

The *European Observatory on Homelessness* was set up by FEANTSA in 1991 to conduct research into homelessness in Europe. It is composed of a network of national correspondents from all member states of the European Union, who are widely recognised as experts in the field of homelessness. Each year the correspondents produce a national report on a specific research theme related to homelessness. The coordinators of the Observatory then analyse those national reports and integrate them into a European research report which focuses on transnational trends.

Contact address: FEANTSA, 194 Chaussée du Louvain 1210 Brussels, Belgium; Tel 32 2 538 66 69, Fax 32 2 539 41 74, e-mail office@feantsa.org, website www.feantsa.org

Coordinators and correspondents of the European Observatory on Homelessness: 2002-03

Coordinators

Bill Edgar, Co-Director of the Joint Centre for Scottish Housing Research, School of Town and Regional Planning, University of Dundee, Dundee DD1 4HT, UK; tel (44) (0)1382 345238; fax (44) (0)1382 204234; e-mail w.m.edgar@dundee.ac.uk

Joe Doherty, Co-Director of the Joint Centre for Scottish Housing Research, School of Geography and Geosciences, University of St Andrews, St Andrews, Fife KY16 9AL, UK; tel (44) (0)1334 463911; fax (44) (0)1334 463949; e-mail jd@st-andrews.ac.uk

Henk Meert, Research Associate of the Joint Centre for Scottish Housing Research (JCHSR), Research Fellow of FWO Flanders, Associate Professor at the Institute for Social and Economic Geography of the Catholic University of Leuven, S. De Croylan 42, B-3001 Leuven, Belgium; tel (32) (0)16 32 24 33; fax +32 (0)16 32 29 80; e-mail henk.meert@geo.kuleuven.ac.be

National correspondents

Austria: Heinz Schoibl, Helix Research and Consulting, e-mail heinz.schoibl@helixaustria.com

Belgium: Pascal De Decker, Antwerp University, e-mail pascal.dedecker@ua.ac.be

Denmark: Inger Koch-Nielsen, Social Forskings Institutet, e-mail ikn@sfi.dk

Finland: Sirkka-Liisa Kärkkäinen, Stakes, e-mail sirkka-liisa.karkkainen@stakes.fi in collaboration with **Anna Mikkonen**, also of Stakes.

France: Elisabeth Maurel, GREFOSS-IEP, Science-Po, Grenoble, e-mail elizabet.maurel@iep.upmf-grenoble.fr

Germany: Volker Busch-Geertsema, GISS e.v., [Association for Innovative Social Research and Social Planning], e-mail giss-bremen@t-online.de

Greece: Aristides Sapounakis, KIVOTOS, e-mail arsapkiv@hol.gr

Ireland: Eoin O'Sullivan, Department of Social Studies, Trinity College, Dublin, Ireland, e-mail tosullivan@tcd.ie

Italy: Antonio Tosi, DISP, Politecnico Milan, e-mail antonio.tosi@polimi.it

Luxembourg: Monique Pels, Centre d'Etudes de Populations, de Paurété et de Politiques Socio-Economiques, e-mail monique.pels@ceps.lu

Netherlands: Henk de Feijter, University of Amsterdam
e-mail h.j.feijter@frw.uva.nl

Portugal: Alfredo Bruto da Costa, Portuguese Catholic University,
e-mail alfredo.bc@mail.telepac.pt and **Isabel Baptista**, Centro de Estudos
para a Intervenção Social (CESIS), e-mail isabel.baptista@cesis.org

Spain: Pedro José Cabrera Cabrera, Universidad Pontifica Comillas 3,
e-mail pcabrera@chs.uplo.es in collaboration with **Graciela Malgesini**,
Spanish Red Cross, e-mail gmr@cruzroja.es

Sweden: Ingrid Sahlin, Department of Sociology, Gotenbourg University,
e-mail ingrid.sahlin@sociology.gu.se

United Kingdom: Isobel Anderson, Housing Policy and Practice Unit,
University of Stirling, e-mail isobel.anderson@stir.ac.uk

ONE

Introduction

In Europe migrants make up around 20 million of the European Union's 380 million people. Immigration has been increasing across almost all member states in the last decade and even countries that historically have been net exporters of people are now net importers. Migration flows include not only economic migrants (permanent settlers, contracted labour and temporary migrants) and those seeking family reunion, but also asylum seekers and refugees and, increasingly, undocumented migrants. This range of migration types is reflected in the increasingly varied social and demographic profiles of migrants. Many of these 'new wave' migrants are more vulnerable in the labour market and the housing market than previous immigrants whose arrival was associated with a defined labour market need. Immigrants with an undocumented or indeterminate status, together with other vulnerable groups such as women and young people, are particularly vulnerable to homelessness and housing exclusion.

The Treaty of Amsterdam established, for the first time, European Community competence for immigration and asylum. The European Council, at its meeting in Tampere in October 1999, agreed that "[t]he separate but closely related issues of asylum and migration call for the development of a common EU policy" and set out the elements which it should include, namely partnership with countries of origin, a common European asylum system, fair treatment of third country nationals and the management of migration flows. The continuing drive for a 'common EU policy' on immigration has arisen from a growing recognition that the policies since the 1970s are no longer appropriate in the changed social and economic circumstances of the late 20th and early 21st centuries. Large numbers of third country nationals have entered the Union in recent years, reflecting both the active recruitment of labour migrants by countries experiencing shortages of skilled and unskilled labour and the arrival of refugees, asylum seekers and reuniting family members; these migratory trends are continuing with an accompanying increase in illegal immigration, smuggling and trafficking. Communication from the European Commission (2000) to the Council and the European Parliament (COM(2000)757) argued that action to integrate migrants into EU societies must be seen as an essential corollary of an admission policy. The 1999 Council meeting in Tampere identified the components of a common European migration and asylum policy that included the fair treatment of third country nationals with a "more vigorous integration policy" (EC, 1999, III(18)) aimed at giving rights and obligations comparable to those of EU citizens. The integration of immigrants into a host society requires access to employment and equality of access to services, including decent and affordable housing.

This book aims to explore the nature and causes of homelessness among immigrants and the implication this has for the provision and delivery of homeless services. In comparison with the indigenous population, immigrants to the EU are more likely to occupy poorer housing and pay a disproportionate share of their incomes to acquire it. Homeless service providers are reporting a significant increase in immigrant and foreign-born residents among their clients. The discussion of these issues is set within the context of the EU strategy to combat poverty and social exclusion, and the search for a common EU immigration policy. The book draws liberally on the 2002 national reports of the 15 correspondents of the European Observatory on Homelessness in order to fashion a European overview (see www.feantsa.org for the individual national reports).

By way of introduction to more detailed coverage in the following sections of the book, this chapter first examines the demographic and economic context of post-war migration to the EU, and then outlines the main dimensions of the relationship between migration and homelessness.

The demographic and economic context of migration in Europe

The European Commission Communication (2000) to the Council and European Parliament (COM(2000)757) summarises the changing demographic and economic character of Europe. In contrast to the overall world situation, two trends are particularly striking: a slow down in population growth and a marked rise in the average age of the population. Regional disparities are a feature of member states where some (Denmark, Italy, Sweden) have already entered negative natural growth (births minus deaths), while others (Finland, France, Ireland, the Netherlands) will continue to experience relatively high natural growth for some years. However, across the EU as a whole, it is net migration that has become the principal component of population growth.

Migration flows to Europe are now composed of a mix of people: asylum seekers, displaced persons and those seeking temporary protection, family members coming to join migrants already settled in the EU, labour migrants and growing numbers of business migrants. Family reunion and the existence of ethnic communities from the countries of origin in a particular host country have become important factors in their size and direction. The flows have become more flexible; in particular there has been an increase in short-term and cross-border movements, with a complex pattern of people entering but also leaving the Union.

It has been argued (Salt, 1997) that the single most important characteristic of the migration patterns and trends identified in the EU states is their variability from country to country. There are certainly marked differences in the migration fields of individual countries, reflecting a range of historical (colonial links) and geographical (especially proximity) processes. The variations that exist make it difficult to classify member states on the basis of migration experience in a meaningful way.

While there has been a trend towards greater harmonisation of migration policy across the EU, there is only limited evidence of convergence in migration experience – unlike other demographic components of fertility and mortality. Limited convergence is in evidence in relation to some elements of migration. This is most clearly seen in the changing demographic pattern of migration. The general trend is towards increased female immigration, towards a higher proportion of immigrants of working age and a decline in the younger age groups. There is some evidence of greater diversification of migrant origins although this is occurring slowly and at varying speeds in different countries. In most countries the same two or three groups dominate both the stock of foreign-born citizens and the flow of immigrants. Diversification reflects the declining importance of these dominant groups. The trend in all countries is towards increased immigration from outside Europe with a growing number of migrants from poor countries.

Three characteristics are said to underlie recent migration experience in Europe (Collinson, 1993):

Escalation: this reflects the increasing level of immigration, albeit with fluctuations in some countries, and the increasing importance of migration in driving population change.

Globalisation: the term 'new migration' has been adopted to reflect the dynamic relationship between geopolitical and geoeconomic change and evolving patterns and processes of migration. According to Koser and Lutz (1998), "[n]owhere have these changes had a greater impact than in Europe".

Regionalisation: migrant flows are highly regionalised in terms of sources and destinations; particular sending countries tend to dominate flows to particular receiving countries.

Migration to EU countries has varied considerably over time in terms of causes, ethnic composition and consequences for receiving countries. Salt (1997) suggests that, within Europe as a whole, population redistribution through international migration gradually declined from the 1960s to the mid-1980s, since when flows have again increased, especially since 1989. White (1993) has made a useful categorisation of this migration into three distinct waves: labour migration, family reunification and post-industrial movement (see Figure 1.1). Very broadly, these waves correspond to Hammar's description of three decades of migration: the 1960s as a decade of labour migration, the 1970s as family reunification, and the 1980s as asylum (Hammar, 1985). We can extend Hammar's description into the 1990s, identifying it as the decade of immigration from Eastern Europe and the poorer countries of Southern Europe.

Figure 1.1: The three waves of international migration

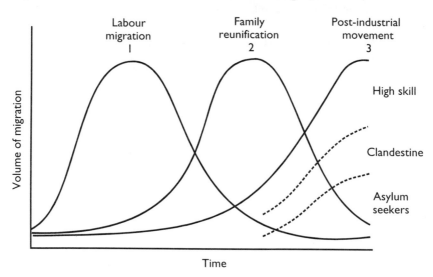

Source: White (1993, p 49)

While White's description of the three waves of migration is helpful at the European level in distinguishing different processes and causes of migration and in deconstructing recent (post-industrial) movement, it is less robust in explaining immigration at the national level. Taking only Portugal as an example, we can see that the demise of the Salazar regime in 1974 created a pattern of waves of migration (that is, returning expatriats) that are distinct in nature and cause from those described by White. Even here, however, it is possible to evince distinct waves of migration and to distinguish post-industrial migration impacts during the late 1990s.

Salt (1997) confirms that most analysis of migration has focused on Northern Europe and relates to individual countries. More recently, however, this imbalance has been redressed by a growing number of studies on Southern Europe, resulting in a significant research series of edited volumes which have been published in recent years (Hudson and Lewis, 1985; Anthias and Lazaridis, 1999, 2000; King et al, 2000). This redress in published research is especially relevant since Southern Europe has undergone a profound change in migration profile in the last 20 years. This is reflected in the research concern that focused on emigration from Mediterranean Europe until the mid-1980s, since when attention has been redirected to immigration to the region, much of it irregular and undocumented. While much research initially focused on Italy, where researchers led the way, more recently studies from Portugal, Spain and Greece have been published. One significant aspect of the new international migration in Southern Europe which has attracted research attention has been concerned with explanations of the high proportions of women in the migrant flows (Ackers, 1998; Anthias and Lazaridis, 2000). This pattern of gender-specific migration cannot be easily explained by 'traditional' theoretical models of push-pull effects. Significantly, however, this aspect of migratory flows is a component that has apparently been largely absent from research in Northern Europe.

The discussion so far reflects the data available on migration; however, part of the migration to Europe takes place outside official channels. Southern European countries (especially Spain, Greece and Italy) have become attractive for clandestine labour migrants. The presence of clandestine job opportunities in the informal economy has attracted many. As 'new' countries of immigration these countries have introduced new admission regulations and these have been enacted in conjunction with regularisation programmes (Muus, 2001). Since 1986, Italy has launched four major regularisation programmes, the last of which in 1998-99 introduced a quota of 700,000 people. The first major regularisation programme in Greece (1997-98) led to 375,000 applications (in a workforce of 4.3 million). Regularisation programmes occurred in Spain in 1991 and 1996.

From the mid-1980s onwards, asylum migration emerged, and by the early 1990s had become a major inflow of immigrants to Europe. However, a number of countries within the EU receive a disproportional share of all asylum seekers. Germany is the dominant destination for asylum seekers (one third of the estimated 300,000 asylum seekers in 1998), while the UK (17%), the Netherlands (16%), France (8%), Sweden (5%) and Austria (5%) soak up much of the remaining number.

As we have seen, immigration to Europe can be traced to a variety of origins and pathways: from the colonial legacy of countries such as France, Britain and the Netherlands, through the return migrants and repatriates of Germany, Finland (Ingrian), Greece (Pontians), and Portugal (African *returnadores*), to the institutionalised labour migration to Northern Europe in the 1960s and 1970s and to Southern Europe more recently. The experiences of these migrants are, perhaps in large part (as we suggest in the next chapter), determined by their ethnicity and by their length of settlement. Arguably, however, of equal importance in determining the status and privileges of immigrants, are the practices, policies and immigration laws enacted by individual member states. Taking this point on board, while understanding that it is important to recognise the complexity of the migration process through time and across space, this book adopts a simple overarching three-fold classification of immigrant categories based on their legal status:

- documented immigrants (including legal labour, family reunion, repatriates);
- refugees and asylum seekers;
- undocumented immigrants.

This classification – frequently in a disaggregated form – is used throughout this book to structure our examination of immigrant vulnerability to homelessness and housing exclusion.

Migration and homelessness

There is an evident paucity of research on migration and homelessness in Europe. Gerald Daly (1996), in one of the few articles that examines the relationship between immigration and homelessness in Europe, argues that the link to homelessness for immigrants is through poverty and xenophobia.

A narrative that runs through this book seeks to demonstrate that ethnicity matters. Membership of a minority group, particularly one distinguished by skin colour, exposes immigrants to racism and xenophobia from the host society. This is tangibly manifest in the discrimination many migrants experience in seeking access to housing – in the difficulties in securing credit and in the higher rental prices frequently charged in the private market to foreigners.

Questions of ethnicity and gender and cultural tolerance are at the heart of debates over social programmes designed to cope with the issue of immigrant poverty and discrimination. The increasing vociferousness of the political right propagating its racist, sexist and xenophobic agendas has worked against attempts to progress 'multiculturalism' and the betterment of conditions for immigrant communities. Daly (1996) argues that "After resorting to the use of temporary hostels, containers and barges to shelter homeless migrants, governments have succumbed to fiscal constraints and right-wing political pressures, restricting immigration and devolving responsibility for homelessness to local authorities and to voluntary agencies. Frequently, this has resulted in neglect" (p 22).

Notwithstanding ethnic origins, the allocation of migrants to categories such as documented (legal) or undocumented (illegal) by immigration laws and policies has a major impact on their settlement experience. Branded as 'illegal' – because a migrant has not conformed to immigrant procedures or has absconded following refusal of asylum or refugee status – an immigrant is condemned to a clandestine existence; seeking work and accommodation while avoiding the authorities creates a very real vulnerability to exploitation by ruthless employers and by unscrupulous property owners. Citizenship, for those who qualify, brings with it enhanced privileges, formally placing the migrant on a par with the indigenous population. But citizenship, while it allows recourse to the rule of law, does not guarantee protection against the day-to-day hostility and prejudice of the host society.

Some members of 'immigrant' communities have faired better than others, managing to secure a toe-hold in the social and economic systems of the 'host' societies. Others, especially among the most recent arrivals but including members of long-established communities, have been disproportionately subject to the negative effects of political, social and economic changes. Having an established community to retreat to may offer some protection against the more overt symptoms of discrimination, but this can also bring its own troubles in the form of intra-community exploitation of newly arrived migrants. Length of stay can, however, have an ameliorating impact with longer-term residents commonly, but not always, achieving a betterment of life chances.

In the context of the uneven economic performance and prospects of several European economies, the situation of immigrants is likely to deteriorate even further. Legal and institutional barriers are being erected, creating enormous disparities between residents with full rights of citizenship and a marginalised class of aliens compelled to work on the periphery, within a shadow economy (Daly, 1996, p 11).

In his study of the situation in the UK, Denmark, Sweden, France, the Netherlands, Belgium, Germany, Ireland, Italy and Spain, Daly demonstrates that, while homelessness among immigrants varies greatly between these countries, the barrier of citizenship is increasingly being called on to justify discrimination and exclusion. Graphically Daly writes of a 'sorting' process which differentiates between the 'excluded' and the 'included', to define who can stay and who must go: "Across Western Europe ... migrants are [being] segregated, confined to menial jobs and relegated to the worst housing in the least desirable districts of large cities. A growing polarisation is evident between average citizens and those without full rights" (Daly, 1996, p 11).

People from minority ethnic communities have long experienced social exclusion in relation to housing (Sim, 2000). Difficulties of access to housing, poor quality of housing and affordability of housing are all problems which people from immigrant and minority ethnic communities share with other vulnerable groups, while "experience, or simply fear, of harassment has led to the tendency of high concentrations of minority ethnic families in relatively few neighbourhoods, often in older inner city housing" (Sim, 2000, p 93). As with so much research on homelessness, while the links that tie immigration with poverty, discrimination and homelessness can be illustrated by anecdote and case study, there is an absence of comprehensive and revealing empirical evidence. However, we can distinguish four sets of issues related to migration and homelessness or housing exclusion.

The problem is socially constructed: immigration laws, which determine the legal status of migrants, establish the extent to which they are provided with social protection and support during the process of reception and settlement.

There are problems of integration and assimilation of migrants: there are two aspects to this. First, past waves of migration have tended to lead to segregation and polarisation of migrants in the (urban) housing markets. Second, 'second generation' migrants, for a variety of reasons, are more susceptible to exclusion from the housing market and hence are appearing as major users of supported housing and homelessness services.

New wave migration is creating new problems: past migration waves tended to follow particular patterns; flows of male, economic migrants often from geographically discrete areas were followed by family reunion migration. Post-1990s, the so-called 'new wave' migration has tended to be female dominated, not to be solely caused by economic push factors and to be more diverse in spatial origin and destination. This new wave migration has tended to bring needs that service providers have not anticipated.

The role of homelessness services has been changing: migrant admission policies do not coordinate action of services to facilitate reception and integration of new migrants. Hence homelessness services may be the front line in dealing with this failure of policy. There is evidence from providers that the scale of migrants in service use has been growing at an alarming rate. However, it is also evident that some migrants are not appearing as clients of homelessness services.

Structure of the book

This book aims to examine these and related issues. The research on which the book is based was undertaken by the 15 members of the European Observatory on Homelessness and hence does not reflect the situation following enlargement of the EU. This enlargement will involve shifts in migration patterns as well as in policies of assimilation and will merit specific focused research.

Chapter Two describes migration trends and controls in the EU and establishes the nature of vulnerability to homelessness and housing exclusion. Chapter Three discusses the experiences of migrants and of the migration process, and emphasises the vulnerability and insecurity that accompanies the volatility and uncertainty of the migration experience. It also examines some of the ways in which the position of immigrants in European society is being recognised, at some levels and by some agencies, and the ways in which immigrants themselves are attempting to claim the right to fair and equal treatment for themselves. Chapters Two and Three provide the historic, social and political background for a more focused examination of the housing vulnerabilities of immigrant groups in present-day Europe. Access to the housing market in examined in Chapter Four. This discussion is set within the context of the commodification of housing, and examines the diverse strategies that immigrants employ to gain access to, or maintain a foothold in, the housing market in often precarious and unsustainable situations. Detailed evidence is drawn from the National Reports of the researchers of the European Observatory on Homelessness to demonstrate the effects of policies on social mix and social balance (available at www.feantsa.org). This chapter concludes with a discussion of the role of discrimination and racism in perpetuating the exclusion of certain groups of immigrants from adequate and affordable housing.

The extent and nature of homelessness among immigrants is the main focus of Chapter Five. This discussion is set within the context of the understanding of the factors that may create or perpetuate vulnerability to homelessness and housing exclusion. Evidence is drawn from across Europe to examine the extent of homelessness and the vulnerability of particular groups of immigrants. A key finding of our research is the extent to which homeless services are left to mop up the failure of immigration policies. Hence the next chapter (Chapter Six) examines the issues related to immigration and homeless services. The chapter begins by examining the profiles of immigrant users of homeless services. The effects of national legislation and policies that exclude non-citizens from services and related factors that may exclude some immigrants from services or lead to them to turn to other solutions are considered. The issues related to service provision are also examined, and these include: the development and adaptation of existing services, access to services, the experiences of immigrants, and existing and emerging management issues and problems. It is apparent from the evidence available that some immigrants are more vulnerable to homelessness than others, and the next section of the chapter considers the experiences and needs of these particular groups. There is a diversity of experience across Europe both in the extent to which immigration is putting pressure on homeless services and in the reaction of services to emerging immigrant needs. The chapter concludes by undertaking a comparative analysis of this experience.

In Chapter Seven we provide an overview of the findings of our research and identify some of the unresolved issues and emerging problems and debates, and make some suggestions as to the focus of future research. While this book presents a European perspective on the nature of the dimensions of the housing and homelessness problems and dilemmas experienced by immigrants in Europe, we are acutely conscious that while we may have identified the nature and dimensions of a problem, we have provided little by way of suggestions as to how these problems can be resolved. Perhaps this defines the most urgent work for the future.

TWO

Migration trends and control in the EU

Introduction

A defining characteristic of the present phase of globalisation is a heightened level of mobility in all sectors of society[1]. Changes in the world economy which began during the last quarter of the 20th century have seen an acceleration and intensification in the flows of capital, in the exchange of commodities, in the transference of information and in the movement of people. While these characteristics are sometimes exaggerated, especially in comparison with preceding historical periods (Hirst and Thompson, 1996), increasingly, it seems, economic and social interactions are less and less constrained by the territorial divisions of the nation state. The rigidities and restrictions imposed by political boundaries are being surmounted. The world economy has entered "a phase of flexible production and accumulation in which business operations are increasingly connected by formal and informal alliances to networks of other agencies including firms, governments, and communities" (Agnew, 2003, p 5). These global networks provide the organisational basis for worldwide operations and transactions which flow from city to city and region to region, jumping nation state boundaries with increasing alacrity.

In the terminology of Manuel Castells (2000), the organisation of the world economy is perhaps now more accurately depicted as a 'space of flows' than as a 'space of places'. In this 'space of flows' capital seeks out the most profitable locations, having little consideration for national origins or regional loyalties; financial networks draw in national and regional stock exchanges and fiscal institutions to a global system of financial interaction and speculation, and global trading systems scour the world for cheap raw materials and profitable markets. In a parallel and often deeply interrelated development, formal and informal migration networks traverse the globe, connecting skilled and unskilled labour with distant job markets, and the destitute and oppressed with places of potential refuge and safety. These capital and trading networks and, to a much lesser extent, migration networks, blithely cut across national boundaries, apparently little influenced by interference from the states whose borders they transcend.

In this emerging 'space of flows', capital transactions, trading and migration have all experienced a quantitative leap and take on ever more diverse forms. The value of foreign direct investment is now matched by portfolio investment and exceeded by financial speculation on the world's currency markets. Foreign exchange trading on the world markets had an estimated daily average value of US$1,500 billion in 2002, compared with US$80 billion in 1980. The expansion in the trade of merchandise and commercial services similarly reflects quantitative increases and a proliferation in the diversity of goods and services exchanged. According to World Trade Organization (WTO) statistics, world trade, as a ratio of world GDP, reached 29% in 2000, an increase of 10% compared with 1990. In 2000 alone, the volume of merchandise traded increased by 12%, the highest rate of annual growth for over a decade (WTO, 2001, p 1).

The flows of people, however, although growing, are much less footloose than the flows of capital and trade. International migration still strongly reflects geographic proximity and the ties of colonial history. Movement beyond these traditional conduits continues to be significantly constrained and confined by political barriers and border controls. However, and especially although not exclusively in its clandestine form, migration finds ways of circumventing the impediments of state boundaries. Through the agency of 'tour' operators, 'traffickers' and 'snakeheads', formal and informal networks link origin and destination in ever more complex ways, facilitating negotiation through, or avoidance of, barriers to entry. The emerging 'space of migration flows' transcends the linearity of traditional migration patterns where one-way passages were the norm; today migration is increasingly transnational. The term 'transnational' refers to communities (individuals or groups) "settled in different national societies, sharing common interests and references – territorial, religious, linguistic – and using transnational networks to consolidate solidarity beyond national boundaries" (Veenkamp et al, 2003, p 57[2]). There is an obvious overlap here with 'return' and 'circular' migration'; yet while back-and-forth flows certainly existed in the past, the scale of such movement, as Mitchell (2003, p 80) argues, "has now reached a critical mass justifying the transnational label as a new social phenomenon" (see also Basch et al, 1994).

Recent United Nations estimates indicate that one in every 35 people, approximately 3% (175 million) of the world's population, live outside their country of birth. The number has doubled in the last 30 years and is likely to grow further (UN, 2002). Migration flows include not only economic migrants (permanent settlers, contracted labour and temporary migrants), but also asylum seekers and refugees, those seeking family reunion and, increasingly, undocumented migrants. This range of migration types is reflected in the increasingly varied social and demographic profiles of migrants themselves: women migrants equal, and sometimes exceed, the number of male migrants, young people and unskilled workers are as likely to be moving as adult skilled and professional workers, and undocumented and clandestine migration represents a rising proportion of total moves. In Europe migrants make up around 20 million of the EU's 380 million people. Illegal or unauthorised migrants comprise an estimated 10-15% of this total, and 20-30% of incoming flows (Veenkamp et al, 2003, p 2).

The rising levels and diversity of capital transfers, trading and migration reflect an accelerated process of what David Harvey has called 'time-space compression'. This is a process in which, as Harvey puts it, the rapidity of time annihilates the barriers of space: "the time horizons of both public and private decision making have shrunk, while satellite communication and declining transport costs have made it increasingly possible to spread those decisions immediately over an ever wider and variegated space" (Harvey, 1989, p 147). Powerful computers process information at lightening speed, satellites facilitate immediate and constant communication around the globe, and miniaturisation make this computational and communication power cheaply and universally available. The revolution in communications technology (especially the mobile phone and the world wide web) has permitted the easy transfer of information between global traders and investors and facilitated communication between migrants and their families. Such technological developments permit not only virtually instantaneous capital transactions, allowing financial speculation on an international scale, but also the relatively straightforward transfer of migrant remittances to home towns and villages. Advances in the development of cheap and fast transport by land, sea and air facilitate the rapid movement of commodities and people across the globe. All these modernisations serve to make the world a smaller place, and have made possible an unprecedented level of interaction between disparate markets creating, in effect, "a world market with global producers and global consumers"; it has become increasingly feasible for corporations and migrants alike to become transnational, to "transcend spatial bottlenecks like the nation" (Agnew, 2003, p 11).

But this is not a simple case of technological determinism. While powerful and cheap technology aids and supports globalisation, the prime driving force is to be found in the structural changes in the world economy which followed the economic crisis of the early 1970s and brought to an end 25 years of post-war economic boom. OPEC oil price rises and the overheating of the US economy precipitated the rejection of the rules of economic engagement drawn up at Bretton Woods, leading to the divorce of the US dollar from the gold standard, followed by its devaluation, and the world-wide adoption of a global system of floating exchange rates. These developments were the precursors to the abandonment of Keynesian checks and balances on national and global economies and the aggressive pursuit of a free market, neoliberal ideology by the US and Britain. Through the course of the late 1970s and 1980s neoliberalism became embedded in most of the world's core economies and, with the aid of international agencies such as the International Monetary Fund (IMF), the World Bank and the General Agreement on Tariffs and Trade (GATT) (later WTO), quickly penetrated the periphery. With China's declaration of a commitment to 'market socialism' and the collapse of the former Soviet Union in 1989, followed by the enthusiastic adoption of capitalism, first by some of its former satellites and then by Russia itself, the global triumph of neoliberalism seemed secure, leading at least one commentator to proclaim 'the end of history' (Fukuyama, 1992).

A central precept of the neoliberal pursuit of a 'regime of free market-access'

(Agnew, 2003) is the need for a fundamental change in the role of the state. The image of the state, cultivated, particularly in Europe, through the decades following 1945, as the protector of society from the ravages and excesses of the market[3] is rendered redundant under neoliberalism. In the neoliberal agenda, the market is the agency through which prosperity is secured; it becomes the friend of the people, to be cultivated and cherished, rather than treated with suspicion and mistrust. Free trade, unfettered investment, deregulation, balanced budgets, low inflation and privatisation are the mechanisms through which efficiency and wealth are achieved (Ellwood, 2001, p 19). The market is, however, a tough friend, especially for the most vulnerable in society, rejecting lame-duck enterprises, challenging the positive role of welfare and state benefits, and requiring the adoption of profit-oriented, bottom-line accounting in virtually all aspects of life. Through the agency of ruling political parties, states across the world have succumbed, for the most part, to the dominance of the market, deregulating financial interactions, removing barriers to free trade and privatising state-owned assets and public services[4]. This shift in the role of the state under neoliberalism has been portrayed as one of retrenchment, involving not just a withdrawal from direct involvement with the production process, but also a change in orientation from a market-hostile, or at best market-neutral, position, to a more market-positive stance in which its role is reconfigured to that of enabler and facilitator, coordinating rather than containing economic activities (Sassen, 1999, pp 150-1; Peck and Tickell, 2002).

With the adoption of a neoliberal ideology, decisive steps have been taken by state governments towards the liberalisation of the exchange of capital, goods and services over the past three decades. Paradoxically, however, there has not been a similar level of equivalent change in the field of migration. In contrast to the demolition of trade barriers and controls on financial markets, state governments have shown a marked reluctance to remove the inhibitions on the free movement of people into their territories. Migration, to a greater extent than either capital or trade, still takes place within the orbit of a 'space of places', in the arena of state activity and state control. In contrast to the rhetoric of commitment to free trade policies and programmes, states across the globe tenaciously hang on to the principle of immigration control, maintaining and updating existing legislation to deal with new developments. The reasons for this commitment to migration control are manifold, and at base are to be found in the specificities of the history and social make-up of individual countries. However, some common threads can be deciphered.

Most governments are wedded to the notion of migration as a self-motivated, individual action, rather than as a structurally induced phenomenon. They are disposed to consider migrant decision making as driven by ill-considered, perhaps even irrational, individual acts. In this context immigration controls are seen as the tools by which governments provide the checks and balances that ensure that their countries are not overrun by an unwanted and surplus population. As Sassen observes,

The receiving country is represented as a passive agent; the causes of immigration
appear to lie outside the control or domain of receiving countries; immigration
policy becomes a decision to be more or less benevolent in admitting immigrants.
(Sassen, 1999, p 151)

An alternative understanding of migration, and one which focuses on its
structural roots, calls on complex historic trends to demonstrate that migration
streams are not simply the result of autonomous individuals acting independently,
but are closely related to and determined by economic and social conditions in
both origin and reception countries. Indeed, many, if not all, labour migrations
to Europe in the 20th century were initially stimulated by the direct recruitment
of migrants by state agencies or private enterprise during periods of labour
shortages. Such alternative views do, of course, have some impact on government
actions (as is indicated by the selective permissions to enter issued to migrant
workers with skills perceived to be in short supply), but more commonly and
fundamentally migrants are regarded with suspicion and mistrust, to be controlled
and curtailed. Even in those circumstances where governments might be disposed
towards more lenient and relaxed immigration regulations, the pursuit of such
policies is problematic. The argument that migrants (including refugees and
asylum seekers), on balance and over time, make a positive contribution to the
receiving societies requires patience and perseverance to deliver. Persuading
parliamentary decision makers, who have an eye to their constituents and the
next election, and the wider public of this positive interpretation, is fraught
with difficulties. Against the sound bites of the anti-immigrant lobby such
arguments, however logical and reasoned, stand little chance.

State commitment to the maintenance and tightening of immigration controls
can also be attributed to the lack of powerful advocates or lobby groups, at
either a national or international level, campaigning for governments to remove
restrictions on immigration; this stands in marked contrast to the pressures put
on state governments to remove the barriers to capital transactions and trading
relations. Despite the avowed championing of untrammelled migration by global
corporations and their neoclassical economic advisers, at best business canvasses
for selective relaxations associated with periodic shortages of particular types
of skilled labour. Humanitarian pressure groups also have a selective focus in
that while they lobby vociferously for asylum seekers and refugees, they rarely
take up the wider cause of opening borders for the free movement of all people.
It is a truism of human rights declarations that while people (mostly) have the
right to *leave* anywhere, they do not have a concomitant right to *go* anywhere.
The voices in favour of open borders and free migration, whether from left or
right of the political agenda, are few and scattered and carry little weight with
state governments (see Ford Foundation, 2000; Hayter, 2000; Harris, 2003;
www.noborder.org)[5]. Indeed, the most vociferous voices raised in relation to
migration are in the contrary direction, arguing for the imposition of tighter
and more stringent controls. In this context we can identify a range of voices:
from the racist outpourings of long-festering and newly emerged neo-fascist

organisations and political parties, through the jingoistic and chauvinistic utterances of the tabloid press, to the periodic warnings of anti-immigrant campaigning organisations[6]. The alarmist messages of such groups impact on public opinion, encouraging governments to kowtow to anti-immigrant demands.

The attitudes and behaviour of European states towards migrants has changed during the decades since 1945. Although there are important variations between countries, for the most part through the 1950s and of the 1960s Europe had a relatively open door policy with regard to third country migrants; the 1970s saw that door gradually close until, in the 1980s and 1990s, it was barred, creating what some have labelled 'Fortress Europe'. Entry to the EU for work and residence is now closely monitored and controlled with individual member states seemingly vying to outdo one another in imposing the tightest restrictions. It is our contention that the way prospective immigrants are categorised and treated during the process of entry in large part determines the nature of their reception within the host society. The skilled or professional worker seeking entry as a refugee or asylum seeker has a fundamentally different experience from a similarly skilled or professional migrant entering with a work permit officially confirming legitimacy of residence; both in turn can be distinguished from clandestine migrants who circumvent all checks and controls on entry and, lacking any official status, occupy the liminal spaces of society with all that implies in terms of potential exploitation and oppression. In Europe today, migrant status is one of the main predictors of social and economic vulnerability.

This chapter has two aims: first, to identify current migration trends in Europe and, second, to examine the ways in which member countries and, especially, the EU have responded in terms of changes in immigration legislation. In conclusion, and by way of introduction to Chapter Three, we attempt an assessment of these trends and responses in terms of their impact on migrants and especially the ways they define vulnerability to social exclusion.

The geopolitics of migration

> ... migrations do not simply happen. They are produced. (Sassen, 1999, p 155)

Prior to the Second World War Europe experienced mass out-migration to the Americas, Africa and Asia. From 1850 to 1940, some 60 million left Europe, over half migrating to the US (King, 1998; Boeri et al, 2002). After the war, although there were and indeed continue to be considerable variations between countries, Europe became one of the major destination areas for immigration. Today Europe is characterised by a high degree of internal mobility (25 million people change their place of main residence each year) and this is accompanied by high levels of emigration and immigration. In 1994, the population of the 15 member states of the EU grew by 1.3 million, the bulk of this attributable to net migration (Rees et al, 1996[7]). A similar trend was recorded nearly a decade later: in 2002-03 the population of the EU-15 grew by 3.6 per 1,000 inhabitants, a total of 1.34 million; one million (75%) of this was accounted for by net migration (www.ibeurope.com).

Commonly four phases of post-Second World War immigration are identified in Europe. The first period, from the end of the war to the early 1960s, was a period of immigrant absorption following the disruptions of the war and rapid decolonisation. The second period, which lasted until the oil crisis of the early 1970s, was a period of economic expansion and labour recruitment. Net migration during these two periods averaged 2.6 per 1,000. The third period, characterised by stagnation, the end of full employment and general economic uncertainty, stretched through the 1970s and into the 1980s; net migration dropped back to 1.7 per 1,000 during these years. The fourth period, dating from the end of 1980s and continuing until the present, saw a revival of net migration to 4.7 per 1,000, and coincides with selective economic recovery, the social, economic and political ramifications following the collapse of the Soviet Union and other political upheavals, not least the Balkans war (Salt, 2001; Boeri et al, 2002). The geopolitics of migration patterns which characterised these four periods demohstrate clear trends in terms of their geography and duration: colonial and neo-colonial ties, geographic proximity, and labour recruitment[8].

According to Eurostat (2001), the population of the EU at the start of the new millennium was over 376 million people. Approximately 5% had a citizenship different from their country of residence; of these, 1.6 % were citizens from other EU member states, while 3.5% were citizens of non-EU countries. Luxembourg had the highest share of other EU nationals (31%), followed by Belgium and Ireland. In Greece, Spain, Italy, Portugal and Finland, however, less than 1% of the population was from another EU country. More than 30% of all EU nationals residing in the EU, but outside their home country, live in Germany; a further 20% live in France, and 15% in the UK. The most numerous groups of EU nationals living in the EU outside their country of birth are the Italians (1.2 million, mostly in Germany) and the Portuguese (0.9 million, mostly in France).

Luxembourg (37.5%) has the highest proportion of foreign population in the EU. Austria (9.4%), Germany (8.9%), and Belgium (8.2%) follow in rank order. Four countries recorded over 5% foreign residents: Greece (6.9%), France (5.6%), Sweden (5.3%) and Denmark (5.0%); the rest had less than 5%, with Portugal recording the lowest percentage (2.2%). For most countries the number of foreigners has increased significantly in recent years, particularly in the new immigration countries of Southern Europe, all of which recorded an increase in excess of 5% from 1996 to 2000. In the north of Europe, the UK, Ireland and Finland also recorded annual increases of 5% during this period see (Table 2.1).

For most countries, non-EU nationals make up the largest group in immigration flows. Germany, France and the UK (as the most populous of the EU member countries) have the largest absolute numbers of non-EU immigrants; Austria, Germany and Denmark, however, emerge as the countries

Table 2.1: Foreign-born and non-EU nationals in the EU

	Number of foreign-born (1999)	% foreign-born	Number of non-EU nationals (2000)	% non-EU nationals
Austria	765,160	9.4	748,880	9.2
Belgium	907,016	8.2	288,596	2.8
Denmark	263,032	5.0	203,984	3.8
Finland	88,315	2.9	72,730	1.4
France	3,323,264	5.6	2,077,040	3.5
Germany	7,336,359	8.9	5,522,877	6.7
Greece	158,970	6.9	116,578	1.1
Ireland	120,404	3.9	34,956	0.9
Italy	1,276,396	2.4	1,102,342	1.9
Luxembourg	160,560	37.5	16,502	3.7
Netherlands	660,100	4.3	450,800	2.8
Portugal	196,384	2.2	134,368	1.3
Spain	808,180	2.7	484,908	1.2
Sweden	489,995	5.3	311,815	3.5
UK	2,284,332	4.4	1,623,078	2.7
Total	**18,838,467**	**5.0**	**13,189,454**	**3.5**

Source: SOPEMI (2003)

with the highest proportions. France, the UK, Belgium, Luxembourg, Sweden and the Netherlands occupy a middle position (less than 3.7% but more than 2.3%). Finland, with under 2.3%, joins the Mediterranean countries in recording the lowest percentage of third country nationals (Figure 2.1). Looking at each of the EU-15 in turn, we can identify the following characteristics of their third country immigrant populations.

Figure 2.1: Non-EU nationals in the EU

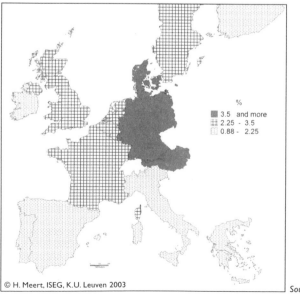

%
- 3.5 and more
- 2.25 - 3.5
- 0.88 - 2.25

© H. Meert, ISEG, K.U. Leuven 2003

Source: Eurostat (2003)

- In the UK, third country migration is predominantly from the former colonies of south Asia (Pakistan, India and Bangladesh particularly), and the West Indies[9]. Smaller recruitments from Cyprus and Malta and from Australasia are also observable. Immediately following the Second World War, under the European Volunteer Workers scheme, Polish workers were recruited to industry and agriculture (but today have little visible presence); until recently few Turks or Yugoslavs or other Central and Eastern Europeans figured among the UK immigrant population.

- In Germany 3 million displaced Germans relocated in the FDR following the Second World War before the Berlin Wall was erected in 1961, and in the immediate aftermath of the fall of the Berlin Wall and reunification some 600,000 moved from east to west (Burda et al, 1998). Two million Turks (75% of all Turkish immigrants to Europe) live in Germany, as do 1.2 million immigrants from the former Yugoslavia (65% of the total in the EU). More recently Germany has seen labour recruitment from Algeria, Morocco and Tunisia.

- For a long time, France was Europe's main immigrant destination country, and now it is second to Germany. Following decolonisation some 2 million emigrated to France from French overseas territories in North and West Africa and the Caribbean. Most Algerian, Tunisian and Moroccan immigrants to Europe live in France.

- A similar pattern of immigration from former colonies is evident in the Netherlands (for example, Surinam). More recently the Netherlands and Belgium have both attracted foreign workers from labour exporting countries such as Morocco and Turkey. Luxembourg's very high proportion of foreign-born populations is predominantly from other and neighbouring EU countries.

- While the number of third country migrants in other European countries is quite small, the proportion they make up of the total populations can be significant. A case in point is Austria where 9.4% of the population is foreign-born, 8.4% from outside the EU. Most of Austria's third country immigrants are from geographically proximate countries in Central and Eastern Europe: Croatians, Bosnians and Turks.

- The make-up of immigrant populations in Sweden has also been largely and until recently dominated by recruitment from neighbouring countries in the Baltic region, mostly Finland. More recently Sweden has seen an influx of immigrants under asylum and refugee provisions from Afghanistan, Iraq, Somalia and Pakistan. Historically Finland has been a country of emigration. Immigration (mostly of asylum seekers) is a more recent phenomenon, but remains at a very low level.

- Denmark's immigrant population is small in absolute terms, but in relation to the country's total population relatively large. Migrants from the former Yugoslavia and Turkey make up the bulk of non-EU immigrants. However, since the 1990s immigration from developing countries, such as Somalia, have grown (from a very low base) by some 40% (SOPEMI, 2003, p 186).

- The Southern EU countries of Spain, Portugal, Greece and Italy were until recently countries of emigration – many moving north over the years to Germany, France, the Benelux countries and the UK. More recently and especially since the late 1980s and early 1990s, these countries have also experienced immigration. Much of this is from neighbouring countries in North Africa as well as from the Balkans. In Spain and Portugal immigration from Latin America and Africa reflect former colonial ties. In Greece, Pontiac Greeks from Albania and elsewhere accounted for 7.5% of immigration during the 1990s (SOPEMI, 2003, p 203).
- Ireland, like the countries of Southern Europe, has only recently switched from a country of emigration to one of immigration; approximately one third of immigrants in the later part of the 1990s were from countries outside the EU and the US. Third country immigrants (Eastern Europe, the former Soviet Union, South Africa and the Philippines) now form the second largest group of foreign-born residents after those from the UK.

Recent trends indicate that third country nationals now dominate immigration for all EU countries, with the striking but not unexpected exceptions of Luxembourg and Belgium; for these countries other EU nationals account for 69% and 44% of all immigrants (SOPEMI, 2003). In Italy third country citizens made up 71% of all immigrants in 2000; in Denmark 70%, in Austria 66%, in Germany 57%, in Sweden 56% and in the Netherlands 52%.

From 1960 to 1973, the number of foreign workers in the EU doubled, from 3% to approximately 6% of the workforce. The UK and France, with relatively open access for citizens of their former colonies, experienced some of the highest increases. In Germany the number of foreigners, nearly half of whom were from Turkey, rose by 4 million in the 25 years after 1960. But primary immigration into Europe, driven by labour needs, all but ended with the oil crisis of 1973. However, as detailed below, the foreign-born population has continued to grow largely because of the several thousand residency permits issued each year for family reunification and to skilled workers. The aging profile of the population of all EU member states and the demand for labour replacement (high while economic growth continues), and the associated pressures for family reunification, create the conditions for continued growth in the numbers and proportion of foreign-born residents in the EU. On the other hand, the tightening of border controls and the attempts to clamp down on clandestine migration and restrict the influx of asylum seekers and refugees – to the extent that they are successful – will act as a break on growing numbers. The growth in transnational migration, with all that this implies in terms of transience, may also inhibit the rate of long-term growth. For the moment, however, the proportion of foreign-born residents in the EU remains relatively low, ranging from around 9% in Austria, Belgium and Germany, to under 2% in Spain (Hall, 2000).

Current trends

Despite fluctuating economic fortunes in some European countries, the upward trend in international migration observed since at least the middle of the 1990s has continued into the 21st century, although the source and type of migrants has become ever more diversified. As in earlier periods, there continues to be considerable variation in patterns of migration between countries. The OECD (SOPEMI, 2003) observes that the composition of migrant populations has undergone significant changes since the 1980s, with the result that, along with selective labour recruitment, family reunification and refugee migration now constitute the bulk of recorded international migration flows, with both family-related and refugee migration in particular contributing to a significant 'feminisation' effect. The proportional contribution of each of these migration streams varies from country to country and indeed from time to time, with the numbers of labour migrants, controlled through work permits, reflecting fluctuations in the fortunes of national economies. In 2001 in Portugal, Ireland and the UK, for example, labour migration dominated, while in Sweden, Denmark and France, family reunification was the most important. Significant though it is, asylum and refugee migration presently occupies third place in all EU countries (SOPEMI, 2003, p 33).

Family reunion

Following the restrictions placed on primary migration during the course of the 1970s and 1980s, the pattern of migration for most EU countries switched significantly to that of family reunification. Primary migrants, threatened with permanent exclusion if they returned even for short periods to their countries of origin, were now being joined by their families as permanent settlers. Family reunification by third country migrants was a major contributor to European migration throughout the final quarter of the 20th century and has continued into the early years of the 21st. In France, for example, family reunification accounted for 79% of migrant inflows in 2000, the highest level ever recorded, and an increase of nearly 23% over 1995. In Sweden and Denmark this component of migration is similarly significant, exceeding 50% of migration from all sources in recent years. However, more recent figures suggest a proportional decline in family-related migration (although not necessarily in absolute numbers); this is largely a consequence of increases in other categories of migrant. In the UK, family reunification declined from 46% of all immigration in 1999 to 34% in 2000, and even in France it fell from its 2000 peak to 72% in 2001. It is too soon to distinguish this as long-term trend, yet some countries (Italy, the Netherlands and Denmark) have recently introduced measures to limit family-related inflows and 2002 data suggests that these measures have, to some extent, been successful (SOPEMI, 2003).

Labour-related migration

Of the three main recorded sources of migrants (labour, asylum and family reunion) labour-related migration, whether of a temporary or permanent nature, has increased most noticeably in recent years. The renewed interest in labour recruitment is in part a reflection of the changing demographics of EU society, especially the growth in dependency ratios with the aging of the population. More directly these increases, for the most part managed through national work permit systems, are related to the needs of particular growth sectors of the economies of individual countries. Recruitment since the early 1990s has been particularly buoyant in information and communication technologies and in the health and education sectors. Much of the managed immigrant flow is to highly skilled jobs in these areas, but there has also been an increase in the recruitment of seasonal employees, trainees and working holidaymakers. The UK and Ireland, both experiencing periods of sustained economic growth, have noticeably relaxed recruitment conditions in recent years and this has been reflected in the granting of a growing number of work permits. In Ireland, 36,400 permits were issued in 2001, doubling the number for 2000. In the UK 81,000 permits were granted in 2001 compared to 67,000 in the previous year and 53,400 in 1999; this growth was sustained in 2002 with in excess of 86,000 permits issued[10]. The issuing of permits reflects the changing structural needs of national economies; in this respect the recent removal of information technologies, which has experienced a recent downturn, from the 'Shortage Occupation List' in the UK is indicative of attempts at fine tuning. Elsewhere in the EU the growth in skilled worker recruitment has been less dramatic, reflecting the less buoyant economies of countries such as Germany and France (SOPEMI, 2003).

According to Salt (2001, p 18) there is increasing 'evidence of polarisation' in the pattern of labour recruitment, "with large numbers of jobs being filled at relatively low skill levels, especially in labour intensive occupations such as catering and cleaning", and, we can add, agriculture. In some countries the level of seasonal recruitment associated with relatively unskilled occupations dwarfs that of skilled worker recruitment: in Germany, for instance, nearly 300,000 seasonal workers were recruited in 2001, the majority from Poland under the provisions of the 1990 German–Polish agreement on the employment of seasonal labour. Elsewhere the numbers are significant but more modest: Austria, 11,000 in 2002; Italy, 30,000 in 2000/01; France 13,500 in 2002; and the UK 25,000 in 2003. An apparently growing trend in the category of seasonal workers is the tendency to recruit working holidaymakers; the UK, for instance, received 41,700 in 2002.

Asylum seekers and refugees

Although still below the peak levels of the early 1990s, which were associated with the crisis in the former Yugoslavia, asylum seeking is also presently on the increase in many EU countries reflecting, in particular, regional conflicts in the Middle East and sub-Saharan Africa. OECD analysis indicates that asylum applications to the EU grew from 50,000 in 1983 to more than 684,000 in 1992. After 1993, as increasingly restrictive measures were adopted throughout the EU, the numbers steadily declined, dropping to just over a quarter of a million in 1996. Since then, the total has slowly climbed again to almost 382,000 in 2002 (SOPEMI, 2003, p 33) – a level, however, that is still only 56% of the 1992 peak. Over the past decade Germany experienced the highest absolute numbers of asylum seekers (averaging 170,000 per year), followed by the UK, the Netherlands and Sweden. However, in 2000-02 Finland and Luxembourg also experienced increases of over 50%, although from a small base. Asylum applications increased in 2000/01 especially in the UK, Austria, Portugal and Sweden, and since 2000, the UK has replaced Germany as the leading recipient of asylum flows to the EU. The 111,000 applications to UK in 2002 was the highest recorded in any EU country for that year[11]. In contrast, Germany, Belgium, the Netherlands, Italy, Denmark and Spain all experienced significant decreases of between 20% and 45% in 2001-02, attributable perhaps to the introduction of strong deterrence programmes. However, it is important to note that while Germany has experienced a recent decrease, and now occupies second place to UK, it still has 40% more applicants that France and double that for Austria[12].

Böcker and Havinga (1997), in their research for the European Commission, suggest that the majority of asylum seekers are not necessarily exercising a conscious, rational choice in choosing their country for asylum based on a comparison of the advantages and disadvantages between various options. Rather, as with other migration streams, former colonial and post-colonial ties and knowledge of the language are among the main determining factors; however, the increases recorded for Sweden clearly reflect other factors at work, possibly associated with the perceived willingness of reception countries to receive asylum seekers. According to Salt, chain migration effects are also important, especially in terms of friendship and kinship networks (Böcker and Havinga, 1997; Salt, 2001).

A relatively small number of nationalities account for the majority of asylum applicants in the EU. The leading source countries for asylum seekers have remained the same for some years: the former Yugoslavia and Turkey have been among the top three every year since 1990, except for 2000, and Iraq has consistently figured in the top five, rising to number one or two in more recent times (SOPEMI, 2003, p 35). During 1990-99, the top four source countries of asylum seekers and refugees were: the former Yugoslavia 25% (1,043,800), Romania 9.4% (392,200), Turkey 8% (335,900), and the former Soviet Union 4.7% (196,600). Following the civil disturbances and the ethnic cleansing pogroms of 1991-92, Yugoslavs came to head the list of asylum seekers, and this despite the fact that many of those fleeing the former Yugoslavia, particularly from Bosnia and Kosovo, did not appear in the asylum statistics, but were frequently given a temporary protected status (Salt, 2001). From the turn of the century, Turkey, the former Yugoslavia, Iran, Iraq, Afghanistan, Somalia and Sri Lanka have become the major sending countries, "all of them having sources of conflict likely to create populations in need of protection" (Salt, 2001, p 23).

These statistics indicate that many asylum seekers who have arrived in Europe since the early 1990s have come not simply to escape poverty, but frequently to escape civil war and severe oppression. The break-up of Yugoslavia in 1991 and the subsequent conflict and ethnic cleansing led to a marked increase in numbers of refugees, while human rights abuses connected to the repression of demands for regional autonomy among Kurdish minority populations led to increased flows from both Turkey and Iraq. Similarly, conflict and persecution in Afghanistan, first by warlords and then by the Taliban, resulted in an outpouring of refugees, while civil war and insurgency in Sri Lanka have resulted in a steady outflow of Tamil asylum seekers (Loescher, 2003[13]).

Clandestine migration

Virtually all commentators indicate that clandestine migration is on the increase, although of course by its very nature this claim is difficult to confirm numerically. According to International Labour Office (Stalker, 1994) estimates, in 1991 there were 2.6 million undocumented non-nationals in Europe (the figure includes seasonal workers and those asylum seekers whose applications had been turned down but had not departed). Drawing together data from border control authorities on the numbers of apprehensions, illegal trespassing and detentions, the International Centre for Migration Policy Development (ICMPD) estimated that in 1993 illegal inflows in Europe totalled around 350,000 (Widgren, 1994). The periodic amnesties issued by some countries for illegal workers provide a further indicator of the extent of irregular migration and working. These were a fairly common feature in Mediterranean countries during the last two decades of the 20th century. Particularly notable were the regularisations of the 1980s, the early 1990s and since 1996. Over the period as a whole around 1.45 million regularisations have occurred, 1.12 million since 1996. Recent amnesty figures for individual countries suggest the numbers of clandestine migrants continue to rise. For example, the 2002 regularisation in Italy attracted 700,000 applicants, 340,000 of whom were domestic workers, and in Spain, 340,000 were regularised as part of the 'Araigo' (settlement) process in 2001; 30% of these were domestic workers (SOPEMI, 2003, p 30). Recent estimates suggest that there are now at least 3 million illegal migrants in Europe, and that, each year, clandestine migrants make up between 20% and 30% of the new migrant arrivals (Veenkamp et al, 2003, p 58).

'Fortress Europe'

Unlike the US, Canada or Australia, no European country views itself as a immigrant society, yet the cumulative immigration flows of the post-war decades suggest that this image may have to be revised. The need for compensatory immigration to balance an increasingly uneven age structure in all EU countries and to fill the gaps in the labour market especially after 2010 when the post-war 'baby-boomers' reach retirement age, imply that immigration pressures will continue for the foreseeable future. A tension between the 'image' (of the insignificance of immigration) and the 'reality' (of substantial and continuing immigration) pervades recent national and EU debates on the development of immigration policy and legislation. While demographic and economic conditions suggest that immigration should be welcomed and encouraged, the inclination of national governments, spurred by expressions of public hostility towards immigration and by fears that immigrants will impose another burden on severely pressed social welfare budgets, is to batten the hatches and resist all but the most selective influx of newcomers. The imposition of work restrictions on migrants from the 10 new EU states following their accession in May 2004 by all of the EU-15 countries[14] is a reflection of the way issues of migration have risen up the EU political agenda and an clear indicator of the 'paranoia' which surrounds the whole issue[15].

Recent reinforcement of migrant controls by EU countries at their borders and the expansion and strengthening of the monitoring and surveillance of migrants once they have entered, can in part be seen as a response to security issues in the context of the so-called 'global fight against terrorism'. But principally they are designed to inhibit and dissuade asylum seekers and counter irregular migration by confronting the networks that deal in the trafficking of human beings. Several states – Denmark, Germany, Portugal and Greece – have recently passed new laws regarding the entry, stay and employment of foreigners; others, such as the UK, have adopted measures which limit admissibility and at least one country (the Netherlands) has taken the unprecedented step (in recent times at least) of expelling long-stay immigrants[16]. Alongside the actions taken by individual member states to guard their borders, attempts have also been made to harmonise migration policy across the EU by way of the development of what Leitner (1997) calls 'a supranational migration framework'. These attempts have been intermittent and only partially successful. However, what is important about these harmonisation measures is not their inclusiveness or comprehensiveness, but rather that they embrace and reflect the apprehension and wariness of individual national states with regard to the arrival of new migrants. Their focus is very much on articulating the problem of migration, their intent is one of enhancing control through the efficient policing of borders and the checking and surveillance of would-be migrants. Labour migration and family reunification have not been of particular concern in the development of a EU framework, both these remain the province of national governments and are not regarded as particularly problematic at the scale of the EU, or at least not as problematic and unpredictable as asylum seekers, refugees and clandestine migration. The relative neglect by the EU of problems faced by immigrants in relation to their integration in the frequently hostile environments of reception countries – an issue which was established as part of the EU migration framework's remit following the meetings on asylum and clandestine migration at Tampere in 1999 – serves to further emphasis the pervading 'frontier' mentality and obsession with issues of controlling and inhibiting entry.

Over the past 20 years EU member states have gradually increased cooperation in an attempt to establish a common approach to immigration and asylum. Successive agreements, treaties and directives have led to the creation of what some refer to as 'Fortress Europe' (but see Mitchell and Russell, 1998). The Schengen Agreement of 1985 was one of the first steps in this process. The declared aim of the Agreement was to facilitate movement between the signatory countries by removing controls on their contiguous borders, but as a corollary it also established a common policy for the establishment of procedures to control migration into the newly created Schengen area. The importance of the latter is indicated in the balance of the articles of the agreement: four articles on open borders, 138 on increased immigration control (Hogan, 2004). Common rules regarding visas, asylum rights and checks at external borders were adopted and measures for the coordination of the police, customs and the judiciary were introduced. Initially comprising five EU states (France, Germany, Belgium, Luxembourg and the Netherlands) and the European Economic Area (EEA) states of Norway and Iceland, the Schengen area was subsequently extended and now includes all member states, with the exception of the UK and Ireland.

In 1992, the Maastricht Treaty formalised European cooperation on immigration matters. Title VI of the Treaty brought immigration policy into the institutional structure of the EU along with combating drugs and fraud, asylum, external borders policy, customs cooperation and police and judicial cooperation. As Veenkampf et al (2003, p 105) observe: "The inclusion of immigration alongside illegality and criminal activities demonstrates how, since its inception, the European policy discourse on immigration has been shaped by security concerns". These concerns were further emphasised in 1999 when the Treaty of Amsterdam incorporated the principles of the Schengen Agreement (common visa lists, abolition of internal border checks, and so on) into the legal and institutional framework of the EU, and immigration and asylum became formally a subject for EU procedures of cooperation. The Amsterdam treaty additionally called for the establishment of policy directives on the crossing of external borders, on the provision of temporary protection for refugees, on conditions of entry and residence of third country nationals, asylum procedures, and on combating undocumented immigration. The call for the strengthening of cooperation was made in the face a 'major public concern' regarding the rising number of immigrants and asylum seekers arriving at EU borders. However, it can also be seen as an attempt to develop and strengthen the association between European identity and regulation of migrants: "[t]he re-establishment and strengthening of European and national identity politics in opposition to the threatening presence of foreigners underscored the rhetoric of security, inclusion and exclusion" (Veenkamp et al, 2003, p 108).

Meetings of the European Council on asylum and immigration at Tampere in 1999 and at Seville in 2002 considered further the issue of an EU common migration framework. At Tampere, the principles of such a framework were articulated: partnership with origin countries, a common EU approach to procedures for asylum, fair treatment of third country nationals and management of migration flows. At Seville, these principles were given articulation in a series of substantive measures. It was agreed, for example, that all EU agreements with non-EU states should include a clause on joint management of migration flows and on compulsory readmission to the country of origin in the event of illegal immigration. If the non-EU state does not fulfil its obligations in these respects, the EU can apply direct pressure through agreements on trade, aid and assistance coupled with political and diplomatic sanctions. At the Seville summit it was also agreed to establish an EU border police force to be drawn from among all member states (to be called the European Union Corps of Border Guards) to patrol shores, ports and crossing points to apprehend illegal immigrants. Two models of the sort of high-tech border controls envisaged had already been set up prior to the Seville meeting. The first was on the Spanish south coast and the Straits of Gibraltar were a 'Surveillance System for the Straits' comprising radar systems and infra-red cameras was established to monitor 115km of coastline checking for illegal immigration from the north coast of Africa. The second was installed on Hungary's border where the EU (at the cost of 30 million euros) equipped guards with everything from uniforms to thermal imaging cameras to monitor and control migration from the former Yugoslavia and the Ukraine. The EU migration framework also extends to data gathering and to surveillance. The proposal for a system for the identification of asylum seekers (EURODAC), which involves taking and comparing fingerprints of asylum seekers, was formally adopted by the European Council in 2000 and became operational in 2003; asylum seekers can now be more easily identified as they move from state to state.

The cumulative reinforcement of screening and vetting procedures for third country would-be migrants at Europe's national borders and the attempts (however incomplete) to develop a common migration framework for the EU, can be interpreted as emanating from deeply conservative motives designed to bolster the notion that Europe is not an immigrant community and a desire to retain the essence of the 'European national character' (Haynes, 1999). That this notion of a non-immigrant Europe is easily challenged by historical reference is not the point. Throughout the post-war period vocal and tacit opposition and resistance to immigration has been a universal feature of all EU member states. The political legitimacy of governments as guardians of domestic stability and preservers of public order has frequently been secured by their readiness to control and block inward migration. Against this predisposition to close-off routes of entry, to create a 'Fortress Europe', are arrayed two counter pressures: first, pressures to comply with humanitarian imperatives and universal notions of social justice, and second, pressures emanating from the forces of economic globalisation. Responding to these pressures, the drawbridge of Fortress Europe is grudgingly lowered to facilitate family reunification and to provide refuge for the oppressed; it is also selectively lowered to assuage the economic demands of domestic business for flexible skilled and unskilled labour. Within Fortress Europe, as a consequence of exclusionary immigration policies which permit only selective and discriminating in-migration, a new "social hierarchy is being engineered" (Klein, 2003) in which a person's position is determined by mode of entry and right to residence.

A hierarchy of vulnerability

John Gubbay, in his consideration of European migration policy, identifies eight categories of migrant, each of which, he argues, defines a certain status level based on differential access to rights in seven domains: (i) right of residence in the destination country (indefinite, conditional, limited); (ii) right to employment or self-employment; (iii) right of access to welfare (education, contributory and non-contributory benefits); (iv) right to political participation (for example, voting); (v) right to claim naturalisation; (vi) right to travel within the EU; and (vii) rights of dependent family members (Gubbay, 1999, p 49). On the basis of access to these domains, Gubbay produces a ranked listing of migrant types, starting with the most privileged. The top four types in what we might call this 'hierarchy of vulnerability' are virtually guaranteed maximum rights across the seven domains. First on the list are 'returnees', individuals and households returning after a period (perhaps a near life-time) abroad; returnees are not seen as immigrants because they already have citizenship as a consequence of blood or birth line (for example, the Pontiac Greeks and Germans from the former GDR). The second type is made up of those who are entitled to entry, residence, work and social benefits by virtue of citizenship of another EU state; in some instances (for example, the Irish in Britain) these cross-state rights reflect an historic special relationship that preceded the formation of the European Community. The third of Gubbay's migrant types is comprised of reuniting family members of EU citizens. This type of family reunification, in which the primary migrant is a citizen of the EU, forms a fraction of a larger family reunification process that in Europe today represents, as we have seen earlier in this chapter, a significant percentage of the total migration flow. Family members (when they are not EU citizens in their own right) do not, however, always have the same privileges of residence as the original migrant: family rights are sometimes dependent on the continuation of the family unit and can be threatened following divorce or the death of the primary migrant. Gubbay's fourth category is comprised of 'other legally resident third country citizens'. Many migrants in this category will have entered as skilled and professional workers through some kind of work permit system. Some of these are migrants form part of a growing transnational migrant group for whom geographic movement is a characteristic of their career paths. They are often actively recruited by large firms in need of special technical expertise and managers, and include specialist professionals hired as consultants on a contract basis.

In contrast to the above, the remaining four of Gubbay's migrant groups exhibit many signs of vulnerability in that their right of residence, of employment and so forth, are limited or non-existent. Thus, the fifth type is made up of third country citizens given leave to stay as refugees on grounds specified in the Geneva Convention, and the sixth is made up of non-EU citizens asylum seekers who have permission to stay for humanitarian reasons. Unlike the refugee whose right to stay is not generally conditioned, the asylum seeker's right of entry is can sometimes be time-limited or subject to specific conditions of stay. Asylum seekers awaiting decisions on their applications make up the seventh of Gubbay's types; the eighth and last type is the clandestine migrant who has no legal rights at all except those minimum rights specified in universal declarations to which the reception country may be a signatory.

The differential access to rights conferred by migrant status is manifest in the poorer housing conditions of those on the lower levels of this hierarchy, in their social segregation, and in their low pay and poor working conditions. Their lack of assured rights and their relatively deprived status in comparison to those with full citizenship (actual or implied), also mark them out for racial harassment and xenophobia. As Gubbay observes, it is the "clandestine immigrants and supposedly bogus asylum seekers" who are the "target of disprivileging"; they are stereotyped as "driven by the pursuit of personal gain, deceitful, mendacious and unable or unwilling to integrate" (1999, p 49).

EU and national immigration policies and border controls have determined the construction of this 'hierarchy of vulnerability'. As it becomes more difficult for would-be migrants to access right of entry and residence through the legal channels of work permits or asylum status, or indeed through family reunion, migrants are forced down the hierarchy into the clandestine category with all that implies in terms of exposure to exploitation by traffickers on the migrant journey, and by gangmasters after entry. Clandestine migrants having achieved entry merge into the shadows of society, into the liminal spaces of the informal economy and are joined there by other irregular migrants such as temporary and seasonal workers who have over-stayed their delimited period of residence, and by absconding asylum seekers fearing that their application for residency will be rejected.

Conclusion

In this chapter we have argued that the obsession of member states, and indeed the EU itself, with border controls and immigration restrictions, has had a detrimental effect on the experience of migration for many groups in that the legislative determination of mode of entry and right to residence are crucial factors in determining a migrant's position in the social structures of the reception society. Discriminating legislation which values some categories of migrant above others cultivates and promotes a negative reaction to, and treatment of, the devalued groups, effectively relegating members of these groups to a precarious and vulnerable existence within the society of their chosen destination country. The nature of that precarious and vulnerable existence is the subject matter of the next chapter.

Notes

[1] Hirst and Thompson (1996) are among several authors who identify two phases of globalisation in modern times. The 'first' globalisation is identified as peaking at the turn of the 19th/20th century. The present phase is variously dated, but 1970s onwards is coincident with rise of neoliberal political and economic ideology.

[2] This recalls Anthony Giddens' concept of 'time-space distanciation' referring to the lifting of social relations from their immediate setting, stretching them over time and space (Giddens, 1990).

[3] This is, of course, a contested image, but one which had some claim to at least nominal legitimacy (see Jessop, 2002).

[4] Of course the process has been very uneven. Subsidies for steel and cotton in the US are matched by Common Agricultural Policy (CAP) subsidies in the EU. In the world economy today, the protection of national economic interests against foreign and overseas competition is rife.

[5] In this context, the voices of trades unions are muted. Nominally 'freedom of movement' is espoused by most, but these sentiments have had little impact on international affairs and indeed are frequently belied by the actions of national trades unions protecting the 'rights' of domestic workers.

[6] More reasoned, but muted voices are to be heard in the ranks of liberal orientated academics; see for instance, Salt (2001); Piracha and Vickerman (2002); Veenkamp et al (2003).

[7] In 1994 4 million babies were born and 3.7 million people died, 1 million people emigrated and 2 million immigrants entered from outside (Rees et al, 1996, p xix).

[8] As examples of the latter we can cite: the labour migrations of the late-1960s and the refugees flows of the mid- and late-1950s from Hungary and Czechoslovakia, the 1962 migration to France of *pieds noirs*, the 1972 Ugandan Asians migrations to the UK following their expulsion by Idi Amin, and the return of Portuguese from Africa in the 1960s and 1970s during the wars of liberation in Angola, Mozambique, Guinea Bissau and Cape Verde.

[9] Ireland, a former colony and now a member of the EU, has long been the main source of immigrants to Britain.

[10] This figure includes renewed permits as well as new issues.

[11] On a per capita basis Britain still receives fewer asylum seekers than many other EU states. When the number of asylum applicants is considered in relation to the country's total population, the UK ranks at tenth place in the EU. At the global level the UK ranks very low on the league table, far behind the world's largest refugee hosting countries, all of which are found in the poorest countries of Africa, Asia and the Middle East.

[12] The current volatility in the number of asylum seekers is well illustrated by the Netherlands which has seen a sharp fall since 2000, when 43,560 people applied for refugee status. Data from the Central Bureau of Statistics showed that 18,670 people sought asylum in 2002. The Dutch Refugee Council estimated that the number had fallen to about 10,000 in 2003 (see De Feijter, 2003).

[13] The estimated US$10 billion spent each year by the industrialised states on their asylum systems is substantially greater than the modest US$800 million that the United Nations High Commissioner for Refugees (UNHCR) spends on the 19 million refugees and displaced persons in less prosperous countries around the world (Loescher, 2003). A recent report indicates that the world's five richest countries (including Germany, France and the UK) spend US$17 billion a year on enforcing immigration controls, approximately two thirds of their entire expenditure on overseas aid (*The Guardian*, 28 July 2004).

[14] Each country has imposed its own specific restrictions, with the UK and Ireland being among the most 'open' in that new state nationals will be free to enter, but unable to claim benefits until they have been in work for at least 12 months.

[15] The imposition of migration restrictions have been motivated by the assumption that the conjoining of 10 'relatively poor' countries with the existing 'relatively rich' 15 member countries would engender massive cross border migration. Alternative scenarios, based on Eurobarometer surveys and published by the EU Commission itself and by the EU Foundation for Improvement in Living and Working Conditions, which indicated that over five years the likely level of migration would be perhaps 200,000 (1% of the working population of the 10 accession states), have been ignored. The argument for low levels of migration from East to West also cite the historic evidence of the non-occurrence of mass migration when Spain and Portugal joined in 1986.

[16] Up to 26,000 asylum seekers are to be deported, a significant proportion of whom have lived for many years in the Netherlands and have children born and educated in their chosen country of residence.

THREE

The experience of migration

Introduction

> The decentring and dematerialisation of economic activity have summoned
> the spectre of 'placeless capital' and the 'homeless subject'.... In this context,
> the experience of migration may well be even more precarious than we have
> yet been able to imagine. Despite the rhetorical appeal of multiculturalism and
> the intellectual popularity of concepts like diaspora and hybridity, the horizon
> of the migrant's imaginary is increasingly filled with experiences of itinerancy,
> ghettoisation and illegality. (Papastergiadis, 2000, p 20)

In the above quote, Papastergiadis deploys the concept of the 'homeless subject'
to capture the trauma of the migration experience, both during the period of
transition from origin to destination and during the time of settlement in the
reception country. 'Homeless' for Papastergiadis embraces not just dislocation
from a place of secure and adequate shelter, but the severance of emotional and
practical support provided by home-based social and cultural networks. The
emphasis of his analysis, and of this chapter, is on the vulnerability and insecurity
that accompanies the volatility and uncertainty of the migration experience in
a world hostile to the unimpeded movement of people. Some migrants survive,
of course, and seemingly relish exposure to the migration process. Indeed, for
professional transnational migrants, equipped with appropriate documentation,
their very existence and identity is embedded in and conditioned by the
displacement and relocation that migration entails. For others, however,
migration can be a hazardous experience bringing with it uncertainty and
insecurity, which may or may not be alleviated over time. Increasingly rigid
border controls, whose rules selectively filter and regulate in changing and
apparently unpredictable ways, induce stress and ambiguity on the journey,
while the xenophobia and racism of the reception society bring into question
the hoped for outcome – whether that be the kinship and security of the
diaspora, the mutual tolerance and cooperation of the multicultural community
or the 'utopia' of the hybrid society.

In this chapter we focus on the experiences of those at the nether end of the
hierarchy of vulnerability: on the low-skilled and unskilled economic migrant,
the asylum seeker and the clandestine migrant. We first attempt to expose the
vulnerabilities which come with the migrant journey and second, the
vulnerabilities associated with the process of reception and settlement. The
attempts of immigrants to secure their rights through citizenship and the

problems of social integration are the topics of the final sections. This chapter provides the background and context for a more detailed examination of the housing and homelessness experiences of migrants in the following chapters.

The migrant journey

International migration is popularly explained in terms of push and pull factors, a binary which is closely linked with another, that of core developed countries and peripheral, underdeveloped countries[1]. Economic migrants and asylum seekers are portrayed as fleeing the 'war-torn', 'crisis-ridden' or 'poverty-stricken' regions of the periphery, joining global migration streams that have the economically and socially stable countries of the core as their destination. Such a characterisation ignores or is ignorant of the fact that the majority of those engaged with international migration actually move from peripheral country to peripheral country (see Stalker, 2001); it also diminishes and underplays, as Anderson (2004: forthcoming) among others has pointed out, the importance of pull factors, of the need and demand for labour, skilled and unskilled, in the ageing societies, of the core of which the EU is part. To draw attention to the importance of pull factors is, of course, not to diminish the underdeveloped character of many of the origin countries. The underdevelopment of origin countries is well documented and explained in large part by the combined impact of colonialism and the present-day processes of neoliberal globalisation which subject peripheral countries to 'structural adjustments', thereby exposing their fledging enterprises to international competition, destroying public services, imposing detrimental trade agreements, and entangling their economies in debilitating debt repayment. Rather, to focus on pull factors is to highlight the need in the growth economies of the core, many of which are undergoing a 'second demographic transition' (Lesthaeghe, 1995), for a replacement labour force and a replacement population. In many European countries an ageing population threatens the so-called demographic balance, increasing dependency ratios and undermining the ability of welfare states to sustain health and pension benefits (Eubusiness, 2003). The demand for labour – although varying from time to time in response to the vagaries of overall economic and sector cycles – is across the board: from IT experts and professional managers to unskilled agricultural workers and domestic servants. For Europe, as for other developed economies, the labour resources of what used to be known as the second and third worlds form a vast 'international reserve army' to be tapped into at times of expansion and shed in times of recession; a surplus, just-in-time labour force providing flexibility for just-in-time production and service delivery. For Peter Stalker, "[i]nternational migrants have become the shock absorbers for the global economy in that by matching demand and supply they operate to keep capital accumulation on an even keel" (Stalker, 2001, p 121; see also Stalker, 1994, 2000).

The international reserve of labour includes not only regulated and documented economic migrants at the top (for example, IT specialists, medics) and the bottom (for example, temporary, seasonal agricultural workers) of the labour market, but also, by default, asylum seekers and migrants engaged in family reunification. Asylum seekers (except in the period when their applications are being considered, during which they are subject to severe restrictions in terms of accessing benefits and welfare services and are officially unable to work) move into the labour market once accepted for entry, often experiencing severe deskilling in the process. Asylum seekers whose applications are rejected frequently abscond and join the ranks of the clandestine migrants adding to those who work in the liminal spaces of society without official documentation. Migrants engaged in family reunion, when they are able to satisfy immigration officials of the authenticity of their claims, variously contribute to the labour force, either indirectly by providing support for existing labour, or directly in providing labour in their own right or contributing to the reproduction of labour in situ when settlement is permanent or near permanent. Clandestine labour, composed of those who gain entry illegally by avoiding border checks and evading internal surveillance, is a growing and important part of the international reserve of labour, supplying unregulated labour for a variety of tasks in food processing, cleaning, agricultural work and construction, where wages are low, working conditions poor and few questions are asked.

The international reserve of labour is then highly segmented. For the professional trans-migrant providing skills in short supply, the migratory journey to find work and residence is relatively untroubled. Disappointments are to do with the nature of the work, personal preferences and exposure to sometimes strange cultures and ways life; with institutional and professional support, exposure to xenophobic and racist behaviour is eased[2]. For others who make up the international reserve of labour – skilled and unskilled workers under temporary contracts, refugees and clandestine migrants and others at the bottom of the hierarchy of vulnerability – the migrant journey from origin to destination is an altogether much more perilous undertaking.

Reflecting an 'exclusionary rationale' (Gubbay, 1999, p 48), tighter border controls and restrictive residency regulations drive those denied the right of entry and residence into the ranks of the clandestine migrants or, when already within the borders of the reception country, encourage asylum seekers to abscond and temporary workers to overstay. The increasing militarisation of border controls, the enforcement of demanding asylum rules and detention policies, the enactment of deportation orders and carrier sanctions have led many thousands of asylum seekers to attempt to enter Europe covertly, forcing them into the arms of people traffickers and necessitating the adoption of ever more dangerous avenues and methods of entry which frequently prove fatal[3]. According to 'UNITED', a European anti-racist network, from 1993 to 2001 approximately one person has died every day as a result of the policies of 'Fortress Europe', while another organisation, 'Anti Racist Initiative, Berlin' (www.berlinet.de/ari), has documented 3,400 deaths and injuries of refugees which have resulted directly and indirectly from Germany's refugee policy: of these, 121 asylum seekers killed themselves in the face of their pending deportation or died in their attempt to flee, and a further 47 died while in prison awaiting deportation[4]. Other would-be immigrants have drowned in the Mediterranean and suffocated in containers. The most serious single instance occurred in June 2000 when 58 Chinese suffocated in the back of a lorry bound for Dover from Zeebrugge. Having paid considerable amounts of money to Chinese snakehead traffickers, in the final and the fatal stage of their journey, they were handed over to a Dutch-Turkish criminal gang based in Rotterdam (Lawrence, 2004b). In another incident, eight Romanian refugees were found dead inside a shipping container at Waterford, Ireland in December 2001, after being trapped for nine days. A refugee hiding on top of a train bound to Britain from France was electrocuted and killed in January 2002. In December 2003, a small wooden ship smuggling 70 people to Greece sank off the Turkish coast, only one person survived. For significant numbers, the experience of migration is truncated before reaching their destination. For those who get through – legally or illegally – the experience of settlement is fraught with its own difficulties and challenges.

Vulnerabilities of settlement

In the EU, notwithstanding considerable variation from country to country, significant numbers of immigrants experience deprivation and discrimination leading to their disproportionate representation in menial jobs and relegation to some of the worst housing. Several factors combine to determine the condition of immigrant settlement; we will consider these under two broad headings: mode of entry and context of reception.

Mode of entry

A migrant's place in the hierarchy of vulnerability identified in the preceding chapter is a principal determinate of the experience of settlement as it is of the migration journey. At the top of the hierarchy, the international executive in a contractually secure job will have access to adequate and secure housing of the highest quality. Documented migrants with skills to offer will access jobs of variable security and pay, and will secure housing of uneven quality across the spectrum of tenures, from home ownership to private renting and the tenancy of social housing (see Chapter Four). At the bottom of the hierarchy, however, the clandestine migrant, smuggled in with false or no documents, will be dependent on irregular work, with erratic and long hours and low pay and, in extreme circumstances, will have an overcrowded room, a rural shack or rented mattress for a home. The vulnerability of those at the lower end of the hierarchy has recently been vividly revealed by Felicity Lawrence in her extensive research into British and European agricultural practices (Lawrence, 2004a). She reports that "… hot-bunking, dozens to a small flat, inhumane working hours, pitiful pay" is the typical fate of the undocumented worker. In Britain today she says,

... gangmasters house twentieth century workers in squalor. Right round the country, I have come across cases from Bristol to Sussex to East Anglia, from the 65 migrants living in an old 10-bedroomed hotel with no kitchen and no heating to the 27 camping in a small house without sanitation. Extortionate rents are deducted from wages for this housing to disguise the fact that migrants are being paid less than the minimum wage. (Lawrence, 2004a)

Cheap immigrant labour, much of it clandestine or undocumented, characterises the economies of all EU countries. The use of gangmasters and illegal labour has a long history but has grown significantly in the European economy in recent decades. From the illegal workers in the textile workshops in the Sentier district of Paris to the clandestine agricultural labourers toiling in the fields of Norfolk and the greenhouses of Andalusia, migrants now account for a considerable proportion of the workforce in many key industries, and tales of violence, exploitation and violation of basic health and safety regulations are increasingly common. In Spain undocumented immigrants dominate agriculture work in some regions. In 2001, for instance, it was estimated that 150,000 clandestine immigrants from Ecuador alone worked in the Iberian peninsula. In the Netherlands, a third of agricultural workers, especially in market gardening, are estimated to be illegal. A Rotterdam University study puts the current number of illegal agricultural workers in the Netherlands at around 100,000. In Britain, the Home Office estimates there are at least 1,000 illegal gangmasters (out of a total of about 3,000) who cost the British Treasury £100 million a year in lost tax and National Insurance contributions (*Observer*, 15 February 2004). They operate in food packing plants, building sites, catering, educational establishments, hospitals, fish and chicken processing factories, textile workshops, contract cleaning, and the sex trade. Today's food and manufacturing sectors are dependent on hidden armies of cheap migrant labour, both legal and illegal: "[t]hey cut daffodils in Cornwall, pack carrots in Lincolnshire, pick fruit in Kent and fillet fish in Scotland. They piece together microwaves in the north and build electrical goods in the south" (Lawrence, 2004c). Agriculture, however, with an estimated total of between 60,000 and 100,000, is by probably the largest employer of undocumented migrants in Britain as in several other European countries.

Economically vital, but socially marginalised, undocumented migrants live in the shadows of European society, often apparently invisible until social unrest or tragedy strikes and they become newsworthy. The cockle pickers of Morecambe Bay, the agricultural workers of Andalusia and the textile sweatshop workers in Brussels provide illustrative case studies.

Case Study 1: The 'greenhouses' of Andalusia

In February 2000 in the Andalusian town of El Ejido, vicious race riots drew attention to the concentration of Moroccan labourers working, mostly illegally, in the 30,000 hectares of greenhouses in the area, producing up to 3 million tonnes of fruit and vegetables, half of which is exported to northern Europe, mainly Germany. The European Civic Forum sent an international commission there to investigate. The commission of enquiry identified the presence of thousands of illegal immigrants working and living in intolerable conditions, making up a flexible cheap labour force hired on a daily basis as the level of work in the 15,000 farm businesses demanded. According to the Office for the Social Integration of Immigrants in Almeria, almost 92% of the region's agricultural workers are immigrants, 64% of them Moroccans. In 1998 the Office estimated the number of legal immigrants at 15,000 and the number of undocumented migrants at between 15,000 and 25,000. The municipality of El Ejido has courted notoriety in adopting a deliberate policy of segregation and makes a point of harassing immigrants with the aim of discouraging them from 'colonising' the town centre. Most of them have to live in old shacks abandoned by the rural population; 55% of them have no drinking water, 57% no washing or toilet facilities and 31% no electricity. Hundreds of people squat in huts made of old wood and plastic. The region's officials put the number of immigrants living in unfit conditions at 17,000. These immigrants also have to put up with unacceptable working conditions, including heat of up to 50°C in the greenhouses and contact with huge amounts of pesticides. Needless to say, they are poorly paid. The producers are squeezed by bank loans, the farm supplies industry and marketing firms, so they try to survive by making savings in the only area they control, namely employment.

In recent years Central and Eastern European undocumented migrant labour has been increasingly recruited in the region to replace "troublesome Moroccans" (Bell, 2002, p 44) who had over the years become organised and were responsible for calling several strikes. Many claim that this was the true background to the El Ejido riots in 2000. The 'regularisation' of the immigrant status of 5,000 Moroccan workers in 2002, following a campaign by the social movement 'Sans-Papiers', led to a further deterioration. Spanish farmers were reluctant to employ Moroccans with legal status since they were more likely to claim their rights to pay and housing. To replace them hundreds of Polish and Romanian women were recruited at less money (about 18 euros a day) than the Moroccans would have expected (about 27 euros). According to Bell (2002, p 44) this left them "in a state of total poverty and despair in the streets without shelter, food or even water". The consequence is that many Moroccans are living in conditions of desperate poverty, six or seven people to a shack with only one working. The situation, according to Bell, is "becoming increasingly explosive" (Bell, 2002; Cabrera, 2001).

Case Study 2: The cockle pickers of Morecambe Bay

In their morning editions of 6 February 2004, British newspapers reported the deaths by downing of 20 Chinese cockle pickers in Morecambe Bay on the North West coast of England, half a world away from their home in southeast China:

> At least 19 people died when they were trapped by rising tides as they picked cockles on the notoriously dangerous mudflats at Morecambe Bay, Lancashire, last night. The victims ... were believed to have been Chinese. They were part of a group of more than 30 cockle pickers who had apparently been working in the dark. The police are investigating why the group were working in such perilous conditions, and said that criminal charges could follow. (*The Guardian*, 6 February 2004)

By the time the authorities were alerted it was already night-time. A major rescue operation was launched and 16 people were saved from the party of 36; two women were among the dead, all the victims were in their teens or 20s[5].

Located in the county of Lancashire on England's North West coast, the 9km sweep of Morecambe Bay has a magnificent backdrop formed by the hills of the Lake District and Bowland Fells. The picturesque setting, however, disguises hidden dangers for the uninformed and the unsuspecting. Morecambe Bay is the largest area of inter-tidal sand and mudflats in the UK and is well known in the locality for its treacherous surface and fast-moving incoming tides. Formed from sediments dumped by retreating glaciers at the end of the last ice age which were subsequently drowned by tectonic sea level rises, Morecambe Bay is now broad and undulating, with a spring tidal range of 10.5m and an ebbing tide that retreats for 12km. Tidal bores race over the sands and mudflats at speeds of up to 17km per hour, moulding the soft sediments, piling them into sand banks, and scooping out dangerous quick-sand filled holes that change position daily. It was a combination of a ferocious incoming tide and rapidly rising floodwaters that trapped the Chinese cockle pickers on the night of 5 February.

Harvesting the cockle beds of Morecambe Bay has long been part of the local economy; public right of access to the Bay for cockle picking is said to date back to the 13th century. Today the harvesting of cockles is regulated by the North East England and North Wales Fisheries Board. At the time of the tragedy 800 permits for cockle picking, issued by the Board, were in circulation. The anticipated value of the cockle harvest for the 2003/04 season has been variously valued at between 9 and 12 million euros on the European market. This is big business. Chinese cockle pickers, organised by five gangmasters[6] in teams of 20-30, had been working the cockle beds since December, the beginning of the harvest period. Arriving in the late afternoon to avoid conflict with local pickers, unable to read, or ignoring, prominently displayed signs warning of fast rising tides and quicksand, the Chinese pickers headed for cockle beds 3km out in the treacherous Bay. Working past sundown into the dark night in near freezing temperatures, they were caught by the rapidly rising tide, silent and invisible until it was too late.

Most of the 20 dead were from the Fujian region in southeast China, a region long associated with out-migration and overseas working. The community is geared up for migration, with overseas family contacts, a money-lending system to fund expensive illegal trips (13,000 euros to Western Europe), and a network of 'snakeheads'[7] to arrange transport and illegal entry to a variety of European destinations. Fujian, while not the only source of Chinese migrants to the UK, is now identified as the origin of the largest wave of undocumented Chinese migrants to Britain.

The tragedy in Morecambe followed complaints from local workers about Chinese cockle pickers in the Bay area in the previous July, leading to a police raid during which 37 Chinese were arrested on suspicion of illegal entry. There is circumstantial evidence of systematic intimidation of the Chinese workers by British cockle pickers. David Eden, director of the Liverpool Bay Fishing Company, briefly arrested (and subsequently charged with facilitating illegal immigration) in junction with the Morecambe Bay deaths, declared that he was threatened and intimidated by other cockle pickers after having agreed a supply deal with a Chinese gang. He further claimed that Chinese cockle pickers were the victims of racist violence and abuse by British fishermen, recounting that petrol and diesel had been poured on their bags of cockles and that scuffles were a common occurrence. Eden himself had received 'in excess of 10' threatening calls on his mobile phone from British nationals, one of the callers threatening to burn down his factory (*The Guardian*, 14 February 2004). It is assumed that the Chinese cockle pickers worked at night to avoid conflict with other gangs operating during daylight hours.

The rewards for workers from the backbreaking work of cockle picking are meagre. In a good week, at 13-16 euros a bag, individual cockle pickers can earn 450 to 600 euros; more frequently a week's taking would be valued at less than 400 euros. From these earning deductions are routinely made by the gangmasters for 'administration costs', for debt repayment, for transport and equipment costs, for room rent and even for tax and National Insurance that, of course, is not handed over to the authorities. The take-home pay of a cockle picker after these deductions can be reduced by half.

The cockle pickers who drowned at Morecambe Bay lived in sordid, overcrowded conditions in Kensington, an inner-city slum area of Liverpool. In seeking out their place of residence, newspaper reporters found a house with "a dingy hallway" and "an ill-furnished room no bigger than two square metres, the largest in this two-storey home. Here 13 people were watching television sitting on plastic chairs or on the floor against the wall; the TV was shared between this house and another down the street where some other Chinese live" (*The Guardian*, 14 February 2004); as many as 60 people were thought to be living in the 11-room property. In the world of the low-paid, migrant labourer there is nothing unusual about the conditions in which the Chinese workers and their compatriots were living.

Six months on from these events (July 2004) it appears very little had changed in the lives of the exploited labourers. A recent investigation by the Liverpool's *Daily Post* discovered

40 people living in a single terraced house, in squalid conditions that "shame a civilised 21st century society". When the seven-bedroom house was raided by police and immigration officers, 31 men and one woman were discovered inside. "The house was a filthy hovel with one toilet, one stained bath and a small kitchen. A musty odour permeated the dank house, and the second floor corridor and rooms near the toilet reeked of urine. There was not a single bed in the property, only a handful of mattresses. The majority of the workers slept on roll mats with sleeping bags and blankets. Blankets were hung against the windows to deter prying eyes" (reported in *The Guardian*, 15 July 2004).

Case Study 3: Textile sweatshops in Brussels

Kuregem is one of the most impoverished Brussels neighbourhoods, close to the Gare du Midi, where high speed trains connect Europe's capital with London, Paris and Amsterdam. This 19th-century neighbourhood is densely settled with 18,000 officially registered residents. More than two thirds of the inhabitants have parents with a non-Belgian nationality, the largest single group in the neighbourhood is Moroccan. Before the First World War, Kuregem accommodated mostly Jewish households, fleeing from pogroms in Germany. During the inter-war years and through the immediate post-war decades, Italians, mostly from the south (especially Sicily), and Greeks settled in the area. The first Moroccan households arrived in the early 1960s. From the late 1980s and early 1990s, immigrants from Central and Eastern Europe have moved into the district and the most recent arrivals are Asians from countries as far apart as Bangladesh and the Philippines.

In Kuregem, the textile industry has always been important, its roots dating back to the Middle Ages. With the onset of the deep economic crisis of the mid-1970s, the labour-intensive textile industries – along with other labour-intensive industries linked to the slaughterhouse of the neighbourhood and to the trade in second-hand cars – looked to replace relatively expensive domestic labour with cheap labour from overseas (Kesteloot and Meert, 1999).

Belgian workers were first replaced by Moroccan households (some of whom engaged in home work, sewing garments) and later by even cheaper immigrants from Central and Eastern Europe. While Moroccan households took up permanent residence in Belgium and thus needed a purchasing power adjusted to the Belgian norms of consumption, the new European immigrants came mostly with a short-term tourist visas and were prepared to accept as little as a quarter of the official minimum wage. The money earned was mostly remitted back home to their families living in impoverished regions such as that around Bialystok in Poland. These workers were very poorly housed, and were frequently reduced to renting of mattresses at 75 euros a month (mid-1990s prices).

Despite a couple of police interventions during the 1990s, the exploitation of this largely undocumented and very cheap labour force still continues. Nowadays, however, illegal employment is focused on people arriving from Asia. One of the most spectacular cases was discovered in the course of 2000, when four 'textile barons' were arrested, together with several dozen illegally employed people. During the course of their investigations, police discovered several sweatshops, consisting of a room with sewing machines and an adjacent narrow room where the workers ate and slept. All of these 'wage slaves' were recruited by a Belgian–Italian Mafioso club with the promise of interesting work and high wages. Once these people arrived in Belgium, their passports were removed by their employers, under the pretence of being necessary for their visa applications; they were never returned. In order to keep their operation hidden the noise of the sewing machines was minimised by the hermetical sealing of every crack in the building. In one of these sweatshops, people lived in the cellar boiler room: during the winter when the boiler was operating to its maximum, they had to live permanently in 50°C. The inspectors' reports record that all these illegally employed people worked at least 14 hours a day and that they earned starvation wages. Moreover, they had to return a large share of these wages in order to refund the loan (about 3,750 euros) that they taken out to finance their journey to Belgium. In order to survive, they were obliged to borrow again from their employers, plunging them into a hopeless morass of debt repayment and dependency. Further investigation has demonstrated that the final destination of the clothing produced in these sweatshops were the retail outlets of well-respected Belgian textile traders. The Belgium daily paper, *De Standaard*, reported on this case continuously for several days; however, it is far from unique in the Brussels milieu of illegally employed and exploited immigrants.

The living conditions experienced by clandestine and illegal migrants are predominantly conditioned by their migrant status. Their illegality necessitates that they remain invisible, that they occupy the margins of society, avoiding social contact, except with their fellow workers. They constitute a dependent community whose working and living conditions are determined by gangmasters and ruthless employers.

Context of reception

For other immigrant groups, legal entry allows ostensible admission to a wider society and access to regular employment. The settlement experience of these groups is, however, extremely variable; a variability determined in part, as we have indicated in the preceding section, by their mode of entry (for example, transnational executive versus refugee), but that clearly is not the whole story, since immigrants with the same mode of entry can have significantly different experiences. An important additional component to take into consideration in this context is what we might call, after Portes and Rumbaut (1996), their 'context of reception'. There are at least three interconnected issues here: first, the climate of reception – the prevalence of anti-immigrant feeling and the extent to which it permeates and conditions behaviour in the workplace and the neighbourhood; second, institutional issues – in particular the extent to which state interventions, at various geographic scales, act to ameliorate or exacerbate the nature of the migrant settlement experience; and third, networks of association – the social support that immigrants might derive from links with the communities of previous immigrants.

Climate of reception

As with all social phenomena, the terms 'immigration' and 'immigrant' are social constructs in that an appreciation of the multiple meanings with which these terms are invested requires an understanding of their role and place in society and the varying levels and degrees of importance attributed to them by different segments of that society. Significant sections of the European public, it appears, have a view of immigration and immigrants imbued with xenophobic prejudice and race bias[8], a view cultivated and embellished by sections of the news media and neo-fascist political organisations. In this view immigration is constructed as an 'invasion' whereby 'hordes' threaten to 'swamp' indigenous and local customs and ways of life. Immigrants are represented as 'alien', as 'criminal', as 'dangerous' and 'threatening'; accused of taking 'our' jobs and 'our' houses; they are 'scroungers', 'benefit tourists' and even 'sexual predators'. Such negative and hostile imagery is, of course, confronted and challenged by a variety of alternative voices both public and private, and there is a considerable body of research that gives the lie to these stereotypes. However, negative constructions of the process of immigration and the characterisation of immigrants are rarely adequately countered by the voices of tolerance and reason. Certainly governments engage in ritual condemnation of discrimination and hostility towards immigrants, and some individual politicians are undoubtedly motivated by strong anti-racist sentiment. Notwithstanding the passage of legislation that outlaws discrimination, such messages of tolerance are to a large extent contradicted by the louder and more vociferous message of suspicion and hostility sent by the dogged exercise of the exclusionary principles embedded in state-inspired anti-immigration legislation and controls. In juggling immigration laws and conjuring up ever more punitive reprisals for offenders and generally vying with opposition parties to establish their credentials in taking a resolute exclusionary stance, state governments feed the fires of racism and xenophobia; by criminalising and demonising asylum seekers and undocumented migrants, they create a climate of suspicion which embraces all immigrants, legal as well as illegal. Legislation designed to block and control in-migration contributes to a social environment in which immigration is defined as a problem, and contributes to the widely held conviction that immigration is to be resisted, curtailed and avoided – defined as a problem in legislation, immigrants become a problem in the real world of housing estates and job markets. As Le Voy and her colleagues conclude, "[d]iscrimination and outright violence against foreigners are encouraged by the language of illegality" (Le Voy et al, 2003, p 14). The exclusionary principles underlying European immigration policies cultivate a 'them' and 'us' posture, an 'othering' of the immigrant as a stranger and foreigner cloaked with suspicion, giving rise to tension and conflict between host and newcomer; throughout the EU hostility to immigrants is rife. In the lexicon of the xenophobe, the descriptor 'immigrant' applies to all who share or are suspected of sharing their stereotypical characteristics – ethnic appearance, skin type, clothing, behaviour, religious affiliation, and so forth. Established ethnic communities comprising second and third generations are thereby caught up in the anti-immigrant hysteria, ratcheting up the hostility already directed towards these communities by some sections of society.

Zygmunt Bauman, in his wide-ranging consideration of what he labels 'the human consequences of globalisation' (1998a, 1998b), links these issues of xenophobia and racism to a wider picture, and in the process reveals himself as one of the inspirations for the analysis advocated by Papastergiadis in the quotation cited at the beginning of this chapter:

> ...the mysterious 'global financial markets' are much less visible to an unarmed eye than are ostensible threats to collective security: in our world of massive migration, in the world increasingly populated with voluntary tourists and involuntary vagabonds, it is difficult not to notice the stubborn and vexing presence of foreigners, aliens and strangers.... And since invisible, difficult to grasp phenomena tend to be explained by the tangible, close-to-hand experience – the mysterious and elusive threats to individual identity tend to be placed at the doorstep of an all too tangible enemy: the stranger next door. It matters little that the deepest causes of the erosion of collective identities lies elsewhere. (Bauman, 1998a, p 8)

For Bauman, "[e]nforced localisation [that is, immigration control] guards the natural selectivity of the globalising effects" (1998b, p 93). The 'tourist' is the welcome immigrant, the executive and the skilled labourer as well as the affluent holidaymaker; the 'vagabond', in Bauman's vocabulary, is the unwelcome visitor, the poor and the destitute, to be allowed in only on sufferance. Among the uncertainties of globalisation, says Bauman, "governments cannot honestly promise its citizens secure existence and certain future; but they may for a time ... unload at least part of the accumulated anxiety (and even profit from it electorally) by demonstrating their energy and determination in waging war against foreign job-seekers and other alien gate-crashers" (Bauman, 1998a, p 11).

Institutional interventions

While xenophobia and racism provide an encompassing and influential backdrop in determining the conditions of settlement among immigrant communities – albeit varying in intensity from place to place and from time to time – of arguably equal importance is the degree and form of institutional intervention; in particular the extent to which the state intervenes (alone or in conjunction with non-governmental organisations [NGOs] and other agencies) to facilitate and smooth the integration of foreigners at a national and local level.

Fred Boal (2000) has recently joined several other researchers in speculating how differences at the macro-institutional level can affect settlement experience (see also Musterd and Ostendorf, 1998; Baldwin-Edwards, 2002). Specifically, these researchers have suggested that there is a strong relationship between the extent to which states have developed their social security and welfare systems and levels of social polarisation and immigrant exclusion and that, in this respect, a broad distinction can be discerned between different welfare regimes. Following Esping-Andersen (1990, 1996), Boal argues that the key issue here is the level of decommodification of social welfare provision. He hypothesises an association between high levels of state welfare provision and low levels of immigrant segregation and discrimination; theoretically, at least, the higher the level of egalitarian state intervention, for instance in the housing and job markets, the less the degree of spatial segregation and discrimination. Boal cites the relative lack of ethnic segregation in Paris and Amsterdam as evidence, but his comparisons are with cities in the US and Australia; whether such distinctions explain the nuances of difference between the member countries of the EU is questionable[9]. As Musterd and Ostendorf have observed in reflecting on such an association "[r]eality proves to be much more complicated than this simple continuum [of welfare state regimes] suggests" (1998, p 7). Yet, in their country-by-country examination of the relationship between institutional structures and the integration of immigrants, Dörr and Faist (1997) conclude that, "the degree and kind of regulations" are indeed crucial for the integration of immigrants and that "far-reaching public commitment offers the best chance to integrate migrants into welfare state provisions" (p 423). For example, in their consideration of immigrant access to housing, Dörr and Faist, imply that the housing needs of immigrant and ethnic groups have been best served in the UK and the Netherlands, where they have access to public housing provided by local authorities and housing associations in the context of anti-discrimination legislation. However, as we argue in the next chapter, whatever initial advantages this might have conferred on immigrants to the UK and the Netherlands, they have been eroded by the residualisation of public housing consequent on its progressive commodification since the 1980s (see also Murie, 1998). Wusten and Musterd (1998) conclude in their overview of urban segregation in western cities with the observation that:"welfare states are multi-dimensional and they do not necessarily change in all respects in the same direction at the same time. They also create their own reality and scale of evaluation" (p 242). The implication of this comment is that the experience of settlement by different immigrant groups varies from country to country, with immigrants who enter countries characterised by entrenched and pervasive welfare states faring better, on average, than immigrants entering countries with less well-established welfare provision. But the association is not consistent across time or space – as with so many social welfare issues, a detailed understanding of processes and outcomes requires a careful investigation of the specific histories and trajectories of change in each country.

In considering the 'context of reception' and the impact this has on the integration of immigrants, it is perhaps institutional interventions at the meso- and micro-levels of the municipality and neighbourhoods that have some of the most tangible and immediate effects on immigrant experience. As Body-Gendrot and Martiniello (2000, p 4) argue, the growing complexity of society is reflected in the difficulty central governments have in effectively "impos[ing] rules from the top". In their view this leads to the "hyperlocalisation of the social" and the "relegation of the treatment of complex social problems to the local sphere". Certainly at this level the engagement is with the practicalities of everyday life. While general policies and legislative measures are devised mostly at the national or regional level, it is at the local authority level that the economic, social and cultural problems of migration are experienced on a daily basis. It is here that migrants end up, this is where the problems of housing, employment, and of promoting coexistence and integration are directly tackled. It is at this local level that the pressures on resources and capacities of public social services and NGO service providers are most immediately felt.

While local level initiatives have long characterised areas of immigrant settlement, for the most part these have been low-key in terms of local authority investment and, often, largely the product of the initiative of NGOs and charitable organisations. A consequence of this historic and sometimes wilful neglect, is that many local authorities are now faced not only with the problem of the integration of recently arrived immigrants, but also with the alienation and exclusion of long-standing, former immigrant communities. In recent years several cities have developed initiatives designed to tackle some of these issues. These 'integration pacts', as they have been labelled (Council of Europe, 2003a), are to found across Europe: for example, in Italy, Bologna has its 'Convivere la citta' ('Living together in the city'), in Spain, Barcelona has developed a 'Municipal Immigration Plan', while in France, Paris set up in 2001 a 'Conseil de la Citoyennete des Parisiens non Communautaires' ('Council for the citizenship of Parisians from non-EU countries') and in Germany, Stuttgart initiated its 'Ein Bündnis für integration' ('A pact for integration') in 2002. These 'pacts' are of course tailored to the particular requirements of the localities in which they operate, but they share a number of common objectives and procedures. Their prime goal is the promotion of social cohesion, integration and peaceful coexistence between immigrant and local populations. These objectives are achieved by, variously: promoting the equal access of immigrant and ethnic communities to housing and employment throughout the locality, providing language and vocational training for immigrants, and by educating and informing the local population about the social and economic realities of immigration and cultural diversity. Importantly, they all stress and devote considerable resources to the establishment of participatory forums for discussion, debate and negotiation between interested parties from the public, private and civil sectors of society.

Given that most of these pacts were established in the late 1990s and early 2000s, it is perhaps too early to evaluate their effectiveness. However, the success or otherwise of these 'pacts' is clearly dependent not only on their adoption as "a vital aim of municipal policy" (Council of Europe, 2003a, p 111) and on their ability to shape local services and support structures to the needs of immigrants (White, 1999, p 217; Chapter Six this volume), but also on the support and backing they get from central and federal state governments and indeed, perhaps increasingly, from the EU itself, in terms of the legal establishment of the rights of immigrants regarding their access to public services such as social housing, and concomitant legislation regarding the outlawing of discriminatory action. National interventions in this respect tend to take the form of 'equal opportunities' and 'anti-discrimination' legislation, and in the setting up of 'social funds' to support positive interventions in the education and training of immigrants. However, there are clear tensions and frictions between, on the one hand, national policies which attempt to inhibit immigration in the name of perceived national interests and the consequent demonising of immigrants (as we have stressed in the previous section) in the eyes of the host society, and on the other hand, national and local policies which, in pursing integration objectives, are in effect attempting to compensate for the consequences of these exclusion measures. Recent proposals which attempt to reconcile these conflicting goals and outcomes by marrying control with integration, seem to rely on a combination of relocating and distancing control functions, as with the establishment of 'European Union mobility service points' in the origin countries, and the softening of the 'Fortress Europe' image by re-casting the language of exclusion such that the negative imagery of 'immigration control' now appears in a more positive light as 'people flow and management' (see Veenkamp et al, 2003; Open Democracy, 2004). Whatever the eventual impact of such proposals, in the wake of the consequences of 9/11, they seem spectacularly out of touch with prevailing political realities. As a recent Council of Europe report observes:

> Since 11 September the immigration debate has been dominated by security and border control concerns. Governments have changed their political priorities: the legitimate aim of the fight against terrorism has been accompanied by a tightening of immigration policies while integration has taken second place. Besides, 11 September has affected the public's perception of foreigners and national and religious minorities ... who are now often seen as a potential threat to national security and to [the] fundamental values of host societies. (Council of Europe, 2003b)

In such a context, 'immigration' and 'immigrant' are imbued with strong negative imagery fostering at best ambiguity and at worst hostility on the part of sections of reception societies, and cultivating fear and uncertainty among migrants and their communities.

Networks of associations

Notwithstanding the lure of "cosmopolitanism and adventure" (Papastergiadis, 2000, p 51), migration can be an alienating experience – even for the documented economic migrant with prearranged job and accommodation – challenging norms of behaviour, testing accepted values and calling into question a migrant's sense of self and the coherence of personal and social identity (see Chambers, 1994). For those at the nether end of the hierarchy of vulnerability, such challenges and tests threaten estrangement and isolation. Having survived the rigours and hazards of the migrant journey and caught up in the ambiguity of settlement created by an often deeply suspicious host society, asylum seekers, refugees, and clandestine migrants together with those legal migrants who lack the immediate wherewithal for survival, find in the comfort and support offered by a community or network of kin or ethnic associates an essential lifeline. These networks of association offer a vital connection for the transient, linking origin and destination, re-territorialising the temporally de-territorialised (Appadurai, 1997; Papastergiadis, 2000, ch 5) through the reassurance of familiar customs and milieu.

Migration is rarely an individual act; rather it is a social undertaking, a process facilitated by a variety of formal and informal networks which provide information on possible destinations, on the likelihood of entry, on the routes to follow and the contacts to make as well as providing finance (in the form of credit) to resource the journey[10]. For the professional economic migrant, such networks are typically highly formal and institutionalised; for the refugee and asylum seeker, the unskilled migrant and the undocumented, these networks are often informal and frequently operate on the margins of legality. On arrival at the destination country, networks of associates in the form of already established kin or ethnic communities, can offer emotional and material support, providing the reassurance of a familiar culture and language, of customary behavioural practices and religious observance. The networks of association in such communities can smooth entry to a wider society, instructing the new migrant in what to expect and how to cope, in facilitating access to education and benefits, in securing work and somewhere to live. This role of communities sometimes receives support and encouragement from central and local governments. The attempt during the 1990s to develop 'empowerment zones' – a concept imported from the US – in France and the UK is a case in point. Within these zones community residents were encouraged, with the minimum of state intervention, to get together to formulate solutions to their problems, although, in the case of France's *zones franches*, the autonomy and self-help focus of the transatlantic model was subverted in favour of a more top-down, interventionist formulation, with city mayors cooperating with central government in defining objectives and guiding process (Body Gendrot, 1996; Body Gendrot and Martiniello, 2000, p 86).

In providing a secure base for settlement and access to the support networks that they provide, ethnic communities can certainly ease the process of negotiation with, and integration into, the wider society. However, it is important not to over stress the benefits of such communities. Many are riven by internal divisions relating to class, gender and other subtle and not so subtle hierarchies of power and influence, which can work to the disadvantage of certain immigrants such as, for example, female migrants caught up in disputes about 'appropriate' behaviour. They can also operate to inhibit integration by encouraging what Stuart Hall (1978) once described as 'a retreat to ethnicity', a way of avoiding or minimising contact with the reception society, particularly if that wider society manifests high degrees of hostility and enmity. Whether a migrant uses such communities as a launching pad into wider society or as a base for retreat, might reflect intentionality: whether a migrant views his or her stay as permanent or transitory, whether the goal of migration is to seek the long-term establishment of a new home or merely, in the shorter term, to accumulate remittances. Further, association with particular communities may inhibit integration in that migrants can be 'tarred' with the stigma and negative stereotyping that is often attributed to such areas, inhibiting access to jobs and credit. In the context of reception, networks of association provided by ethnic communities can empower or enfeeble (see Crisp, 1999).

Rights and resistance

The vulnerability of immigrants in their chosen country of settlement is further highlighted by the absence of citizenship. The social, civic and political rights accruing to citizens as members of a bounded nation state, define the line which divides resident from stranger, native from foreigner, 'us' from 'them'. Some categories of non-citizens may be granted certain rights and protections under domestic law, but these are distinguishable from the privileges granted to citizens by being selective and frequently time-limited. Variously immigrants do not qualify for certain basic freedoms and rights which are taken for granted by citizens of most EU countries: the right to non-conditional residence; the right to freedom of movement within individual member states and between EU countries; the automatic right to benefits and other welfare services; the right to vote and to participation in the democratic process; the right to family reunification and to marry citizens. Some migrants after appropriate periods of residence, which vary from country to country, have the opportunity to apply for naturalisation, but as the 'tests' of citizenship become more rigorous and demanding, even this right is being eroded. Lack of citizenship rights are a legal expression of social and political exclusion, an exclusion which is compounded and exacerbated by racism and xenophobia.

Rights, the EU and the Council of Europe

At the supranational level the concern with immigrant rights and integration has been uneven and lacking in focus in that it has been caught up in a wider concern about more general issues of rights and inequalities. In recent times the EU, in line with its attempts to develop a 'people flow and management programme', which seeks to marry immigration control with integration, has nominally, at least, been busy trying to ensure that immigrant rights (once they have taken up residence in the EU) are guaranteed and indeed expanded. The context of this concern with the fair treatment of immigrants is the belated recognition that immigration (albeit controlled and selective) is increasingly a necessity for the economic and social well-being of European society: as a recent report of the European Commission observed, "it is clear from an analysis of the economic and demographic context of the Union and of the countries of origin, that there is a growing recognition that the 'zero' immigration policies of the past 30 years are no longer appropriate" (European Commission, 2000, p 6). Indicative of these concerns are the institutional changes that accompanied the 1997 Treaty of Amsterdam, which saw certain migration issues (the granting of visas, asylum, immigration, and the free movement of persons) transferred from the third pillar to the first pillar of EU operations. Following this change, immigration was no longer a matter solely for intergovernmental coordination, but for action by the Council of Ministers based on proposals from the European Commission. The level of Commission activity in response to these newly bestowed powers has, however, been modest. Several declarations and guidelines have been issued relating to, for example, equality between people irrespective of racial or ethnic origin, the elimination of discrimination in employment and occupation on grounds of religion or belief, disability, age or sexual orientation, and the legal status of third country nationals who are long-term residents. In 2000 the Charter of Fundamental Rights – building on the 1989 Charter of Fundamental Social Rights of Workers, which required member states to guarantee to workers from non-member countries living and working conditions comparable to those of EU nationals – drew together in a single document the full range of civil, political, economic and social rights of European citizens and all EU residents. Constrained by the remit of its founding documents and by the principle of subsidiarity, the Commission's direct involvement in issues of immigrant rights and integration has so far been confined to politico-bureaucratic activities manifest predominantly in terms of exhortation and encouragement, rather than in terms of decisive intervention. In the area of immigrant affairs, as with so many other social and political issues, EU commissioners seem reluctant to expand the scope of their operations beyond those traditionally ascribed.

The Council of Europe's substantive commitment to immigrant rights and the combating of discrimination are of an altogether of a different order. From the establishment in 1953 of the European Court of Human Rights through to the setting up of the European Commission against Racism and Intolerance (ECRI) in 1993, the Council has consistently demonstrated its commitment to issues of social justice and equality of treatment, and its determination to fight racism, xenophobia and anti-Semitism. This concern reflects, of course, the very different remit given to the Council in comparison with the European Community at the time of its establishment. Nevertheless, ultimately the

Council's influence, as with the EU, is determined by the willingness to comply on the part of the participatory and signatory states.

One of the earliest acts of the Council was the establishment of the European Convention on Human Rights (1950) which focused on securing civil and political rights for residents of signatory states; in 1961 The European Social Charter added social and economic rights. The European Convention on the legal status of migrant workers, which came into force in 1983, was designed to complete the protection granted to migrants by the European Social Charter and was based on the principle of equality of treatment between migrants and nationals. In 1997 the European Convention on Participation of Foreigners in Local Public Life extended civil and political rights (freedom of opinion, assembly and association at the local level to foreign residents, as well as the right to vote and to stand as candidates in local authority elections). The Council has also been responsible for launching many other initiatives including the setting up of a Community Action Programme to combat discrimination.

While the attention paid to social and civil rights by supranational organisations may aid in the acceptance of these norms by national governments, it is still the prerogative of each government to decide whether or not to comply with international standards. As Julia Gray (2000, p 32) has observed, "[c]onsidering that individual rights are one of the primary characteristics of the classic citizenship model, the fact that their guarantor and provider continues to be the nation-state is crucial to our understanding of the implications of international migration. We may be witnessing a deterritorialization of social identity, but the locus of power in terms of citizenship rights still rests primarily with the nation-state".

Immigrant empowerment

Operating at a local, national and pan-national level, there are a plethora of pressure and lobby groups that address issues of immigrant rights and offer substantial challenges to racism and xenophobia. It is through membership of such organisations that immigrants get the opportunity to struggle directly for the betterment of their conditions. Scores, even hundreds, of such organisations can be identified in each member state of the EU. Their roles vary from the relatively modest – providing information and advice to immigrant groups in a local community, through to the more ambitious – bringing about change through lobbying and pressurising state authorities on behalf of migrants. The larger groups include the European Human Rights League, Amnesty International, the Council of Immigrant Associations in Europe, SOS-Racisme, and the Federation des Droits de l'Homme and Platform 'Fortress Europe'. All are concerned in various ways with monitoring rights, immigration legislation and discrimination, and acting as advocates for immigrants and as pressure groups to improve the conditions of settlement, especially of refugees, asylum seekers, and undocumented migrants and displaced persons (Leitner, 1997, pp 136-7).

One of the best known of these campaigning groups is Sans-Papier. What is notable about this organisation is its independence and autonomy; it was set up by and continues today to be run by the members of Sans-Papier themselves. Since its establishment in 1996, Sans-Papier has grown and expanded from a relatively small, local group to an international organisation with membership in all EU countries. The movement dates its origins to 18 March 1996 in Paris when 324 Africans, including 80 women and 100 children, occupied the church of Saint Ambroise (Hayter, 2000, p 142). Sans-Papier campaigns for the regularisation of all migrants who have no documentary proof of their right to residence, whether they are migrants who have entered 'illegally' or asylum seekers who have absconded or migrants who have overstayed their officially allotted time.

The importance of this movement is encapsulated in the terminology used, namely 'undocumented' rather than 'clandestine' – a deliberate choice reflecting a decision to 'come out from the shadows' where they lived in fear of discovery and of deportation, and declare themselves to the authorities and demand regularisation. In the time-honoured way of social movements, Sans-Papier has publicised its cause by marching, by organising petitions, through the occupation of key buildings, and by lobbying governments and legislatures. While tangible achievements at a European level has been rather modest, Sans-Papier has been successful in securing the regularisation of significant numbers of undocumented migrants in individual countries, and has even been persuasive enough to influence judicial outcomes; Body-Gendrot and Martiniello, for example, cite the French judges who ruled in favour of undocumented North African migrants to exercise their right to housing by occupying vacant public buildings (2000, p 85).

The Sans-Papier movement has been through lean phases, but its campaigns have nevertheless spread from France to neighbouring countries, especially Belgium and Italy. The European-wide demonstration on 31 January 2004 provides a good illustration of its international influence and its capacity to organise over the longer term. Pulling together over 50 organisations in the European Network of Migrants, Refugees and Sans-Papier, two years' work culminated in simultaneous protests and marches in 11 countries and 30 cities: Germany (Berlin, Frankfurt, Munich), England (London, Oxford, Liverpool), Austria (Vienna), Belgium (Brussels), Spain (Barcelona, Madrid, Malaga), France (Paris, Lille, Toulouse, Marseilles, Lyons, Rennes, Grenoble, Calais), Greece (Athens), Ireland (Galway), Italy (Rome, Turin, Bologna), Portugal (Lisbon), Switzerland (Geneva, Fribourg, Lausanne, Bern, Basel). The opening paragraph of the manifesto produced for the occasion captures the intent of the event and indeed the motivation that drives the entire movement:

> Facing the development of Fortress Europe which denies the most fundamental rights of immigrant and refugee people (housing, healthcare, financial support, paid work, education, citizenship, freedom of movement and of settlement...), it has become essential to bring together the struggles of people who have no

rights. Everywhere in Europe, victims of repressive European legislation are fighting for their basic rights and survival. The perspective of a network crossing national borders aims to create a collective, autonomous, mutual accountable force, led by the protagonists themselves, and capable of responding to the increased economic and political attacks in Europe that governments are promoting. (European Network, 2004)

The specific demands of the manifesto included: freedom of movement and settlement, the closure of all detention camps in all European countries, an end to all deportations and the right to citizenship and permanent residency for all, the unconditional regularisation (right to stay) for all undocumented migrants and the right for children to live with their families.

The activities of Sans-Papier in facilitating the empowerment of immigrants and demonstrating their capability for resistance and unwillingness to accept their lot, questions the assertion of Gubbay that those who are least privileged tend to "accommodate to their subordination, both because resistance appears impossible and because of the hope that compliance might earn them increased rights" (Gubbay, 1999, p 49).

Conclusion

Immigration highlights some of the most important and pressing ethical and moral dilemmas of modern society. The declarations and enactments of the EU and the European Council reveal the uneasy conscience of Europe. They provide an explicit recognition of the plight of immigrants, refugees and asylum seekers and give expression to a set of remedial targets and objectives. The failure to translate these targets and objectives into political and social practice, however, belie their intent. Interventions on behalf of immigrants by state governments through the enforcement of anti-discriminatory legislation and the enactment of effective inclusionary policies are at best fragmentary and always contradicted by the aggressive pursuit of policies and programmes designed to block entry and eject the unwanted.

The position of immigrants (especially those who make up the bottom tiers of the hierarchy of vulnerability: refugees, asylum seekers, temporary workers and undocumented migrants) is similar across all EU member countries. Variable national dispositions towards the treatment of immigrants, from the assimilationist standpoint of France, through the pluralist position of Scandinavia and, until recently[11], the exclusionary stance of Germany (Cesari, 2000, p 93), have had little impact in differentiating the treatment of immigrants. Caught in the crossfire between, on the one hand, the bureaucratic hostility and suspicion of the state, and, on the other hand, the racism and xenophobia of their reception societies, the fate of immigrants in every EU country has been remarkably similar. As the following chapters show, especially in relation to housing and homelessness, the mistreatment and exploitation of immigrants at the hands of the political, social and economic institutions and gatekeepers of society have been replicated across Europe. In this context, the relative ease or difficulty in accessing citizenship has had little impact on their experiences. In and of themselves the politico-bureaucratic formalities of citizenship, while arguably an important first step on the road to possible integration, are of little consequence beyond the official acquisition of the right of residence and the right to vote. Formal integration into the body politic, however, is rarely if ever matched by integration into the social fabric of European society.

Across Europe immigrants are welcomed (selectively) as workers, but rejected (mostly) as citizens. The explanation of this situation is complex and the subject of considerable ongoing debate and dispute. In this chapter – as elsewhere in this book – we have touched on elements of that debate, but in a rather instrumentalist manner. What we have not done, for it is beyond the scope of this text, is to explore the relationship between state ambiguity (welcoming some immigrants, rejecting others) and the prevailing, and increasingly vociferous[12] levels of societal racism and xenophobia. As the hate and antagonism of the far right melds into apparently respectable (for some), liberal misgivings about the goals of multiculturalism and the detrimental impact of immigration on the coherence of community and nation (for example, Goodhart, 2004), the prospects of the alleviation of the plight of immigrants seem as remote as ever. The remainder of this book considers the consequences for immigrants in relation to their housing conditions and vulnerability to homelessness.

Notes

[1] The usefulness of such binaries have, of course, been challenged from a variety of perspectives: by Castles and Kosack (1973) from political economy; by Phizaclea (1983) from feminism; by Abu-Lughod (1978) from a geographical and political perspective; and by Piore (1979) from a cultural/social perspective. See Cohen (1996) for an overview.

[2] Even for the professional migrants, however, migration is not without its perils. Wren and Boyle (2002), for instance, cite a growing body of evidence that suggests that "migration itself can be considered a pathogenic stressor causing ill health" (p 35).

[3] Information on the geographical pattern of migrant route ways to Europe suggests five main trajectories: three of these are land routes from the East. The most northerly goes through Russia, the Baltic and Poland. To the south a route winds through Ukraine, the Balkans and the Czech and Slovak Republics. The third route goes through Bulgaria, Romania and the Balkans. A fourth route transits the Middle East and Eastern Mediterranean. The final path crosses the Mediterranean from North Africa, mainly into Italy and the Iberian peninsula (Harding, 2000).

[4] www.united.non-profit.nl/pages/List.htm

[5] The following account has been compiled from newspaper reports in *The Guardian* (6-20 February 2004) and *The Scotsman* (6-13 February 2004) and from the following web

pages: www.morecambebay.com/ and news.bbc.co.uk/1/hi/england/lancashire/ 3465109.stm

[6] A gangmaster is someone who supplies casual labour to industry, taking on immigrant workers, often for an agency fee, and regulating everything from their accommodation to their place and conditions of employment. Many operate legally, others illegally and unscrupulously.

[7] Called snakeheads because a so-called 'snake of migrants' winds behind them, often illegally, across the world on the promise of employment.

[8] Eurobarometer 59.2, May-June 2003.

[9] There is, of course, some empirical evidence that might challenge this generalisation. In social democratic Sweden, for instance, where state equalitarian interventions are among the strongest in Europe, segregation of immigrants is still manifest (see for example, Özüekren and Magnnusson, 1997).

[10] Such networks have their down-side as well, especially for the most vulnerable, in the form of exploitive people traffickers and gangmasters (see Morecombe Bay case study).

[11] In May 1999 Germany removed many of its long-standing barriers to citizenship for former immigrants with a major reform of the regulations governing the naturalisation of foreign nationals.

[12] As manifest in the recent proliferation and political success of anti-immigration (immigrant) and racist political parties: for example, Vlaams Bloc (Belgium), BNP (UK), People's Party (Denmark), Freedom Party (Austria), National Front (France), Law and Order Offensive Party (Germany), National Alliance and Northern League (Italy), Pim Fortuyn List (the Netherlands).

FOUR

Immigrants and European housing markets

Introduction

Over the past decade there has been a profusion of publications focusing on the housing and living conditions of immigrants in European countries, and in particular, in the larger cities. These studies have focused on a variety of topics: the spatial pattern of their settlement (for example, Kesteloot and Van der Haegen, 1997), the pathways they develop through the housing market (for example, Bolt and Van Kempen, 2002), the quality of their housing (for example, Drever and Clark, 2002), self-help and housing (for example, Kreibich, 2000) as well as issues of citizenship (for example, Faist and Häubermann, 1996), racism (for example, Daly, 1996) and purchasing power and social status (for example, White and Hurdley, 2003). Only a minority of these publications, however, adopt a comparative European perspective (for example, Musterd and Ostendorf, 1998)

This chapter attempts to develop a European-wide perspective on the present housing circumstances of immigrants in Europe. It seeks to develop an understanding of these circumstances in terms of several interrelated processes, operating at variety of scales: the state, the region, the neighbourhood and the household. When examined in this way it becomes readily apparent that, in a post-war timeframe, the present precarious housing situations of many immigrants in Europe are not unusual. It is also clear that, in general, a process of progression through the housing market is recognisable for many migrant households who have arrived since the Second World War. Understanding this process of slowly improving housing circumstances may provide important insights for a European policy designed to fight housing exclusion and homelessness among immigrants.

This chapter is structured around three particular aspects of migrant housing circumstances in Europe. The first of these is the restructuring of welfare states, especially the ongoing process of commodification, which fundamentally influences the operation and organisation of the European housing market (see Edgar et al, 2002). Second, there are the housing strategies of immigrants themselves. It is important to recognise that poorly housed people are not passive victims responding to macro-social processes; when denied easy access to the private housing market or to social housing, immigrants can call upon reciprocal arrangements embedded in the social networks of their communities

(Granovetter, 1973) to access housing in the informal sector. The third component determining the nature of immigrant housing is the socio-spatial context in which immigrants live and work. The socio-spatial context refers to the tangible environments in which houses are located, in which they are purchased or rented, in which people live, in which social capital is developed and in which the services of the welfare state are redistributed. The interplay between these three components gives rise to the diversity of current immigrant housing circumstances, which vary from the palatial housing of the international executive on the one hand to the rented mattresses of the undocumented migrant arriving from the developing countries on the other.

In a further section of this chapter, in the context of examining the socio-spatial characteristics of immigrant settlement, we develop a critique of the concept of 'social mix' (sometimes called 'social balance'). For many central state and local state governments the mixing of immigrants with the local population to avoid undesirable 'ghettoisation' of immigrant communities has been a central concern of policy decisions and resource allocation – the dispersion of asylum seekers from concentrations near their point of entry is one of the latest manifestations of this policy. Following this, we examine the relation between racism and access to housing for immigrants. One of the focal points here is the systematic charging of higher rents in the private market for immigrants, a feature prevalent throughout the EU. Finally, a set of conclusions is presented: this includes a comparative analysis of the 15 EU member countries, which are divided into four subgroups based on their migration history (recent or established) and the present capacity of the state to intervene in the housing market through the allocation of social rented housing.

Commodification of housing in Europe

Since the mid-1980s, European housing markets have undergone considerable changes. In general, two important trends are recognised. The first concerns the so-called process of commodification, referring to the increasing dominance of the market in the provision and distribution of housing. The second important trend relates to the changing role of the state: from a provider of housing to a provider of opportunities, enabling different housing initiatives relying on decentralisation and the involvement of NGOs and private sector initiatives.

Commodification and access to housing

The growing importance of the market in the provision of housing is apparent in all European countries, albeit unevenly. Before explaining in more detail this trend of commodification, we briefly point to three important contextual developments, that is, the post-Fordist restructuring of the labour market, the new spatial organisation of cities and the ongoing regionalisation of housing markets.

First, the post-Fordist restructuring of the labour market has seen an expansion in the number of high-salaried occupations, involving an increasing demand for expensive, high-quality dwellings in inner-city locations and a diverse range of rural settings. Given the more global and flexible organisation of the labour process, cities all over the world (including Europe) compete to attract affluent inhabitants, while the provision of public housing for the poor is frequently neglected. Second, new modes of economic regulation associated with globalisation and post-Fordist capitalism have also brought about major changes in the built environment of many European cities. Two important processes are at work: on the one hand, the reshaping of the commercially built environment, entailing the construction of new hotels and other infrastructure to accommodate mobile professionals and executive workers; on the other hand, the selective building of dwellings for the highest income classes. The disappearance of hundreds of thousands of cheap dwellings is an important consequence of this gentrification processes; in France, for instance, it has been estimated that since the mid-1980s, about 100,000 cheap private dwellings have disappeared from the market (Betton, 2001). However, this 'new spatial logic' of the city is not confined to the central city, it affects entire urban areas. One of the results is the increasing spatial segregation of the different classes (Donzelot and Jaillet, 1997). This is clearly illustrated by the social housing estates in Porto; many of these developments, as well as the typical Portuguese slums in the metropolitan peripheries, are built in inaccessible areas, cut off from the rest of the city (Bruto da Costa and Baptista, 2001). Although the layout of cities clearly varies between Southern and Northern Europe, the chief principles of the new urban-spatial logic is to be found in all major cities of Europe. The recently performed cross-European URBEX-research has illustrated this very well (see Musterd and Murie, 2002).

Third, in the context of increasing commodification, the growing economic competition among regions and cities has led to a more pronounced regionalisation of housing markets; there does not exist one unified European market, nor even national housing markets (Saey and Van Nuffel, 2003). These regional housing markets not only reflect present-day socioeconomic and socio-political factors, but also the historical legacy of regionally differentiated housing provision. In the case of Belgium, for example, lower house prices and lower housing quality are associated with 19th and 20th-century developments. In contrast, regions in the vicinity of Brussels (the economic core of the country) have been characterised by much higher housing prices. Another factor at play is that Flanders is in general wealthier than Wallonia, leading towards higher housing prices in the north of the country. Taking into account all these factors, access to housing, particularly for those people living on the official Belgium minimum income, differs strongly from region to region (De Decker, 2001).

These three trends reflect the new growth cycle of the post-Fordist economy and are crucial in understanding growing home ownership in most European countries since the early 1980s. Specifically, the growth in home ownership has been encouraged by various subsidies and by the ready availability of mortgages. Households with sufficient purchasing power can afford to own their own dwelling, thereby escaping from increasing rents in the private market (because of the continuous inflation) or from poor quality housing. The effect of this trend has been most clearly visible in those countries with a less pronounced tradition of home ownership.

The deep economic crisis of the 1970s and early 1980s also encouraged the state to slow down its direct intervention as a provider of housing and shifted state expenditure towards supplementing incomes and other social issues. It is within this context that the 'right to buy' (a specific housing policy enabling sitting tenants in the social rental sector to purchase their dwelling) should be understood. The impact of this policy has been considerable across Europe. In Scotland for instance, the share of social rented dwellings declined by 34% between 1979 and 1999, with over 400,000 properties sold off, and in England the effect has been equally dramatic: between 1991 and 2002 over 1 million dwellings were lost from the public housing sector, a reduction of 30% (Wilcox, 2003). Also, in the city of Copenhagen, 7% of the municipally owned dwellings were on the free market between 1993 and 2000.

However, increasing ownership has not only to do with the sale of social housing. It also points to a remarkable trend among low-income groups who buy their own dwellings in order to escape from dramatic rent rises or to find an alternative to the shrinking stock of public housing. This ownership, known as 'enforced home ownership', frequently leads to poor housing conditions as the concerned households purchase low-quality dwellings that they cannot repair because of lack of sufficient funds. Enforced home ownership is mostly found in countries with a long tradition of home ownership (such as Italy; see Tosi, 2001a), in both rural and urban settings (see Meert et al, 2002).

Enforced home ownership and gentrification processes illustrate that the owner-occupied housing market is clearly bifurcating. On the one hand, the lowest income groups own their dwelling, sometimes in very uncomfortable circumstances, such as Belgian and Dutch households living in owner-occupied caravans or chalets; on the other hand, the high-salaried groups own expensive and opulent dwellings. However, as most European countries have further deregulated the private housing market, this bifurcation is also seen in privately rented accommodation, reflecting both rack-renting at the bottom and high-cost privately rented apartments at the top. The case of Brussels demonstrates that immigrants are well represented in both segments of the rental housing market: on the one hand, asylum seekers and undocumented migrants are victims of rack-renters, while international executives, lobbyists and European civil servants occupy the most expensive segment of the rental housing market on the other.

Access to housing and the changing role of the state

Most European states have not only restyled their social housing policy, but have restructured it fundamentally. This is illustrated by the fact that everywhere in Europe housing expenditure has declined since the 1980s as a share of national budgets and that private housing outlays have increased in virtually every country as restraints have been imposed on public spending. Almost everywhere the production of new social rented housing has declined consistently since the early 1980s. This is even the case among the most robust welfare state regimes of Europe. Indeed, in the past, the Scandinavian welfare states have been largely characterised by access for all to wide-ranging social security, social welfare and social housing provision. However, budget constraints have also affected these Nordic welfare states and have resulted in severe cutbacks in spending.

Throughout Europe the erosion of housing subsidies and the privatisation of the existing social rental dwellings have increased the pressure on a diminishing stock. At the same time, the reduction in benefit levels has meant that fewer people are able to meet the rising cost of housing (Edgar et al, 1999). The process of a narrowing welfare state has coincided with a gradual increase in the number of immigrants from a wider range of countries than in the recent past. In general, changing housing policy is reflected in three interrelated trends. First, responsibilities have been decentralised from central government to regional and municipal layers of government. Second, the changing role of local government to 'enabling authorities' is reflected by a move to non-governmental institutional structures to meet social housing objectives. Third, as Ball and Harloe (1998) have argued, changing housing policy is also reflected in a decreasing political priority for (social) housing which is itself reflected in a shift towards 'weakly regulated market structures' and a greater reliance on private finance to meet social housing objectives. These trends should be considered within the context of the Maastricht Treaty, which compelled member states to pursue a social policy more reliant on market-oriented approaches than previously. The collective outcome of these trends, including more insecurity and vulnerability in the housing market, is also strengthened by the historically weak welfare role of housing in the development of social welfare regimes in most European countries (Edgar et al, 2002).

With the exception of Sweden and Denmark, a European-wide trend identified by several authors (see Oxley and Smith, 1996; Van der Heijden, 2002) is the shift from supply-side to demand-side subsidies. This trend is seen as one of the most important reasons explaining increasing housing costs. Indeed, the growing importance of demand-side subsidies enables the private housing sector to play a more prominent role as the provider of bricks and mortar and in determining rents and selling prices. In contrast, in the case of supply-side subsidies, the state provides cheap and affordable housing for the lowest income groups. Those households who are nowadays no longer eligible for social housing (because of the commodification of the stock and the decreasing supply by the state), will have to rely on the private rental sector as home ownership is not a feasible option. This will also include those who do not have residence or citizenship qualification, such as asylum seekers and undocumented migrants and others at the lower end of the hierarchy of vulnerability (see Chapter Two).

From a broader time perspective, we notice that this changing role of the state in housing policy has developed at a time when it has been perceived that crude housing shortages have largely ended. However, the re-emergence of shortages of affordable social housing, the re-establishment of the link between poverty and poor housing and an increasing segment of households at risk of homelessness or living in precarious circumstances has again emerged in Europe (see Ball and Harloe, 1998). Historically, governments have tended to intervene in the housing market to break the link between poverty and poor housing when it was perceived that this could damage social, political or economic stability (Malpass and Murie, 1997). While recent changes in the housing market in Europe indeed suggest that the link between low income and poor housing is being re-established, direct intervention by the state fails to occur.

Summary

Since the late 1970s, access to the different European housing markets is almost everywhere embedded in a context of increasing commodification. This has gone hand in hand with a changing role of the state: from a provider of housing towards that of an enabler, allowing other and (new) key players to allocate housing in a context of growing economic liberalisation. From a broader sociological perspective, it has become clear that these housing-related trends are accompanied by other contextual developments, such as the restructuring of the labour market and the new logic of spatial organisation of our cities.

Immigrant strategies in accessing European housing markets

As access to housing is more and more arranged by principles of the free market and since the state is no longer the central distributor of housing resources for low-income households, community networks and reciprocal arrangements come to the fore in providing low-income households with an alternative strategy for finding a place to live. This is particularly the case for immigrants from 'Third World' countries and from transition states. They do not have the purchasing power to own or to rent decent dwellings on the private market, nor are they eligible for housing allowances or other public housing initiatives. In this context, their housing strategies should be understood as individual or household undertakings designed to cope with increasing housing costs and declining public initiatives. The current European housing markets are thus characterised by significant marginal and informal housing initiatives. These initiatives often rely on the principles of the free market, an extreme example of which is the hiring of beds and sofas in Madrid that are rented for eight hours, three times a day to immigrants from South and Central America. Such housing circumstances bear witness to an extreme exploitation of these vulnerable households by those who offer these alternative (informal) dwellings and to the fact that access to such accommodation is mostly facilitated by functional social networks among ethnic communities (Granovetter, 1973).

The following section examines the ways, in a variety of European contexts, immigrants access housing, first in the owner-occupied market, second in the privately rented market and third in the social housing sector. We conclude this section with a discussion of the most dramatic housing circumstances of immigrants across Europe, a range of situations that border on rooflessness. While such circumstances are not exclusively linked to strategies relying on immigrant social networks, aspects of civil society and reciprocity (Polanyi, 1944; Kesteloot and Meert, 2000) are more pronounced than in the other housing strategies.

Immigrant housing strategies and (enforced) home ownership

Generally speaking, home ownership goes hand in hand with an increasing purchasing power. However, there is at the same time a lot of evidence to indicate that many immigrants are forced into purchasing a house as a 'last resort' strategy for escaping rising rents on the private market. In **Ireland**, O'Sullivan (2003) shows that returning Irish immigrants and immigrants from the EU have access to the existing range of housing and allied welfare services, restricted only by income and wealth. Although difficult to verify, he writes that it has often been suggested at the level of anecdote, that returning Irish immigrants bring home with them considerable cash reserves earned abroad, thus easing their entry to home ownership and contributing to the escalation of house prices. Moreover, as Barrett and O'Connell (2001) demonstrate, returning Irish immigrants are heavily drawn from those with third level educational qualifications and they earn more than those who stayed in Ireland. On the other hand, clearly not all returning Irish citizens are in a position to purchase their own homes, and many of those who returned may now be on the local authority housing waiting list, although it is not possible to quantify this (O'Sullivan, 2003).

The Belgian housing census of 1991 made it possible to distinguish between three qualitative levels of both the rental and the owner-occupied sectors[1]. Combining the year of construction with the level of amenities within the dwelling allows the delineation of a *primary* sector of comfortable and recently built dwellings (post-1945), a *moderate* sector comprises older dwellings with amenities, and a *residual* sector of dwellings that lack basic conveniences, regardless of the year of construction.

In **Flanders**, the northern part of Belgium, richer foreign nationals often tend to own a dwelling. Their length of residence may also play a role (De Decker and Kesteloot, 2003). Consequently, owing to their socioeconomic position and their longer presence in Belgium, Italians figure prominently among owner-occupiers; some have even built their own houses. As Figure 4.1 shows, their housing situation is similar to that of the Belgians who live in

Flanders. It is remarkable that the share of residual home ownership (or enforced home ownership) is even lower among Italians than among Belgians. In contrast, fewer Spaniards are owner-occupiers, due in part to their lack of residential security. Many returned to Spain following the restoration of democracy in 1975 and the subsequent economic development of the country. Furthermore, Spaniards are established more in the cities than the Italians, where rented dwellings are over-represented and consequently the opportunities for owner-occupation are less. Turkish and Moroccan immigrants have a low socioeconomic status and have been resident for a shorter period of time than either Italians or Spaniards and hence few are owner-occupiers. The lower percentages of owner-occupation among Moroccans than for the Turks are in part attributable to the stricter interpretation of the Koran by the former, which prohibits a mortgage, because interest on loans is considered as theft (Meert et al, 1997). Furthermore, the pronounced rural mentality of the Turks could play a role here, in that investing in real estate is seen an important means of acquiring status. Turkish home ownership, however, is partly due to the application of a need-induced purchase strategy (explaining the relatively high shares of residual home ownership (Figure. 4.1). Under pressure from social displacement and rising rents, they purchase a dwelling in a poor condition, which is cheaper than renting a slum dwelling. In the process, they create relative housing security, but these owners usually have no money to renovate the dwelling. Similar patterns of home ownership are displayed among these immigrant groups in the Brussels Capital Region.

Figure 4.1: Housing market sectors, percentage of households of some nationalities (Flanders)

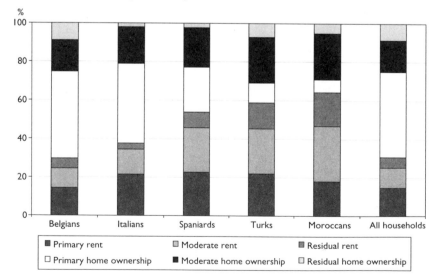

Source: Belgian National Census 1991

In the **United Kingdom**, immigrants from south Asia are more likely to be in owner-occupation than immigrants associated with black or other ethnic communities. However, they often live in relatively poor conditions (for example, older terraced housing in need of modernisation) and have relatively low incomes (Bowes and Sim, 2002). It has been argued that the UK government's social exclusion agenda that targets resources at the most deprived geographical areas will miss impoverished black minority and other ethnic communities living in mixed tenure areas (Gill, 2002). Among Indian households, many have been relatively economically successful, but this is often linked to self-employment and can result in vulnerability to mortgage repossession in the event of business failure (notably where business loans are secured against the family home). However, detailed studies have shown that attitudes of minority groups to owner-occupation and borrowing were very varied (Bowes and Sim, 2002, p 50). For instance, Anderson (2003) stresses a reluctance on the part of some ethnic groups to borrow for mortgage purposes because they view paying interest as immoral; this is also the case with the Moroccan households in Belgium. In both cases this reluctance presents an important obstacle to expanding ownership.

Regarding **Germany**, Busch-Geertsema (2003) found that the ownership levels among foreign residents in West Germany has continued to rise in the past years (from 3.5% in 1972 to 5.9% in 1978, 8.1% in 1987, 11.4% in 1993, to a provisional high of 12.4% in 1998). However, this rate is still very low, and it is even lower in East Germany (1998: 4.6 %; see Stabu, 2000). Moreover, as we have already illustrated for several European countries, home ownership among immigrants does not always equal decent housing circumstances. Moreover, as Häußermann and Siebel (2001, p 22) state,

> ... [the rising share of owners] must not be taken out of context as an indicator of successful integration. One explanation could be that foreigners are excluded from the affordable segment of the higher quality rental market through discrimination. The acquisition of a dwelling is therefore a way out of a dreadful housing situation.

Although there is also no detailed statistical evidence, several studies suggest that home ownership and poor housing quality is also to be found among specific minority ethnic groups in **Austria**. Schoibl (2003), for instance, writes that while 62.2 % of Austrian citizens occupy their own dwelling, this is only the case for 12.9% of all foreign residents, with particularly low percentages among former Yugoslavs (6.8 %) and Turks (2.9%). In an exemplary study of the housing situation of labour immigrants in an urban area of the provincial capital Salzburg, Freudenthaler et al (1994) found extremely overcrowded housing conditions among Turkish and Yugoslavian owner-occupiers of flats.

Contrary to the mainstream development across Europe, in the **Netherlands**, the share of owner-occupiers among Mediterranean immigrants dropped from 19.8% in 1981 to just 5.4% in 1994. During the same period, the percentage

Figure 4.2: Type of immigrant housing in France (1996)

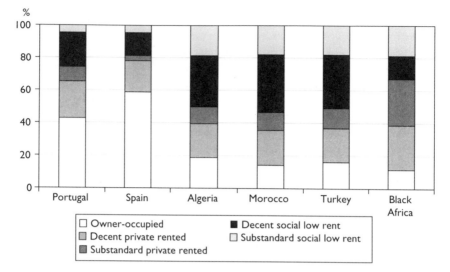

Source: Boëldieu and Thave (1996)

of owner-occupiers among the Dutch population rose from 42.8% to 48.5%. The relatively lower quality of immigrant owner-occupied housing compared to that of the native (Dutch) owners remains a characteristic in the Netherlands as elsewhere (De Feyter, 2002).

In **France**, an INSEE survey dating from 1999 showed that over half of longer-established European immigrants have become homeowners. However, immigrants from the Maghreb who are owners (Morocco 13%, Algeria 17%), Turkey (16%) and Black Africa (10%) are much less well placed and wide equality gaps persist (see Figure 4.2; Maurel, 2003).

Southern European countries have a long-lasting tradition of home ownership. In the Lombardy region of **Italy** (especially around Milan), one of the richest districts of the country, the home ownership rate is nearly 70%, but 40% of the households in this area who are recorded as below the poverty threshold also own their homes (Tosi, 2001a). As Figure 4.3 illustrates, home ownership is not limited to Italian citizens. In 2001, more than 17% of Latin-American immigrants owned their dwellings, while this was also approximately the case for 10% of East European, Asian and African immigrants. Figure 4.4 shows that home ownership also increased among immigrants between 1990 and 2001, especially among the Latin-American immigrants in the Milan area[2], reflecting the home purchase by more affluent immigrants who have succeeded in increasing their purchasing power by successful participation in the labour market or by successful business development. However, as Tosi suggests (2003), home ownership among immigrants does not necessarily mean that they presently all live in decent circumstances.

Figure 4.3: Housing circumstances of immigrants in Lombardy (Italy), according to origin (2001)

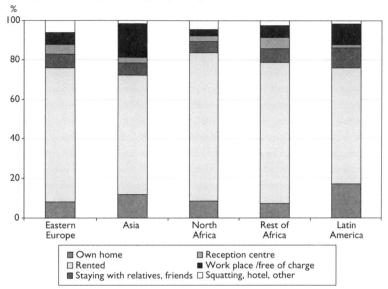

%

Eastern Europe	Asia	North Africa	Rest of Africa	Latin America

■ Own home　　　　　　　　　　　　■ Reception centre
□ Rented　　　　　　　　　　　　　　■ Work place /free of charge
■ Staying with relatives, friends　　□ Squatting, hotel, other

Source: Ismu e Province of Milan-Bicocca (2001)

Figure 4.4: Immigrant housing in the Milan area, by nationality (1990-2001)

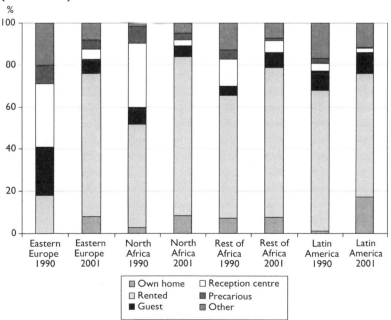

%

Eastern Europe 1990	Eastern Europe 2001	North Africa 1990	North Africa 2001	Rest of Africa 1990	Rest of Africa 2001	Latin America 1990	Latin America 2001

■ Own home　　　□ Reception centre
□ Rented　　　　　■ Precarious
■ Guest　　　　　　■ Other

Source: Ismu e Province of Milan-Bicocca (2001)

In Athens (**Greece**), ownership among all foreign residents amounted to 8.2% in 1999. The Albanians are a case in point. Sapounakis (2003) refers to data of the Albanian Embassy, which state that 30% of Albanians, after 10 years of work, own a small business, while up to 70% have bought a car, and a recent survey for the city shows that nearly 6% of them owned their home in 1999. However, no details about quality are available for this specific group of Albanians.

Home ownership among immigrants has also increased in Scandinavian countries, reflecting the growing commodification of housing in welfare states that were until the mid-1980s characterised by a clear dominance of state-controlled allocation of housing. In **Denmark**, for instance, Koch-Nielsen (2003) argues that home ownership has become more and more important among Yugoslavian, Pakistani and Turkish immigrants. In particular, former Yugoslavs move from the rented to home ownership sectors. Unfortunately, there are no specific data available about the housing quality within this – still limited – ownership sector. In **Sweden**, just 27% of immigrants born outside the Nordic neighbouring countries and the 14 other European member states own their own homes (including Tenant Owners' Societies), compared with almost 63% of Swedes (Figure 4.5). In the case of **Finland**, refugees such as some Vietnamese families who arrived in Finland years ago have also purchased dwellings, although neither in Sweden nor in Finland are detailed data available about the housing quality of these ownership groups.

Figure 4.5: Sweden, population (aged over 18) distributed by country of origin of birth and form of tenure (%)

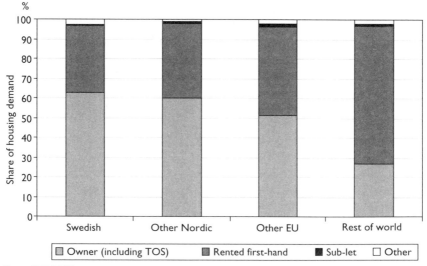

Source: SCB (2002)

Immigrant housing strategies and access to the private rental sector

The rented housing sector predominates as the largest tenure for almost all immigrant groups in nearly all member states of the EU-15; however, distribution between private and public sectors varies among different immigrant groups. In the following paragraphs we deal exclusively with the private rented sector; the next section looks at the public rented sector. As discussed in Edgar et al (2002, p 5), the private rented sector is in general dominant in Southern European countries (Italy, Greece and Portugal) and in Continental Europe (Belgium, Luxembourg, France, Austria and Germany). We start first by addressing access of immigrants in these countries to the private rented sector, followed by examples from countries where the private rented sector has traditionally made up a rather low percentage of the housing stock (such as Ireland, the UK and the Netherlands).

Figure 4.4 shows that there is an increasing trend in privately rented housing in the Milan area of Northern **Italy**. Here, between 1990 and 2001, private renting increased from 18% to 68% for Eastern European immigrants and from about 50% to more than 70% for African immigrants. It only slightly decreased for the Latin-American immigrants, from 67% to 58%. The increasing trend of the private rented sector goes hand in hand with the decreasing importance of reception centres (for all nationalities) and staying with relatives, friends and acquaintances (that is, the 'Guest' category); this is especially so for Eastern Europeans. There is also a clear diminishing trend of visible precarious housing circumstances, that is, squatting, staying in hotels and so on. However, as Tosi (2003) argues, one part of the rented accommodation market falls within the composite informal or semi-informal sector where housing hardship is added to by black market costs that characterise this sector. Nevertheless, as far as housing mobility is concerned, comparison of housing type at the time of arrival with current type of accommodation confirm the upward direction of mobility, a tendency towards less temporary and more satisfactory accommodation (Figure 4.6). Those immigrants in rented or owner-occupied property have generally been in Italy for a relatively long time and to a large extent they have permanent jobs and permanent residency permits (Ismu e Province of Milan, 1997; Tosi, 2003).

The category of so-called economic immigrants, that is, people who have left their country in order to find (better) employment in the country of arrival, constitutes the majority of immigrants in **Greece**. As in Italy, housing problems are particularly acute at the initial stage of arrival in the country. At this stage, immigrants reach Greece illegally or semi-legally, having only enough money to survive their first days in the country. Old, inadequately equipped apartments, basements and ground floors of apartment blocks, as well as decrepit houses, are taken up by them in search of cheap rented accommodation (Sapounakis, 2003). Over time, the overwhelming majority of economic immigrants gains access to regular housing through the formal rental market. Sapounakis (2003) shows that this process, which is standard throughout the country, has certain

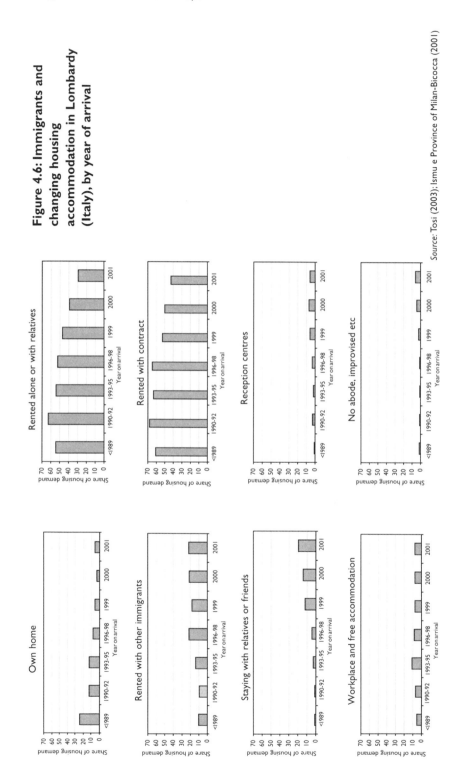

Figure 4.6: Immigrants and changing housing accommodation in Lombardy (Italy), by year of arrival

Source: Tosi (2003); Ismu e Province of Milan-Bicocca (2001)

characteristics that often become critical for its efficacy. The first characteristic pertains to the paucity of small and cheap flats in most urban centres in Greece, particularly in the provinces, where economic immigrants often reach special arrangements with their employers, usually to their detriment. A second characteristic that deserves particular attention is the lack of any advisory support mechanism for drawing up and signing leases. Without legal support, future tenants sign the lease provided by the landlord, not aware of their rights or obligations. A third characteristic element for foreigners is the excessive rent, which to a certain degree is due to the recent abolition of rent controls, an issue of more general significance which we return to later in this chapter.

In a widely discussed report, the national ombudsman of **Spain** warned in 2001 of steep rises in prices on the private rented market, affecting in particular young people and the most needy immigrants (Defensor del Pueblo, 2001, p 186). In Madrid alone, 180,000 flats are vacant and not on the market. Of 2,100,000 housing units in the Madrid hinterland, 283,000 are unoccupied. This has produced a high increase in rents and a hardening of the conditions for renting. According to Cabrera and Malgesini (2003), these conditions reflect an increase in the demand for rented accommodation generated, in part, by immigrants with legal residence whose numbers in Spain have increased enormously in recent years: from 710,647 in 1998, to 1,109,060 in 2001.

As Figure 4.1 shows, the rental sector is predominant among the Spaniards, Turks and Moroccans who live in **Flanders** (Belgium). The residual rental sector is most important among Moroccans and Turks (respectively 17.5% and 13.5%). The better segment of the rental market, the primary rental sector, is the most important for the Italians and the Spanish. The Turks also score higher than the Moroccans, reflecting the latter's relative preponderance in the Limburg mining district – an area of post-war, poor-quality housing. In the Brussels Capital Region, the residual rental sector is also more important among the Turks and the Moroccans compared with immigrants who arrived before these two groups (De Decker and Kesteloot, 2003). Regarding the most recent immigrants, De Decker and Kesteloot also mention that refugees very often end up in urban residual rental markets, where they are housed in distressing conditions. The situation is often so serious that the relevant legislation has in the meantime been repeatedly amended and in certain cities, politicians and the courts are trying to tackle the problem of rack-renting (see also Chapter Six). As can be expected, there is no global summary of these conditions. However, fragmentary reports from the press reveal scandalous practices.

French housing data, provided by INSEE (1999) point to the common trend which can be observed in nearly all countries: the rental sector is most important among those immigrants who arrived most recently in **France**. The substandard private rented sector accounts for 10% for Portuguese, Algerian and Moroccan housing, while this share rises to 12% for the Turks and 16% for people originating from black Africa.

According to the last **German** microcensus of 1998, 83.8% of all foreign residents, compared with 55.8% of Germans, were main tenants and 4%

subtenants, compared with 2.1% of Germans (Busch-Geertsema, 2003). Nearly 90% of all foreigners in Germany therefore live in rented housing. In its survey of the housing situation of foreigners in 1998, the Federal Statistical Office concluded that significant differences continue to persist compared with the German population:

> A greater percentage of foreign households live in rented accommodation than German households. In contrast to most Germans they mainly live in larger buildings (with three or more dwellings), they have been living for a shorter period in their present dwelling than the average population, have smaller dwellings but pay more rent for them and have to spend a larger proportion of their income on housing. (Statistisches Bundesamt, 2002, p 168)

In **Austria** immigrants are in general excluded from municipal housing; they are therefore reliant on the private rental market of older dwellings, the stock of which, owing to the forced slum clearance and renovation, continues to shrink. As a consequence, the foreign resident population is concentrated in restricted segments of the housing market, predominantly in districts or neighbourhoods with old dwellings up for rent (Schoibl, 2003).

In contrast with Austria, legal immigrants in the **Netherlands** have normal access to social housing. Thus rather few immigrants are to be found in the Dutch private rental sector, compared with many other European countries. While Moroccans and Turks are still underrepresented in the owner-occupier sector, the accommodation quality in the private rental sector is reasonable and much better than that of the private rental sector where the first generation had to live. De Feyter (2003) stresses that the progress is all the more pronounced, if the fact that the labour market situation of Turks and Moroccans has worsened since their arrival (see also Bolt and Van Kempen, 2002, pp 415-16).

In the case of **Ireland**, the majority of refugees (once admitted) appear to be living in the private rental sector as evidenced from two small-scale studies by Clann Housing Association (1999a, 1999b)[3], with a small number in accommodation provided by local authority or voluntary sector housing providers. O'Sullivan (2003) emphasises that those in receipt of work visas and those operating via the work permit system are not entitled to social housing and are thus restricted to market-provided accommodation, primarily the private rental sector. Although not empirically verifiable, there is some evidence that employers often provide accommodation along with employment, albeit in some cases at very high costs to the workers (Jennings, 2002).

In the case of **Finland**, where the private rental sector constitutes only 15% of the total housing stock, Mikkonen and Kärkkäinen (2003) write that it is often assumed that the private rental market is not keen to rent to immigrants and that it may even be impossible for immigrants to find a private dwelling (see also Reiman, 1999). In the over-heated housing markets of the Finnish metropolitan regions, landlords can choose their tenants, and they demonstrably prefer not to rent to immigrants. According to the personnel working with immigrants, it is on the whole easier for Ingrian Finns (immigrants of Finnish descent from Leningrad Province, Russia) to find dwellings than for refugees. The rental markets are aware of the desperate situation of immigrants and in some areas they offer immigrants poor dwellings at unreasonable prices. On the other hand, the Unit for Immigrant Services states that private owners rent dwellings to immigrants because the social authorities may pay the immigrants' rent. It seems that private landlords who have valuable dwellings in good condition do not usually want to rent them to immigrants, whereas poorer flats are often willingly hired to them because immigrants will accept such dwellings without complaining.

Immigrant housing strategies and access to the social rental sector

Despite the far-reaching restructuring of the role of the state in allocating housing in Europe, social renting is still important in a wide range of European countries. According to recent data (2000, 2001), the share of social housing in the total housing supply is still more than one fifth in the UK (21%), Austria (23%), Denmark (26%, including cooperative renting), Sweden (38%, including cooperative renting) and the Netherlands (38%). At the other extreme, there is no tradition of social rented housing in most of the Southern European countries (Spain and Greece 0%, Portugal 4%, Italy 6%) (Edgar et al, 2002, p 5). We first review the allocation of social rented housing to immigrants for those countries with a large supply.

In the **Netherlands**, the housing situation of immigrant households is still worse than that of the indigenous Dutch households, despite their access to the social rental sector (De Feyter, 2003). Bolt and Van Kempen (2002), however, do not consider the differences to be very great. Indeed, since the late 1970s – when immigrants were first given access to social housing – Turks and Moroccans have had access to social housing and the quality of this part of the housing supply is reasonable to good. In 1981, 50.5% of the Mediterranean households lived in the social rental sector and this figure had shot up to 85.5% by 1994 (De Feyter, 2003).

In the **United Kingdom**, according to the 1991 Census, some 43-50% of Bangladeshi households lived in the social rental sector, compared with just 10% of Indians and 12% of Pakistanis (Anderson, 2003) However, immigrants still have limited access to social housing and there is a frequent mismatch between household size and property size, while racial harassment remains a key issue inhibiting immigrant access to the social rental sector (Sim, 2000, p 99). Apart from structural obstacles impeding access to the social rented sector, an incomplete understanding of how the social housing system operates within minority communities can also be a disadvantage, as can language issues, resulting in a reliance on informal and not always accurate information within communities (Sim, 2000, p 99).

Meanwhile, social housing in the form of council housing continues to undergo residualisation in the UK. This is shown by Watt (2003) in his recent study of the changing housing circumstances in the London borough of Camden. We present his results here in detail, as they perfectly illustrate this process of residualisation. During the 'Golden Sixties', Camden Town was a rather prosperous municipality, with only 1,000 to 3,000 unemployed people. However, between 1980 and 1983, the number of unemployed increased and reached 12,000. Between 1981 and 1993, another 38,000 jobs were lost, with half of them in the traditional production sectors (London Borough of Camden, 2001). As such, the official unemployment rate peaked at 17.6%. Although the unemployment rate has decreased since the mid-1990s (as elsewhere in the UK), it is still above the national average and is particularly high in those areas of council housing. Ethnic groups are particularly badly off in this respect, being frequently discriminated against in the London labour market (Fainstein et al, 1992). Asian and Black male tenants in Camden have an increased risk for unemployment, compared with white people. In this context, Watt identifies several important processes. One the one hand, those from higher-income groups bought their dwelling through 'right-to-buy'. As such, they no longer belong to the pool of inhabitants who rent a council house. On the other hand, newcomers to social housing were frequently recruited from among homeless people. A third important process concerned the changing ethnic composition of the inhabitants. A survey of 1993 showed that all tenants who entered these council houses between 1939 and 1969 were white, while during the first years of the 1990s, the share of non-whites rose to more than one third. Thus, the population of households inhabiting the council houses of this London borough has changed considerably during the last decade. While this segment of the London housing market was previously dominated by white, married, middle-aged couples, it is now dominated by more young people, female singles and people from minority ethnic groups. These groups face considerable deprivation on the labour market. At the same time, the social housing supply dropped considerably because of the right-to-buy which served the higher-income groups. These trends all erode the local finances, leading to more deprivation in this housing sector (Watt, 2003).

In **Ireland**, the link between social housing and immigration concerns Irish returnees (those with low purchasing power not enabling them to own a dwelling) and refugees (O'Sullivan, 2003). People who are recognised as refugees are entitled to access social housing. However, as already mentioned, the majority of refugees appear to be living in the private rental sector (Clann Housing Association, 1999a, 1999b). In this context, O'Sullivan (2003) writes that refugees who are accommodated in social housing may face problems of acceptance, particularly if it is perceived that they have been allocated accommodation ahead of Irish nationals. However, as noted previously, immigrants in receipt of work visas and those operating via the work permit system are not entitled to social housing and are thus restricted to market-provided accommodation, primarily in the private rental sector.

In **Belgium**, the accessibility of social housing by asylum seekers has also been recently discussed by the different regional authorities (De Decker and

Kesteloot, 2003). On a motion by the board of directors of the Flemish social housing company, the Flemish Minister for Economic Affairs, Foreign Trade and Housing approved a position concerning the registration and allocation of social housing to candidate political refugees and people without papers. It specifies that a candidate tenant, who is (temporarily) residing legally in Belgium and has an official address, can be registered as a candidate tenant, and be accorded social housing. However, the letting of a social housing unit can be stopped when a foreign national loses the right of residence. In the Brussels Capital Region, a person or a family can apply for social housing as soon as they have registered with the foreigners register or as soon as it can be shown that the person has gone through a status regularisation procedure under the 1999 Act. From then on, the conventional allocation procedures come into play (see De Decker, 2001). However, in the third Belgian region, Wallonia, there are no specific measures for receiving asylum seekers in the social housing sector. This sector has some 100,000 dwellings. On the other hand, there is an open demand from 42,000 low-income households. The rule is that whoever files an application must be subjected to the usual admission and allocation procedures. In addition, there are social rental agencies that manage 1,200 dwellings in Wallonia at this time. These are dwellings from the private rental sector that are let, under social advice and guidance, to underprivileged households. The prices are about 20% below the market rate and the region offers the owners premiums to renovate existing dwellings, provided they fit into this system. While there are no data on the presence of asylum seekers in these two housing segments, it is likely that some have gained access. It is however impossible to enter the social rental sector as an illegal immigrant, because of the documents required for registration.

In an extensive overview discussing access of immigrants to social (municipal) housing in **Germany**, Busch-Geertsema (2003) points to a far-reaching cleavage between, on the one hand, repatriates and, on the other hand, asylum seekers. Referring to an extensive local study of Behrendt et al (1996), which deals with the prospects of different population groups in their search for housing in Dortmund, Busch Geertsema argues that repatriates have relatively good prospects. These immigrants have long claimed the mantle of the 'deserving': they were given low-interest loans and subsidies to acquire housing and were also clearly among the privileged groups for social housing. The contrast with foreign refugees and in particular asylum seekers, is enormous. The latter have no access to the social housing sector and many politicians, the population in general and even 'local' homeless people, have considerable reservations as to whether they deserve support. As a consequence, a new group of 'undeserving poor' has been created and legally sanctioned in the German social legislation. Seldom has the differentiation between deserving and non-deserving immigrants been stated as blatantly as by the Bavarian Minister of the Interior: "We need fewer foreigners who exploit us, and more who are useful to us" (*Focus*, 10 June 2000). In more recent debates, however, the new generation of 'deserving and useful' immigrants pertains less to repatriates and far more to computer experts from India and elsewhere who are recruited with green card initiatives (Busch-Geertsema, 2003, p 40).

In **Finland**, approximately 1,000 immigrants a year apply for a municipal dwelling in Helsinki (Mikkonen and Kärkkäinen, 2003). The largest groups are refugees and Ingrians. In 2000, over 50 immigrants, most of them living in municipal dwellings, were interviewed about their housing situation. There were major differences in the supply of general housing guidance and housing information in their own language, since some interviewees did not receive either but others did. It was, however, obvious that much more guidance was needed on a variety of issues (Pärtty-Äyräväinen, 2001). The most frequently cited problem by refugees highlights the issue of overcrowding in the municipal housing sector. This relates to relatively large families who are allocated a rather small houses by the municipal provider. In general, there are not enough big dwellings in the social housing stock to accommodate the demand from larger families (Mikkonen and Kärkkäinen, 2003).

Immigrants and access to informal housing

The previous overview of obstacles which impede the access of a wide range of immigrants to the decent segments of the European housing markets raises the question as to how and which segments of the housing market these specific groups can access. Edgar et al (2002) mentioned the importance of strong social networks among immigrant groups, which may function as safety nets. However, the same overview also made clear that such safety nets are often interlaced with power relations and exploitation of the newly arrived immigrants on the housing (and the labour) market. In what follows we briefly present some of the harshest housing situations of immigrants, as they are reported across Europe. A special focus is on overcrowding, which is present in most of the 15 member states. It should be clear that these inhospitable housing and living conditions are especially applicable to the most recently arrived immigrants, and specifically those who have no 'formal and former' link with the country (the latter being the case for so-called returnees or repatriates).

Our overview starts in the Southern Europe, where Tosi (2003) mentions that in the case of **Italy**, an important share of the rented accommodation market falls within the composite informal or semi-informal sector. Here, housing hardship is added to by the black market costs that characterise these markets. The identifying traits are well known: rent calculated on the basis of the number of beds, subletting, the operation of black market 'rules', the presence of genuine rackets and so forth. A recent national survey by Sunia Ancab – LegaCoop (2000) provided the following data: 72% of rented accommodation suffers from overcrowding (37% overcrowded, 35% extremely overcrowded). The Moroccans, for example, live in different conditions in different regions. While in Veneto there is less housing exclusion and better housing conditions, in Campania the situation appears to be quite critical, with 30% of immigrants living in improvised accommodation and with an average of two people per room for those with less precarious accommodation. The problem of Gypsies constitutes a particular case. Their housing problems were considerably aggravated by the recent migratory inflows that resulted in a number of camps becoming overcrowded and full to bursting point, with a consequent degradation of housing conditions even in many authorised camps. The new inflows also caused an increase in the number of camps that did not provide basic sanitary and safety facilities (around 20 Gypsy children have died in fires over the last 10 years). To alleviate the dramatic conditions in which many Gypsies (including Italian Gypsies) live in 'nomad camps' would require particular effort from public institutions and attention to the specificity of the problems that these populations encounter. In reality, positive action taken by local administrations represents an exception, while there are a large number of law and order approaches. The immigration situation has not only resulted in a progressive reduction in the living conditions in camps but also a growing 'territorial insecurity', a growing difficulty in finding places to settle without being exposed to the continuous threat of being moved on (Tosi, 2001b).

Harsh housing conditions for immigrants are likely to appear also in rural settings in most of the European countries; the case of **Spain** allows us to lift a corner of this veil (see also Case Study 1 in Chapter Three). As Cabrera and Malgesini (2003) mentions, in Spanish rural areas, there is a tendency to live under very precarious conditions, next to farming fields, which do not meet the minimum conditions of habitability. They are occupied only while the work lasts or during the harvest season, thus condemning workers to itinerancy which enhances their sense of being uprooted and forces them to resort to shelters and support institutions during periods of unemployment. There is also a problem in Spanish cities, manifest in cases of 'pre-ghettoisation' that have started to emerge in certain central districts with dwellings in a poor state of repair, where groups of immigrants are concentrated in overcrowded conditions that generate a 'vertical shanty town'. Frequently, overcrowding is a strategy for reducing accommodation costs and it is promoted in part by the landlords themselves. On occasion they ask to be paid per person accommodated, enabling them to extract inordinately high rents for old dwellings that are often in a very bad condition. However, many immigrant workers, relying initially on this strategy, can subsequently leave these transitional dwellings and pay for a new flat of superior quality (Martínez Veiga, 1996, p 92).

In **Greece**, a number of urban areas are characterised by camps with self-designed housing units, created by immigrants where living conditions are appalling. Situations that confirm such conditions are frequently made public. The case of Bulgarian workers in Nea Manaloda, Eleia, who live in their own shanty town at the edge of the city, without electricity, running water or sewerage, can be cited by way of example (Sapounakis, 2003).

Of all Southern European countries, **Portugal** especially had a reputation of poor housing conditions, reflected in the vast number of shanty towns and temporary and illegally constructed huts. Figure. 4.7 shows the gradual decrease of this residual housing sector over 30 years. The accentuated drop in the total

Figure 4.7: Huts in Portugal between 1970 and 2001

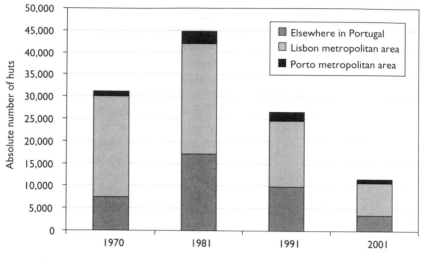

Source: INE-General Census 1970, 1981, 1991, 2001

number of huts since the 1990s reflects, in large part, the results of the Special Rehousing Programme (known by the Portuguese acronym PER), initiated in 1993 and still in progress, aimed at eradicating huts from the Lisbon and Porto metropolitan areas.

According to a 1994 study by Cardoso and Perista, a large majority of the immigrant population in Portugal lived at that time in districts of so-called spontaneous dwellings. Bruto da Costa and Baptista (2001), meanwhile, stipulate that residential mobility is frequent among immigrants, without, in many cases, leading to an effective improvement of living conditions. Most 'residential movements' suggest a path that goes from a transitory initial situation, such as in dormitories, hostels, pensions and the like, up to the occupation of old houses virtually in ruins, or staying with relatives or friends, via the construction of a hut, and then moving to a stone-built shanty. However, those who arrived some time ago have moved on to districts of social housing or even certain suburban areas where more affordable housing can be accessed. It is worth pointing out, at this point, that in recent years, the sharp increase in the rehousing by PER of thousands of families living in shanty towns has also provided access to social housing for many immigrants who were living there.

Although there is no systematic overview available of shanty town settlements in **France**, national newspapers, such as *Le Monde* and *Le Parisien*, frequently report on the appalling living conditions of immigrants, especially Gypsies, in French urban regions. In the winter of 2002, *Le Monde*, for instance, regularly wrote about the three Romani camps in Choisy-le-Roi, close to Paris, while another group of Bulgarian Gypsies, according to the same newspaper, survived in an airport hangar in Bordeaux in the southwest of France. In this last mentioned settlement the Roma who were living there had no water, electricity or heating. There were no toilets in the settlement and inhabitants were reported to sleep on the ground, as well as outside. Other similar Gypsy camps were identified by *Le Parisien* in the town of Lieusant, Seine-et-Marne.

In contrast with France and most of the Southern European countries, such camp-like and rather large-scale settlements of immigrants are not widespread or well known in **Belgium**. Here, indecent housing circumstances mainly occur under the urban form of so called rack-renting. As can be expected, there is no global summary of these conditions. But the fragmentary reports from the press reveal scandalous practices. De Decker and Kesteloot (2003) provide the following examples of a limited selection that demonstrate clearly the extremely poor housing conditions of immigrants in the main metropolitan areas in the country:

* Houses left empty for 20 years occupied by immigrants (Brussels, in *De Morgen*, 31 August 2001).
* Hundreds of premises declared uninhabitable are nonetheless let out predominantly to asylum seekers and refugees living illegally in the country. Rack-renters asking for 400,00 euros for a $16m^2$ room with cockroaches and mildew (Antwerp, in *De Morgen*, 14 April 2002).
* In certain cases, a dwelling is let for a number of hours or per mattress to different families. Three separate families, for instance, can have the premises for eight hours per day, sleeping in shifts. They often use the same mattresses without bedding, which is neither healthy nor hygienic (witnessed by Van Cauwenberghe, Ghent asylum coordinator, in *De Morgen*, 16 November 2001).
* The office of the public prosecutor in Brussels has asked for the detention of a 51-year-old Brussels resident on suspicion of rack-renting. A woman filed a complaint because she paid the man 500 euros a month for accommodation in a converted garage.
* Investigators recently discovered a tenant and her two children living in a covered interior courtyard and sleeping in an upgraded, cockroach-infested garden shed (Brussels, in *De Standaard*, 13 September 2002).

As will be discussed in Chapter Six, the relevant legislation has been repeatedly amended and in certain cities politicians and courts are trying to tackle the problem of rack-renting (De Decker and Kesteloot, 2003).

In **Germany**, similar developments can be found (Busch-Geertsema, 2003). Some immigrants without legal status have to put up with particularly poor housing conditions. Very little is known about the housing situation of stateless immigrants. In one case study for the East German city of Leipzig, Alt (1999) reported, on the basis of many interviews, that only a very small number of 'illegal immigrants' lived entirely without fixed accommodation in cars, railcars, parked caravans, containers, on park benches or in tents. Apart from commuting immigrants from neighbouring countries, nearly all immigrants try to find a fixed abode as promptly as possible (Alt, 1999, p 165). The forms of accommodation that Alt found among immigrants without legal status include houses that are empty or ready for demolition, and 'mass accommodations' that can be rented for between 2.50 and 5 euros per night, with five to ten people in a room. Such accommodation was let out in Leipzig both by employers of illegally employed workers, as well as by private people, who at times housed between 50 and 100 people. Among the most unpopular, according to those interviewed by Alt, were housing alternatives sublet by people with legal residence status, or housing in which people could live in the place of the owner or main tenant officially domiciled there. Many people without legal status have to live with the constant fear that their illegal residence will be discovered through conflicts with compatriots, other foreigners or neighbours, and that they would then be threatened with deportation. As a result, they are exposed to excessive rents and other arbitrary measures without any rights and are often completely defenceless.

In the **Netherlands**, De Feyter (2003) also mentions occupation of caravans and other substitute dwellings by the most deprived immigrants. Those undocumented immigrants who come to the country to earn as much money as possible and then return home often live in very poor circumstances. Here, beds are also rented per shift and wages are very low. At times, immigrant workers live in old caravans, in the back of fruit and vegetable greenhouses, in barns, and the like.

Regarding **Austria**, extreme housing conditions are also registered among the most recent immigrants; however, these circumstances are not limited to these new immigrants, they are also applicable to Turks who arrived in the country in the 1960s. This may point to a more structural prejudice regarding their rights to decent housing. In their study on the housing situation of immigrants in Elisabethvorstadt (Salzburg), Freudenthaler et al (1994) paint an extremely precarious picture, characterised essentially by overcrowding and extreme housing shortage. On the basis of the current definition of overcrowding, more than one person per room, all the households studied were severely overcrowded and none had adequate space. More than half of the interviewed households lived in extremely overcrowded conditions with more than 2.5 people in a room, about half of them are Turks, the other half Yugoslavs (Schoibl, 2003).

As already mentioned, the housing supply for the most recent immigrants in **Finland** is rather good and the only mentioned problem relates to overcrowding, both in the municipal and the private housing sector. However, overcrowded housing conditions among immigrants is a serious problem in **Sweden** (Sahlin, 2003). In a detailed study by Popoola (1998), 35% of the population of Herrgården (situated in the district of Rosengård in Malmö) was overcrowded (here measured as over two people per room, excluding kitchen and living room). Some 20 nationalities were represented among the overcrowded households, although with Lebanon, Iraq and Yugoslavia as the more usual countries of origin. The most overcrowded households found in Herrgården (at least four people per room, again excluding kitchen and living room), exhibited a raft of health problems, such as headaches, disturbed sleep and back pain (from sleeping on the floor) which can be associated with overcrowding.

Summary

This section looked at the different ways immigrants gain access to the European housing markets, by focusing separately on the private sector (ownership and rent in a context of market exchange), the social sector (embedded in the sphere of state redistribution) and different forms of semi-informal to informal housing (with a more pronounced flavour of – exploiting – social relations). Regarding the private sector, we conclude that in several countries, both the ownership and the rented segment are clearly bifurcated when the housing situation of immigrants is considered. Regarding ownership, this is especially the case in those countries where there is a long tradition of immigration (for example, France, Belgium, Germany). Their long stay allows the concerned households to build some private capital and to consider permanent settlement in the country (mostly households with a background of labour migrants). However, as multiple examples from Germany and Belgium have shown, enforced home ownership among immigrants does not equate with decent housing. The private rental sector is bifurcated in those countries that have a rather extended private rental sector (for example, France, Belgium, Germany, Greece, Spain, Austria) and which combine this situation with an inflow of recently arrived migrants from transition and 'Third World' countries. Apart form Portugal and its large-scale Special Rehousing Programme (PER), Southern European countries hardly possess any social housing (although the share of this sector in Portugal is only 4%). In several European countries, documented immigrants (including acknowledged refugees) are entitled to social housing (for example, in the Netherlands, Ireland, Belgium). However, the case of Germany clearly showed that in practice, a clear cleavage exists between subjectively defined categories of deserving and non-deserving foreign residents. Finally, this section has also highlighted that the different obstacles that immigrants encounter lead them towards degrading housing circumstances, ranging from rented mattresses in neglected urban neighbourhoods to uninhabitable stables in the rural south of Europe.

Immigrants and the debate on social mix

Actors in the housing market, such as private and public companies, decision makers and including the inhabitants of housing estates have engaged in a widespread discourse on the topic of what constitutes a desirable 'social mix' between different social groups (ethnicity, class, nationality). Below we briefly consider the ongoing discussion that is being conducted in several European countries. We question the dominant discourse that argues that concentrations of immigrants at the neighbourhood level may destabilise neighbourhoods, that they may impede immigrants in their pathway towards social integration and that they may threaten (mostly subjectively) the local people in their daily lives.

France is one of the European countries where the discussion about social mix (or 'social balance', the literal translation of *balance sociale*) has dominated the housing debate since the 1980s. Social balance has been a recurrent theme of all major housing legislation (Maurel, 2003). The 1990 Besson Act, which gave effect to the right to housing and established the Social Housing Comprehensive Development Plans, the Urban Planning Act of 1991 (sometimes known as the 'Anti-Ghetto' Act), the 1998 Anti-Exclusion Act, and the 2000 Solidarity and Urban Renewal Act (SRU Act), all focus on the idea of 'social balance', the premise of which is that an organised mix of social groups in all areas of a town will improve social cohesion. But the substantive aspects of social balance are nowhere spelled out. The SRU Act lays down a framework for new social housing construction in all municipalities with over 20,000 people. The idea is to spread the cost of low-income housing more evenly across the town, and consequently, as Maurel (2003) argues, it is perhaps more relevant here to talk of 'urban balance' rather than 'balance' at the neighbourhood level. However, the stated aims are nevertheless directed towards preventing ghetto formation and promoting a mix of social groups: this is social balance. While the nature of the 'social' groups targeted is not spelt out, it is implicitly understood that it applies to ethnic groups. This implicit aim is based on two basic assumptions. First, the concentration of immigrants is regarded as a dis-benefit (never a resource) and dispersal of immigrants is a requirement for balance in society. Second, integration of immigrants into the urban community must be a personal process. Fear of the 'ethnic divide' underpins the political consensus on social balance (Maurel, 2003). On this basis, the aim of social balance will be reflected in population redistribution policies, thresholds and quotas, and the unstated use of implicit allocation criteria. What will follow is the demarcation of zones and areas, and a ranked underclass of 'high-risk' social groups. It is significant that the concept of social balance is only ever mentioned in relation to so-called 'sink' neighbourhoods or 'problem communities', never to concentrations of high-income, high-quality housing. In this context it is apparent that social housing actors and landlords will pursue two distinct strategies. The first is a 'reserve strategy', the creation of neighbourhoods in practice reserved almost exclusively for foreign communities. Foreign applicants will be allocated to housing estates with a high ethnic population based solely on their ethnicity. Here, the neighbourhood is the discriminator. It is an 'asset risk' strategy in that the spatial concentration of immigrants is focused in 'written-off' sectors of the built environment in order to preserve the asset values of the rest of the housing stock. It is the 'one for one' technique (one immigrant out, another in). In France, spatial segregation – at neighbourhood, street block or building level – mainly affects Turkish and Maghreb families, half of whom live in communities with high ethnic concentrations. A form of residency hierarchy emerges in which the chances of a transfer or rehousing are slim. A working group on equal access to social housing, set up at the instance of the Federation of Social Housing Associations concluded, in a report published in July 2001, that concentration of immigrant households was due to the concentration of inferior public housing stock, population redistribution policies and the complexity of allocation rules. In such cases, the social balance principle operates not at a neighbourhood level but on a different and broader scale.

The second strategy of social housing actors and landlords is the planned redevelopment of the housing stock to restrict immigrant access to renovated and upgraded buildings or blocks: large apartments divided up into smaller studio flats to rule out large families, demolition of high-rise blocks, and properties left deliberately vacant. Applications from immigrants are not turned down wholesale, but case-by-case according to the housing type, in a calculated minimalist approach to social balance. In this manner, social balance and a spatial population distribution policy are manipulating the right to housing (Simon, 1999)[4].

In the **Netherlands**, the state, being a prominent landlord, has always had the opportunity to exercise supervision over the spatial spread of different social groups in the vast segments of public housing. However, very recently (spring 2004), the debate about social mix emerged with great vehemence. The immediate cause for this discussion was the decision of the Rotterdam municipality to refuse people who earn less than 120% of the minimum wage access to the local housing market (resulting in a monthly income barrier of 1,260 euros). In practice, a wide range of people of non-Dutch origin (regardless of their present nationality) will be targeted with this measure. It is important to note that 55% of the 287,200 dwellings of the city are municipal, meaning that the local government has indeed the opportunity to effectively steer housing allocation in the city. Supporters of the Rotterdam initiative argue that investments to renovate deprived neighbourhoods do not lead to structural improvements or enhance the livability of these neighbourhoods. Therefore, they argue for a selective allocation of the available dwellings in the city. This contested decision is supported by the central government. Moreover, the present Dutch government (a coalition of Christian Democrats and Conservative Liberals) rejected a second, accompanying measure, which argued that neighbouring and more affluent municipalities around Rotterdam take responsibility for housing a share of the poor refused in the central city. This Dutch policy has inspired some local decision makers in the Flemish city of Antwerp (Belgium), where 20 of the 55 council members belongs to the extreme right and racist Vlaams Blok[5], the biggest opposition party in the city. A local alderman (with no competency for housing matters) launched the idea that a similar housing allocation policy could be elaborated for Flanders' largest city, including the spatial dispersal of the lowest income households to more affluent neighbouring municipalities.

The debate on social mix of foreigners and non-foreigners is also prominent in **Germany** (Busch-Geertsema, 2003). Along with other commentators (cf Bartelheimer, 1998; Becker, 1988, 1997; Schubert, 1999), in a report for the

Committee of Enquiry on Immigration established by the Federal Government, Häußermann and Siebel (2001) explicitly oppose influx restrictions and maximums for foreigners. Indeed, such measures have been discussed time and again in Germany, and often put into practice in various places in the 1970s and 1980s, and are still being discussed. They are based on the assumption that a *healthy social mix* could thereby be achieved in *overburdened* areas. Busch-Geertsema (2003) indicates that such practices are reinforced by the findings of social science research. He cites the work, for instance, of Eichener (1998a, 1998b), who has tried to prove through extensive research that foreigners are best integrated in 'German' residential areas if a certain percentage of non-Germans is not exceeded. His work argues that at the 'street' level the mix should be fixed at a maximum of 10% to 15% of foreign households; while the proportion should not exceed 25% to 33% per block of flats. As soon as the proportion of foreigners exceeds these limits, it is argued, there is a danger of the beginning of an uncontrollable 'segregation' process ushered in by the departure of German families, accompanied by a further increase in the proportion of foreigners. Busch-Geertsema rightly states that whereas measures to limit the influx of immigrants and to introduce quotas are in the interest of landlords who have classified all foreigners as 'risk tenants', they are in no way in the interest of immigrants. In an analysis of the segregation debate in Germany, Häußermann and Siebel (2001) come to the conclusion that it is the task of the body politic to both reduce and to allow segregation. Voluntary segregation motivated by ethnic and cultural considerations should be allowed, while forced segregation through discrimination and lack of other alternatives should be reduced.

Contrary to the aforementioned countries where the debate on a desirable social mix is never far away, the **Italian** case demonstrates that the presence of immigrants does not automatically lead to this kind of debate. In this respect, Tosi (2003) argues that the scarce concentration of immigrant settlement (as compared with other countries) within Italian cities can be easily linked with a number of traits typical of the immigrant situation and of urban settlement in Italy: a housing market that is less segregated than in other countries and no ethnic targeting of social housing (one of the main factors affecting concentration/segregation in other countries). One fundamental context factor concerns the geographical distribution of poverty. In Italy as elsewhere, as Tosi states, many immigrants settle in areas that are run down to a greater or lesser degree, but in the majority of cases these areas are neither 'urban ghettos' nor even 'crisis neighbourhoods'. The concentration of poverty on the neighbourhood scale is less frequent in Italy than in other countries. In many regions poverty and social exclusion are (relatively) not very localised.

In **Finland** also no highly segregated housing areas or ghettoes exist (Mikkonen and Kärkkäinen, 2003). And there are few areas with a high concentration of one national or ethnic group, but some areas do have a higher concentration of immigrants than others. Recent studies suggest that the socioeconomic differences between housing areas have been slowly increasing in Helsinki even though the policy of social mixing has been observed for decades (Vaattovaara, 2002, pp 107-23). According to the research, minority ethnic groups have begun to concentrate in almost the same residential suburbs of Helsinki as those inhabited by socioeconomically disadvantaged groups. (Kortteinen and Vaattovaara, 2000, pp 115-24).

Summary

This brief overview of current policies towards social mix shows that there is a dominant and quasi-European-wide discourse that understands concentration of socially disadvantaged groups (in many cases, immigrants) as a difficulty that needs to be tackled. However, it is important to recall here one of the earliest and most fundamental critiques of the concept of social mix, written in a review of the use of this concept in town planning. The author, Sarkassian (1976), argued that people can change their socioeconomic position, not their ethnic background (see also Kesteloot, 1998). The implication of this observation is that policy makers should not confuse the target: it is poverty that has to be fought, not the poor themselves, whether they are white, brown or black. This message was also the focus of a recent manifesto, written by people engaged in housing (NGOs, welfare associations and academics), disputing the current ideas of the Antwerp alderman to copy the Rotterdam policy of enforced social mix (see Inslegers et al, 2004).

Immigrants, racism and access to housing

The previous discussion on social mix includes a somewhat ambiguous component of racist arguments about allocation of housing across the population. As events in the Netherlands (Rotterdam), Finland and Germany have shown, especially in those situations where the proportion of social housing is high, the state can actively intervene and try to steer the composition of the housing market according to desired ratios of foreigners versus non-foreigners. However, in case of the private rental market, an examination of both newspaper reports and existing scientific literature shows that there is a profusion of concrete examples of housing discrimination on racist grounds. In this section, we point to two phenomena: first, the refusal of private landlords to rent (or to sell) their property to foreigners; second the systematic use of increased rents for immigrants who try to access the private rental market. Regarding the first process, we illustrate the phenomenon with the concrete example of private landlords in Brussels who refuse refugees as potential tenants. Regarding the second strategy we have selected a variety of examples that illustrate this trend. Finally, in concluding this section we argue that racism and the power of gatekeepers is clearly more than just some occasional obstacles impeding immigrant access to the decent segments of the European housing markets. Rather, as we will show, calling on the example of the history of housing allocation in the UK, racism and xenophobia is an endemic and systematic feature of housing markets in the EU–15.

"I do not let to foreigners"

In research dealing with the housing circumstances of Turks and to a minor degree Moroccans in Belgium, Kesteloot et al (1997) ascertained that labour immigrants and their descendants are still discriminated against in the housing market. More recently, the same seems to happen with 'new' immigrants arriving in the country. De Decker and Kesteloot (2003) refer to a specific study, elaborated by Alarm, an organisation that represents refugees, asylum seekers and people who have regularised their status, that work in Sint-Jans-Molenbeek (one of the 19 Brussels municipalities). Alarm conducted a study of the willingness of home owners to let to their clients. In the course of 2002, 65 homeowners were approached. The test was always conducted in the same pattern: first, someone from Alarm rang up, immediately gave their name and asked whether the dwelling was still available for let. If the answer was yes, s/he asked if it was possible to see it. If that was also possible, s/he asked specifically whether the owner was willing to let the dwelling to a refugee. Two hours later, the owner received a second telephone call, this time from a Belgian test subject who asked the same first two questions. In no fewer than 58% of the cases, the homeowner refused to let the dwelling to the first caller, while the second caller could rent without any problem. In about half of the cases, the foreign national was sent packing as soon as the owner heard their name or accent. Frequently used excuses were that the flat was already rented, that someone had already had first option, or that the caller should ring back the following week. When the Belgian test subject called just a couple of hours later, there seemed to be no problem at all. In the other cases, the foreign national was refused after s/he expressly asked whether the owner was willing to rent to foreigners (Centrum voor Gelijkheid van Kansen en voor Racismebestrijding, 2003).

Excessive rents in the private housing market are regularly reported in Germany (Busch-Geertsema, 2003). Indeed, various research studies, focusing on German housing markets, have shown that foreigners often pay considerably higher rents for relatively poorer housing than German nationals, because landlords demand 'discrimination supplements' (Häußermann and Siebel, 2001, p 22). According to the microcensus of 1998, despite the often poorer quality of the dwellings, the rents charged to foreign households per square metre are on average significantly higher than those paid by German households: "Nation-wide, German households pay DEM 10.69/m²; non-German households DEM 11.51/m², or nearly one German mark more" (Winter, 1999, p 861). The average rent burden of foreign households (that is, percentage of household income paid in rent) is admittedly – not least owing to the poor housing quality and the higher residential density of foreign households – not very much higher than that of Germans, but it has risen disproportionably in recent years: in 1993, the rent burden of all tenant households in Germany was 19.2%; for foreign households it was 20.5%. In 1998, the rent burden of all households was 23.5%; that of foreign tenants 25.3%. There are, however, clearly more foreign than German households with a very high rent burden of 40% or more. In 1998, 22.1% of all foreign tenants fell in this category, compared with 16.7% of all German tenants (Stabu, 2000).

The already cited research of Freudenthaler et al (1994) in the Salzburg area of Elisabethvorstadt, also mentions the problem of extreme price levels disproportionately affecting immigrants:

> ... in the case of ...'mass accommodations', the value for money is completely distorted and the utilisation relationship is regulated differently by contract. Here, payment or the contract is so structured, that charging is by the bed. The prices for a bed are accordingly high and are almost always above ATS 2000/ bed [approximately 145 euros]. This means that unbelievably high rents are charged for a room or a dwelling. (Freudenthaler et al, 1994)

Many landlords do rent out beds and rooms exclusively to one individual, but on a 'pension' or 'shift' basis, so that the prices are outrageously high, and the rights of 'tenants' are severely restricted. The housing conditions that go hand in hand with these high prices are often shameful. In the Spänglerstraße, for example, sanitary facilities were provided only on each floor to be shared by 12 people and many 'rooms' were in effect corridors.

Systematically higher rents for immigrants who access the private rental market is also a frequent phenomenon in Southern Europe. In the case of Italy, Tosi (2003) writes that one can speak of a 'special rent for immigrants': according to estimates (Ares, 2001) that rent is 25% higher than the average free market rent. Tosi argues (2003) that paying a higher price for accommodation of the same (or even lower) quality is the crucial test for the existence of discriminatory practices towards a part of the population. He also argues that it is not necessary for there to be a high level of racial prejudice for there to be discrimination towards immigrants; it is a phenomenon, inherent in the rental market (Toniolo and Bragato, 1998; see also Bernadotti, 2001). Although there are variations on the theme, which reflect the variety of local markets and types of local immigration, these characteristics of the rental market have been reported practically everywhere in Italy: for example, in Veneto (Criacp, 1992; ORIV, 1998), in Salento (Perrone, 1994), in Palermo (Gruttadauria, 1994), in Lombardy (Bellaviti et al, 2001), in Emilia (Bernardotti, 2001) and in Piedmont (Comitato Oltre il razzismo, 2000).

To conclude this set of examples, we refer to Greece, where Sapounakis (2003) reports similar findings: excessive rents for immigrants, which to a certain degree are due to the recent abolition of rent controls. Here, many landlords also claim that they are obliged to ask for higher rent from foreigners as a guarantee for the risk that they will not pay their rent and other charges in time, an interpretation which stems from smouldering racist tendencies.

Racism and gatekeepers

Over the years, in the UK, many studies have documented the disadvantaged housing position of black minority and ethnic households relative to their white counterparts. Arguably, a large part of this reflects the general economic disadvantage and poverty experienced by these groups. However, there is a very significant body of evidence that economic disadvantage is further compounded by the racialised nature of the housing system. This has been manifested through direct or indirect racial discrimination in the procedures for gaining access to housing in all tenures, combined with 'cultural insensitivity' and a degree of choice or selectivity relating to cultural norms of different minority ethnic groups. Once housed, black minority and ethnic households may be subject to racial harassment or violence in their homes or neighbourhoods that can further compound disadvantage and lead to homelessness (Anderson, 2003).

Patterns of housing inequality in the UK have their origins in the immediate post-Second World War period when significant numbers of black migrant workers arrived in the country (Bowes and Sim, 2002). Discrimination in access to housing was identified in research as early as the 1960s (Rex and Moore, 1967). Aspects of housing disadvantage commonly experienced by black minority and ethnic households have also been documented in research reviewed by Sim (2000). Housing disadvantage may occur in relation to access to housing in different tenures, through interactions with cultural norms and either direct or indirect discrimination on the part of housing agencies. Among Pakistani households, for example, it is common to retain links with Pakistan and space for family visits is a high priority. These sorts of issues have not been sufficiently prioritised in the council sector although some, limited, provision has recently been made through black-led housing associations (Anderson, 2003). Further, various studies over the years have identified both direct and indirect discrimination in housing allocation procedures, with offers of housing often considered unsuitable by black minority and ethnic applicants. For example, Harrison (1999) refers to the widely cited studies by Phillips (1986) and Henderson and Karn (1987), which found substantial evidence of direct negative discrimination in local authority housing allocations, as well as cultural insensitivity.

Summary

Racial harassment and discrimination in European housing markets are not just occasional events. Rather, racism and discrimination are a systematic component of the housing market, with different gatekeepers performing a crucial role in impeding immigrant access to decent housing.

Figure 4.8: Europe and migration history versus share of social rent in the member states (2000)

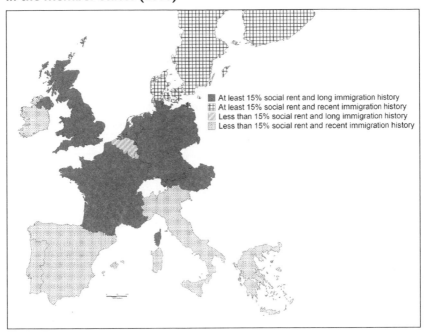

Source: European Housing Statistics (2001) http://mrw.wallonie/be/dgat1/HousingStats; Ball (2002)

Conclusion

This chapter has examined the present housing outcome of immigrants in terms of the interactions between three sets of processes: first, those operating at what we might call the 'macro-social' level, namely the realignment of the welfare states and the associated processes of commodification. Second, processes operating at the 'micro-social' scale – we are here referring to the strategies adopted by immigrants to access housing and to cope with housing stress; and third, those operating within the 'socio-spatial' fabric of society, that is, the tangible environments in which immigrants live and work. The multiple examples cited in this chapter which illustrate the basic facts and trends about the position of immigrants in European housing markets make clear that the period of stay, the circumstances in which immigrants arrived in a country, and cultural aspects all play a key role in determining housing outcomes. To conclude this chapter and as a way of summarising its main findings in a comparative perspective we present a very simple typology of the EU-15 countries. The typology combines two indicators. The first is the proportion of social rented housing in the national housing stock, which reveals theoretically at least the capacity of a state to determine the allocation of dwellings to specific social groups. The second indicator makes a distinction between countries that have experienced relatively recent immigration and those countries that have experienced several post-war migration waves. On this basis we can identify four categories that reveal a clear spatial patterning (Figure 4.8):

- those countries that combine a long tradition of immigration with a sizeable social housing sector (equal to or greater than 15% of the national housing stock): Austria, France, Germany, Netherlands, UK;
- countries with a recent history of immigration and a sizeable social housing stock: Denmark, Finland, Sweden;
- countries with a long history of immigration and a small social housing sector (less than 15% of total stock): Belgium, Luxembourg;
- countries with a recent history of immigration and a small social housing sector: Greece, Ireland, Italy, Portugal, Spain.

Countries with a long immigration history and a large social housing sector

In 2000 nearly 40% of the housing stock was recorded as socially rented in the Netherlands. Since the late 1970s, Turks and Moroccans have had access to this sector and the quality seems to be reasonably good. High shares of housing in the social rental sector are also to be found among, for instance, the Bangladeshi in the UK, while for other 'immigrant' communities (for example, Indian, Pakistani) the proportion is much lower. Based on a detailed study of Watt (2003), we described how the right-to-buy and the commodification of the municipal housing stock in the London Borough of Camden influenced the quality of living in a council block: the share of immigrants as well as the share of unemployed and homeless people increased, while at the same time the capacity of the social landlords to improve the housing quality shrank as a consequence of diminishing resources. The German case also showed how the access to the social rental sector acts as a line of fracture among the newly immigrated groups, with, on the one hand, the 'deserving poor', that is, repatriates, and, on the other hand, the 'undeserving' asylum seekers.

Despite the relative importance of the social rental sector, home ownership among immigrants is a considerable housing segment in the UK, Germany, Austria and France. Moreover, in general the importance of this segment continues to increase. Home ownership is more frequently to be found among those migrant households and their descendants who belonged to the first post-war migrant wave (colonial and labour migrant wave, including family reunion). This sounds reasonable as long-standing immigrants accumulate resources for home purchase. However, there are a number of issues that differentiate immigrant groups in terms of home ownership. First, we noticed clear cultural differences. In the UK and elsewhere, for instance, a reluctance to borrow for mortgage purposes has been identified among specific ethnic groups, essentially related to religious beliefs. Second, not all migrant groups who arrived at the same time were as successful in the labour market or as entrepreneurs. For example, in the UK some Indian households, although relatively successful economically, are frequently linked to precarious self-employment which can result in vulnerability to mortgage repossession when businesses fail. Third, migrant groups have different expectations vis-à-vis their country of origin, and some may have waited longer than others to purchase a dwelling in anticipation (unfulfilled) of returning to their country of origin. As a consequence of all these factors, we identified in some countries a clearly bifurcated ownership sector among immigrant communities whereby homeowners occupied both well-appointed dwellings while others occupied inadequate and overcrowded houses.

While home ownership has increased in France, the UK, Austria and Germany, it dropped among the immigrants in the Netherlands between 1981 and 1994. This reflects interventions on the part of the state to house the weakest and poorest of immigrant households. However, more recent decisions regarding social mix and the role of the state in ensuring ' social balance' – specifically in the context of Rotterdam – suggest that a rupture with the former policy can be expected in the future.

With the exception of the Netherlands, the private rental sector also plays an important role in this first group of countries, especially for the most recently arrived immigrants. Again, this private rental sector is clearly bifurcated, with an important share of poorly housed people among the newest immigrants, including both asylum seekers and undocumented people. One of the most iniquitous strategies of private landlords discussed in this chapter was the systematic charging of higher rents for the weakest groups on the housing market. Strongly related to the previous observation, in the countries that make up this category, the most destitute immigrants are those who rent sofas, mattresses and other basic furniture, mostly on a very short time basis. One should notice that this not only happens in the context of the 'formal' housing market, but is also a characteristic of the 'informal' market operating within immigrant communities where power relations also lead to exploitation of the weakest parties. In sum, regarding housing and immigrants, the countries considered here (Austria, France, Germany, the Netherlands and the UK) reflect a highly differentiated and complex situation: multiple migration backgrounds meet multiple housing segments.

Countries of recent immigration and a large social housing sector

As shown in Chapter Two, immigration has been rather recent, and in terms of absolute numbers, a rather modest phenomenon in Scandinavian countries, compared with many of the other member states of the EU-15. However, as in those countries with a longer tradition of immigration, home ownership has also increased in Denmark, Sweden and Finland[6]. However, despite the commodification of housing, refugees and Ingrians in Finland have both accessed the social housing sector when problems of overcrowding have been identified. However, problems also occur within the privately rented sector, as is illustrated in Finland. Here, private landlords try to rent poor quality dwellings to immigrants, knowing that they can rely on state intervention to pay for the rent. In general the housing circumstances of immigrants in Scandinavian countries can be identified as among the best in the EU.

Countries of long-standing immigration and a small social housing sector

As Figure 4.8 shows, the combination of post-war immigration with low shares of social housing is uncommon in the EU-15. Only the two neighbouring countries, Belgium and Luxemburg, display these characteristics. Compared with the other member states, they have also another specific migration feature. In the Grand Duchy, affluent immigrants, affiliated with the EU, are widespread in the housing market. In Belgium, and more specifically in the Brussels Urban Region which encompasses nearly one fifth of the country's population, affluent foreigners are also well presented in the housing market. By contrast, poorer migrant groups are to be found in 19th-century urban neighbourhoods or specific regions with a clear industrial past.

As Belgium and Luxembourg have a negligible social rental sector, most immigrants have to turn to the private sector. As we have already observed in relation to the first group of countries with a long tradition of immigration, home ownership is particularly important for those people who arrived as labour migrants, combined with family reunion (far more important than the colonial immigration in Belgium). Thus Italians are very well represented on the ownership market, Spaniards to a lesser degree. Further, as also noticed in the UK for instance, cultural aspects and especially religious beliefs also differentiate home ownership among migrant groups. The more secularised Turks are in general better represented in the ownership market than the Moroccans. However, home ownership is frequently a matter of necessity as steeply increasing costs force many households to buy low-quality dwellings in order to escape from higher rents. Hence, ownership does not necessarily equate with decent housing circumstances.

Those migrant groups who do not have enough purchasing power to access home ownership are locked in the private rental sector, where – especially in the Belgian inner cities – very low-quality housing is offered. The most unsatisfactory housing circumstances are to be found among newly arrived migrants, many of whom are obliged to occupy damp cellars and other basic accommodation, with some renting mattresses and sofas by the hour.

Countries of recent immigration and a small social housing sector

This last group of countries has no established tradition of immigration and lacks a significant social housing component in its housing stock. The whole of the Mediterranean belt and Ireland comprise this group. Of these countries, Ireland has the highest share of social renting (10% of the housing market); this compares with 6% in Italy, 4% in Portugal and close to 0% in Spain and Greece.

Despite the recent character of immigration in these countries, home ownership among immigrants is not exceptional. In Ireland, there are even indications that the more affluent repatriates contribute to steep increases on the housing market, because of their high purchasing power. In Athens, 6% of the Albanians, reflecting their success as small entrepreneurs, owned their dwelling in 1999. In Lombardy, surrounding the north Italian city of Milan, 10% of the Eastern European, Asian and African immigrants owned their dwellings in 2001, although available information also makes it clear that enforced ownership frequently appears among these immigrants.

Most immigrants who are not repatriates or returnees, face initial severe housing problems when they arrive in these countries where the private rental sector provides the main route into housing. This has been illustrated in this chapter by the changing housing circumstances of immigrants in Lombardy, where sharing private rental dwellings with other immigrants is very common in the early years after arrival. Moreover, in all of the Mediterranean countries that comprise this group, private landlords systematically charge higher rents to immigrants. In Ireland recognised refugees also tend to live in the privately rented sector; those in receipt of work visas and operating via the work permit system are not entitled to social housing. This contrasts with low-income Irish returnees who have access to, and are heavily reliant on, local authority housing.

Finally, in Southern Europe, where home ownership and privately rented properties are the only housing alternatives available to immigrants, informal housing figures strongly: inhabited stables (Spain), camp locations (especially Gypsies in Italy) and self-built, low-quality housing (Greece and Portugal) are among the most precarious housing circumstances of immigrants. Portugal is the only country where the state is involved in promising programmes of housing redevelopment, as illustrated by the demolition of vast slums and the replacement of this housing sector by decent and affordable social rental dwellings.

We close this chapter with a quotation, taken from two German housing experts. They argue that the housing of immigrants is much more than simply providing them with decent dwellings. Housing also refers to the quality of the neighbourhood, to available public infrastructure, to the possibility of building social capital and so forth. The issue of social mix is at the heart of this debate. Reflecting on the empirical material discussed in this chapter, we can conclude with Häußermann and Siebel (2001) that:

> Enforced desegregation is no better than enforced segregation. The municipal authorities should not fight against voluntary segregation, but should distance themselves from the illusory and harmful goal of dispersing immigrants throughout the city and instead concentrate their social policies in areas where foreigners currently live. Securing affordable housing in as many different locations as possible and supporting the free choice of residence through higher housing allowances would be more helpful to all, especially as they would also neutralise the discriminating effect against immigrants, which is irrefutably

connected with the administrative attempt to isolate and contain them like an infectious disease. (2001, p 81)

Notes

[1] At the time of writing, the results of the recently completed 2001 Belgian National Census were not available.

[2] This data should be carefully interpreted. First, in 1990 the process of recent immigration was just starting and the number of immigrants was very low. Second, the great variations between the two dates are for the most recently arrived immigrant groups – from Latin America and Eastern Europe.

[3] Clann Housing Association was established in June 1998 by the Refugee Agency in collaboration with a range of private initiators, such as the Bosnian Community Development Project, the Vietnamese Irish Association and private individuals within the refugee community. Its aim is to investigate and respond to the housing needs of refugees in Ireland through the provision of secure and affordable housing.

[4] GELD was set up as a partnership between public authorities, social partners, NGOs and researchers, in April 1999; its mission is to conduct research and initiate action on discrimination.

[5] Vlaams Bloc was officially condemned in April 2004 as racist by the Ghent court, citing the Belgium law on racism.

[6] Non-Nordic immigration only became important in the mid-1980s. However, of all Nordic countries, Sweden undoubtedly has the largest known influx of immigrants. In the immediate post-war decades, most of the immigrants to Sweden came from the neighbouring countries, although by that time people also came from all over the world, attracted to sustain the booming Swedish economy. More recently, as in many other European countries, Sweden attracts large numbers of asylum seekers (see also Chapter Two). For these reasons, it could be argued that Sweden should be included in the group of countries with a long immigration history. However, compared with countries such as Germany and the UK, where massive immigration was linked with labour market conditions and post-colonial developments, Sweden associates more with the Nordic countries.

FIVE

Migration and homelessness

Introduction

Communication from the European Commission to the Council and the European Parliament (2000) (COM(2000)757) argued that action to integrate migrants into our societies must be seen as an essential corollary of immigration policy. One of the most important indicators of the incorporation of immigrants into a country is their integration into the labour market. However, the ability to access a job and to sustain a position in the labour market is in itself dependent on access to affordable housing. Hence successful integration into the housing market is also an important indicator of the successful assimilation of immigrants into a host country. This chapter examines the nature and extent of homelessness among immigrants entering the member states of the EU. This examination requires an understanding of the factors that help to create vulnerability to homelessness among different categories of immigrant. It also requires an understanding of the extent to which homelessness is a stage in the integration of an immigrant into society or the extent to which it reflects the failure of integration.

Chapter Two identified the different components of migration and the extent to which immigration into Europe has been changing in recent years. This consideration suggests that the causes of homelessness will vary for immigrants, dependent on their personal situation and the legal status afforded to them by the reception country. In order to provide a context to understand vulnerability to homelessness, Chapter Four described the coping strategies adopted by people to acquire shelter. This chapter therefore begins with a discussion of the factors that may lead to vulnerability to homelessness among immigrants.

Within the context where the scale of immigration into Europe has been increasing and the composition of migrant populations has been changing, the chapter begins by examining the empirical evidence concerning the extent and nature of homelessness among immigrants.

Migration is not a condition but a process. Over the centuries migrants have initially endured hardship and poorer living circumstances than citizens in their host country, but over time have assimilated and improved their lot. Undoubtedly, for some migrants today, homelessness and the experience of poor living conditions is also part of this process of residential and social mobility and integration into the host society. The evidence suggests that, in many countries, young single adults from minority ethnic groups (that is, second generation immigrants) are more vulnerable to homelessness and an unsettled way of living than other groups in society. There is also evidence that recent immigrants are a significant and, in many countries, an increasing proportion of the clients of homeless services. This suggests that policies of integration need to pay more regard to housing requirements and the need for support for resettlement for migrants. This indicates the need for integration policies that address issues of social inclusion for immigrants in the long term as well as in the short term. The final section of the chapter considers the extent to which homelessness is a transitional phase in the process of integration.

Throughout the chapter evidence is drawn from different countries in Europe (using evidence from the national reports of the researchers of the European Observatory on Homelessness – see www.feantsa.org) to illustrate issues under discussion. The conclusions provide a framework for Chapter Six, which considers the nature of service provision and the role of homelessness services in meeting the needs of immigrants and the lessons we can draw from this for policy approaches.

Vulnerability to homelessness

Undoubtedly a key factor affecting the vulnerability of immigrants to homelessness relates to their legal status. In previous chapters we have described migrants in relation to the concept of citizenship. A central aspect for migrants is "the right to enter, or, once having entered, the right to stay" (Anthias, 2000, p 39). Their legal status also infers rights to social or public sector housing, to social protection (for example, minimum income, rights to health services) and their right to work. Legal status can also affect the immigrant's right to access homelessness services.

While legal status is undoubtedly a key factor in creating vulnerability to various forms of homelessness, it has been argued (Schill et al, 2001) that 'race' and ethnicity are at least as significant as immigrant status in determining access to, and opportunity within, the housing market. Thus we may expect that the ethnic mix pre-existing in countries as well as in the migrant streams will pattern the profile of homelessness among immigrants.

One of few published contributions which explicitly examines migration and homelessness is that by Daly (1996). Daly argues that "Questions of race, ethnicity, gender and cultural tolerance are at the heart of European debates over housing and homelessness, social programmes and budget cutbacks" (p 11). Citing evidence of anti-immigration statements by various politicians including EU heads of government, Daly goes on to highlight two parallel trends in the EU (p 12):

- enhancing the rights of some residents (for example, guest workers, longer established migrants);
- raising the gates at ports of entry, so that recent arrivals are increasingly treated as 'shadows' of citizens, likely to suffer racism, disaffiliation and homelessness.

Key arguments are that across Europe, public policy does not sufficiently address multiculturalism and that immigrants lack power and so can be ignored by politicians. There is an enduring publicly perceived conflict of interests between immigrants and nationals. Under pressure from xenophobes, governments have moved to the right on issues of immigration, alongside a more general advance of the political far-right in elections across Europe; a trend continued post-2000. Consequently it is argued that "tension is mounting for newcomers to conform, to speak the national languages, and to integrate into mainstream society" (p 22).

However, Daly's paper has some weaknesses (Anderson, 2003). It does not present any new empirical evidence, but rather draws on published literature to compare a sample of EU countries. The title talks about migration and homelessness, but much of the discussion appears to be about homelessness and 'race' rather than migration. This is a dilemma common to much of the available literature when attempting to examine the links between migration and homelessness. In Daly's paper, the link between increasing homelessness and increasing racism in relation to migration is not robustly demonstrated (although it may well be correct). Daly cites extensive evidence of homelessness and racial disadvantage but presents no specific material on migration and homelessness, and only discusses asylum seeking, which is just one part of the total picture of migration.

In addition to these factors of legal status, 'race' and ethnicity, discrimination and racism, we would argue that structural or institutional factors also play a part in increasing the vulnerability of immigrants to homelessness. There is evidence, cited below, to demonstrate that many European governments have been caught unawares by the rapid increase in asylum migration during the 1990s, and that reception facilities have been unable to cope with the level of demand. Equally, the shift in policies involving the use both of central reception facilities and of dispersed housing has created an increased vulnerability for some categories of immigrant. Immigration policies in many countries prevent immigrants from working (or receiving more than the very minimum of income support) and in this manner make it difficult to access housing.

We may also expect that agency factors as well as structural factors will affect the vulnerability to homelessness. This also suggests that factors of gender and age create specific forms of homelessness, which are often invisible to the traditional nature of service provision or that may require specialist services to accommodate. The situation of women and of young people in particular is cited in much research in relation to homelessness among immigrants.

Finally, the nature of the migratory process may, of itself, create a vulnerability to homelessness. The nature of migration and theories to understand the processes of migration were briefly reviewed in Chapter Two. That review demonstrated distinctive types of migration processes at work and illustrated clearly that immigration is not a simple process of leaving a country of origin to settle permanently in a country of destination. Rather it involves a complex set of processes of movement and adjustment involving relationships to different communities and places that result in a pattern of settlement that may be more or less permanent. A satisfactory understanding of transnational migration requires an integrated approach to the entire social process in which migrants operate. This includes the position of migrant families in their home communities, the specifics of the migratory process itself, the patterns of insertion and adaptation to the receiving societies and the transnational links that may tie some immigrants in a geographically dispersed but integrated community (Pieke, 2002). Studies of 'diasporas' or transnational communities in Europe demonstrate complex interactions between immigrants in different metropolitan areas and regions and complex movements of people between these areas (Kesteloot, 2003).

Equally, our review of migration literature demonstrates that migration from one country to another involves a process of decision making by the individual or household. This decision making is often made under situations of stress and uncertainty and in the face of a lack of knowledge that may be additionally constrained by a lack of language or of understanding of the laws and culture of the host country. Roque (2000) argues that mobility consists of moving, at a certain moment, from one place where a period of time has been spent – be it longer or shorter – to another place where one arrives and will spend another period of time which has yet to be decided. One cannot consider mobility, he argues, without considering the periods of permanence spent in these places. Thus, we move from the classical analysis of migratory movements as discrete, isolated acts by which people change their place of residence because of a series of constraints or decisions, to another analysis of migration as events that take place in time. This considers the whole migratory process as a sequence of movements that are linked to each other by periods of settlement, which entail relationships in socially constructed places. The study of mobility is, thus, "inseparable from the study of permanence, of settlement, of establishment" (Roque, 2000, p 3).

Viewing migration as a process, as a series of interlinked events associated with more than one place and in which settlement involves the development of a sense of place identity (or sense of acceptance) gives a distinct understanding of the role of housing in the migration process, and gives some understanding of the vulnerability to homelessness for some migrant groups. When these different explanations are placed alongside the different categories of immigrant (identified in Chapter Two), it is clear that there are different causes of homelessness or different vulnerability to homelessness among immigrants.

Legal status

Different categories of migrant are determined on the basis of European membership (freedom of movement within the EU) and national legislation which creates a distinction between:

- documented immigrants (including legal labour, family reunion, repatriates);
- refugees and asylum seekers;
- undocumented immigrants.

Each group of immigrants has a different vulnerability to homelessness determined, in part, by their legal status and the rights this accords them in a particular country. The homelessness pathway for new immigrants will be influenced by the extent to which this determines their access to housing and social protection.

Documented immigrants

This is a broad group and includes migrants admitted as workers, repatriated national groups, students or those joining family. Other legal migrants include EU citizens and citizens of former colonies. Generally immigrants are expected to support themselves without recourse to public funds and it is likely that the majority do house themselves in the private sector (renting or in home ownership) possibly with the support of family. Students have access to university accommodation and are supported by scholarships or parental contributions.

Although there is little specific research on the housing outcomes for these groups, a level of homelessness can be expected to occur since access to the housing market will depend on their socioeconomic, family and employment status. Migrant EU citizens appear as a significant proportion of the homeless population in many metropolitan centres. For example, Scottish and Irish people form a substantial and highly visible section of the single homeless in London (Fitzpatrick et al, 2001); a quarter of the reported homeless clients in Stockholm came from abroad, around half of whom are Finnish (Sahlin, 2003). Often a woman's legal status is dependent on that of her husband and will therefore change if she leaves him as a result of domestic violence. Women immigrants are therefore also vulnerable to homelessness arising from domestic abuse and there is evidence in many countries of an increase in immigrants in women's refuge accommodation (Federatie Opvang, 2001; Hemat Gryffe, 2001; Busch-Geertsema, 2003).

There is also evidence across Europe that recent legislation has tightened controls and increased restrictions on legal migrants arriving through family reunion (see Chapter Three). The 2002 Danish Aliens Act is one example of how this process interacts with housing issues. Under the rules on family reunification described in the Danish Aliens Act, aliens with relatives in Denmark do not have the right but the opportunity to obtain a residence permit in Denmark. However, a number of requirements must be met, both with regard to the spouses, partners themselves, children and to their marriage/partnership. There are also a number of specific requirements for the individual already resident in Denmark including a housing requirement. Under the housing requirement, the individual already resident must be able to document that he or she has personal accommodation of reasonable size at his or her disposal.

This means that they must have a place to live that they rent or own (or own cooperatively). If the property is rented, the lease period must be permanent or extend to at least three years beyond the date on which the residence permit application is submitted. A sub-let on a property will not fulfil the housing requirement. Furthermore, the residence must be of reasonable size. Once family reunification is completed there must be no more than two people per room or the total residential area must be at least 20m² per person.

A number of EU countries have experienced a relatively large influx of repatriate immigrants; these include Germany (1980 onwards), Greece (1990s), Portugal (1970s) and Finland (1990s onwards). Repatriate immigrants are relatively well provided for in relation to housing and social benefits and employment training. However, many of the special measures to ease the integration of repatriates have been reduced in recent years. There are thus different pathways to homelessness among repatriates, or at least we can say that the causes of homelessness among repatriate immigrants occur for different reasons. First, legislation may require a reception period that normally means a period of residence in temporary housing. Second, repatriates gain access to regular housing but are often segregated and concentrated in large social housing estates where they experience problems of social isolation, unemployment and poverty which, combined with language difficulties, make it more difficult to integrate into society. This can lead to relationship breakdown or to problems of unstable lifestyles and homelessness among the children of repatriates. These problems have been described in relation to the children of Aussiedler in Germany where research has shown a high and increased rate of young repatriates in the penal system for young offenders (Walter and Grübl, 1999). Walter and Grübl also refer to the segregated housing situation and to social isolation from the rest of the local population as one of the causes of this development. Third, vulnerability to homelessness occurs simply because insufficient housing is provided for the number of repatriates accepted in different periods of time.

Refugees and asylum seekers

Setting minimum standards on the rules on the recognition and content of refugee status was set as a priority for establishing a Common European Asylum System by the EU Heads of State of Government at the European Council in Tampere (Finland) in October 1999. In September 2001, the European Commission tabled a proposal for a directive laying down minimum standards for the qualification and status of third country nationals and stateless people as refugees or as persons who otherwise need international protection.

Immigrants who are accorded a status as a Convention Refugee (that is, under Article 1 of the 1951 Geneva Convention relating to the status of refugees) are generally entitled to access to housing and social benefits on the same basis as citizens. However, structural factors related to a lack of social housing (on which most refugees depend) and institutional factors related to the allocation and waiting times make it difficult to access suitable housing. In addition, immigration dispersal policies can lead to 'secondary migration' within countries of immigrants when asylum seekers are granted refugee status that can lead to their vulnerability to insecure housing or homelessness.

The legislative framework for responding to asylum claims in most European countries derives from the 1951 Convention on Human Rights. Applications for political asylum to all EU countries have increased significantly during the 1990s. Hence there has been significant retrenchment in recent years due to a combination of "self-interest and political expediency" (Pearl and Zetter, 2002), for example, new legislation (referred to in Chapter Three) in Denmark, Greece, the Netherlands and the UK. Although housing is at the very cornerstone of reception and resettlement, the outcome of legislation has meant that "the reality for many asylum seekers is being homeless, stateless and status-less within a system that is far from welcoming" (Pearl and Zetter, 2002, p 226).

The specific detail of the nature of homelessness among asylum seekers in different countries is discussed below. The issue to be drawn out here is that the process of asylum reception and the nature of the accommodation made available create different pathways, which may lead to inadequate or insecure housing or to visible homelessness. Two distinct pathways emerge in each of the two types of reception system in use across Europe:

- Arrange own accommodation (using allowances where available or own resources). Where asylum rules preclude the applicant taking employment they are reliant on black market labour or available allowances for housing costs. They also need support from institutional sources or friends/family to access the rental sector. Allocation rules for social housing normally mean they are dependent on the private sector. Where their private resources or allowances are insufficient to meet market rents then the applicant will be vulnerable to homelessness.
- Sent to reception centre where application is considered. If their application is rejected they may leave, become undocumented immigrants and rely on friends or low-threshold hostels or rooflessness. If the application is accepted they may be sent to a new town (under a dispersal programme) and provided with housing as a refugee. They may subsequently leave this (for example, for reasons of employment opportunity, desire to be close to family and friends, harassment) and then become homeless (rely on family and friends or on homeless services).

Undocumented immigrants

Undocumented immigrants have no legal rights to housing or social support and hence we may expect their position in the housing market to be more precarious than other immigrants. Legislation in all countries excludes undocumented immigrants from the social housing sector. Hence, they are forced to rely on the informal housing market, housing provided by an employer, family or friends, low-threshold hostels or rough sleeping. Even access to homeless services, however, is denied to them by law in many countries (see Chapter Six).

In the face of evidence of growing irregular immigration we may have expected to see a growth in immigrants in homeless services. However, governments have employed a range of policies, including regularisation, tighter controls and penalties on employers and readmission agreements for deportation. In recent years, Belgium, Greece, Italy, Portugal and Spain have regularised the status of substantial numbers of migrants with irregular status within their territories. France, the UK and Germany have increased penalties on employers hiring undocumented workers. Germany and Spain have signed readmission agreements with countries to enable the deportation of migrants without permission to reside (Gibney, 2001).

Undocumented immigration remains a poorly understood phenomenon and the housing circumstances of irregular immigrants have not been subject of detailed research. The vulnerability of undocumented immigrants, however, depends to some extent on the reasons for their undocumented status. The ways in which immigrants become illegal in the eyes of the state are diverse, as are the origins of the immigrants themselves. However, there are two broad groups of undocumented immigrants. First, there are those who have never been given right of entry or residence in a country. These include those entering fraudulently using false documents and those who are trafficked. The growth of trafficking networks means that deliberate acts of illicit entry are on the rise throughout Europe. Second, there are those who enter a country legally but overstay their visa period or otherwise breach their conditions of admission. A third group would include those who lose their rights of residence as a result, for example, of relationship breakdown; this includes women who flee an abusive partner on whom their residence rights depend. This broad categorisation does not capture the diversity of circumstances in which immigrants come to be outside the protection of the law but it does demonstrate that this is a heterogeneous group, that pathways to homelessness vary accordingly and that we should not ascribe characteristics or make assumptions about the totality.

The experiences of undocumented migrants in seeking and keeping accommodation are as diverse as the people within this category (Anderson, 2000). However, even a cursory knowledge of these situations is sufficient to suggest how their housing situation may be affected by the nature of their illegal status. People who enter a country through trafficking may be dependent on the trafficker for access to accommodation. People who overstay their residence rights may have accommodation that they accessed during the legal period of their residence. Women who flee an abusive partner also flee the safety of their accommodation and rely on women's shelters for support. Yet others will sleep rough and rely on low-threshold homeless services for food, clothing and overnight accommodation or otherwise obtain sanctuary from religious institutions and churches.

For many their illegal status means that the accommodation is transitory, at best, allowing them to keep one step ahead of the authorities. Tightening restrictions in most countries increasingly exclude access to social housing and also means that normal private rental contracts are problematic. Hence undocumented migrants have a dependence on fellow expatriates for information on the availability of affordable and accessible places to reside. It also follows that the likelihood is that, where they find accommodation, it will be of the worst kind "in the most run down and shadiest end of the property market" (Gibney, 2001, p 12). Their weak market situation means that, in many circumstances, the undocumented migrants face exploitation in the housing market, not just from unscrupulous landlords but also from fellow expatriates – "the ties of ethnicity and nationality that so often serve to make survival without proper documentation possible can just as quickly turn into fetters that facilitate exploitation" (Gibney, 2001, p 13). Another view of undocumented migrants is given in a Spanish study (Olabuénaga Ruiz et al, 1999). This research argues that irregular migration is rarely a haphazard enterprise and that therefore "a substantial proportion of those who enter as unauthorised immigrants are adventurers or even entrepreneurs, the makers of decisions that reflect calculated risks that make them a desired social type in many countries" (taken from Gibney, 2001, p 35; referencing the study by Olabuénaga Ruiz et al, 1999). German research, on the other hand, suggests that de facto refugees form a substantial proportion of undocumented entrants and residents, boosted by the way in which restrictive measures force legitimate refugees into illegal activities to enter the state (Alt, 1999). On this view the phenomenon of the 'refugee illegal' results in a privatising of the assistance, including accommodation, provided to refugees as ethnic communities, friends, relatives and NGOs become providers of housing and support in lieu of the state.

'Race' and ethnicity

It has been suggested that 'race' and ethnicity are at least as significant as immigrant status in determining access to the labour market and housing market (Schill et al, 2001). It is indeed evident that some ethnic groups are more vulnerable to homelessness and housing exclusion than others. It is difficult, on the basis of existing evidence, to provide a clear or convincing explanation of why ethnicity, in itself, should be an important factor in determining access to and opportunity within the housing market. We may expect that overt and covert racism will play a part, and extensive reference is made in the previous chapter to the discrimination that occurs in the allocation of private and public sector rented housing. Reference is made elsewhere (Busch-Geertsema, 2003) to public attitudes to the 'deserving and undeserving' immigrants; for example, repatriates are generally well provided for in most countries. Hence immigrants who share similarities in language and culture to the host community may find it easier to assimilate.

The existing ethnic composition of the host country may also be expected to be a key factor. For example, in Portugal, immigrants from Eastern Europe who do not have an already established community in the country are reported to have more difficulties accessing housing than immigrants of African origin who can relate to existing communities and refer to immigrant associations run by fellow countrymen (Da Costa and Baptista, 2003). Among African immigrants the consolidation over the years of strong family and other social networks (for example, neighbourhood) and their low levels of unemployment (lower than that of nationals) guaranteeing some 'regular' income have played a major role in preventing homelessness. Eastern European immigrants appear to be more vulnerable to these extreme forms of marginalisation. However, this may also be related to the fact that Eastern European immigrants have arrived more recently and have often come through clandestine channels.

The economic circumstances of migrants at the point of migration and/or differences between sending countries in the level of development can also be posited as an explanation. For example, in the UK, Anderson (2003) summarises research to demonstrate the differences in the housing circumstances of immigrants from India, Pakistan and Bangladesh. Although none of these groups appears in the homelessness statistics there are marked differences between them in their reliance on public sector housing and in the quality and affordability of the housing they occupy. However, it is unlikely that such differences are a consequence solely of ethnic variations. As important is the fact that it is generally poorer and more disadvantaged households who have migrated from Pakistan and Bangladesh while Ugandan Asians and immigrants from India are relatively well-educated and wealthier at the point of migration.

Cultural factors may also underlie apparent differences between ethnic groups in terms of their vulnerability to homelessness. For example, de Feijter (2003) reflects on the fact that relationship breakdown is accepted as a key risk factor in relation to homelessness and points to cultural differences in relation to divorce and family status among ethnic groups in the Netherlands. Divorce plays a limited role in most ethnic communities with an Islamic background. The divorce rate among Turks and Moroccans is about as high as that among the Dutch (CBS, 2000, p 52), while that of the Surinamese and African population is much higher. Special attention must be paid to the divorce risk of ethnically mixed marriages. About 15% of all Dutch marriages end in divorce after 10 years. That rate is 75% among all marriages between Turkish or Moroccan men and Dutch women. There are not many single-person households, and few single-parent families among the Turks and Moroccans, while among the Surinamese, Antilleans and Africans these figures are much higher (CBS, 1999, pp 12, 17-20).

The extent and nature of homelessness among immigrants

Immigrants experience homelessness in all its various forms – rooflessness, houselessness, insecure and inadequate housing (see the FEANTSA definition of homelessness, www.feantsa.org; Edgar and Doherty, 2003). However, there is very little available or reliable data on the extent and nature of homelessness among immigrants in Europe, either because this information is not counted or is not counted in a consistent manner across Europe. Thus while there are statistics from official sources on the numbers of asylum applications and refugees or on the number of repatriates receiving assistance, there remains a lack of data on immigrants in other situations. Equally, there is very little available research evidence to explain how risk factors arising from immigration translate into homelessness. More is known about the traits of housing disadvantage for immigrants with respect to the local population. The housing market situation, variety of housing strategies and case studies of different ethnic and national groups was discussed in previous chapters. In this section we consider the routes into homelessness experienced by immigrants and the nature of that homeless situation.

Asylum seekers and refugees

The situation of immigrants who are 'fortunate' enough to be accepted as refugees or asylum seekers was described above. One situation for these immigrants is a period of residence in reception centres or temporary accommodation. This is often communal accommodation, often of relatively poor quality. The length of time spent in the centres is often longer than originally envisaged when the centres were established. The availability of this accommodation is often insufficient for the demand and priority may be given to families over single people. Finally, the temporary nature of this accommodation and the inability to enter the labour market during that period creates additional problems for the asylum seeker in establishing a firm foothold in the housing market unless some form of follow-on support is provided. These issues are exemplified here using evidence from Belgium, France, Sweden and the UK. Similar examples could be cited for other countries.

Although France ranks only fifth in Europe after the UK, Germany, the Netherlands and Belgium, the numbers of asylum applications has tripled over the past four years with an estimated 70,000 applications in 2001. There are two legal bases for claiming asylum in France: Convention Asylum (under the 1951 Geneva Convention) and Territorial Asylum (introduced in 1998 by the

Table 5.1: Estimate of accommodation needs for asylum seekers in France (2001)

Asylum category		Low estimate	High estimate
Convention (arrivals)		47,291	
Territorial (arrivals)		17,270	31,206
Sub-total	A	64,561	78,497
Convention (pre-determination)		80,000	
Territorial (pre-determination)		31,000	
Sub-total	B	111,000	
Statutory refugees (adults)	C	102,000	
Failed asylum (overstayers)	D	100,000	
Total		377,561	391,497

Chevènement Act). Maurel (2003) estimates the demand for housing or accommodation arising from all forms of asylum in 2001 to be between 375,000 and 400,000 (see Table 5.1).

There are two forms of accommodation for asylum seekers in France: reception centres (CADA) and transition hostels (centres provisoire d'hébergement, CPH). The reception centres (CADA) provide accommodation from the time of being granted temporary leave to remain until the final decision (including any appeal to the refugee Appeals Board). This provision has increased 182% in six years, in response to the increase in asylum claims (from 3,470 to 9,782 places). Nevertheless, supply is heavily over-subscribed and may meet only 20% of asylum application demand. Convention refugees, who arrived with the prior agreement of the French authorities, can find accommodation in one of 28 temporary centres (CPH). These centres provide statutory refugees with accommodation for six months (renewable) and support for the integration process (for example, help in finding housing and work). However, the number of centres has remained the same since 1998 and no additional places have been provided since 2000. Government plans to launch a programme of low-rent transit apartment homes partly explains why this provision is stagnating. Although statutory refugees have access to public housing on the same terms as French nationals, and rights to housing subsidies, they find housing difficult to access. A recent survey by France Terre d'Asile (2001) describes these difficulties to include housing costs, unsuitable location and discrimination. The consequence of this lack of access to social housing leads to CPH residents overstaying their six-month period and hence causing blockage of access to CPH places. A number of pilot projects have recently been developed to facilitate access to rehousing but it is too early yet to evaluate the effectiveness of all these initiatives in meeting the need for accommodation.

Ordinary publicly funded temporary shelter and emergency accommodation is being used to plug some of these gaps for asylum seekers and statutory refugees. First, this accommodation is being used to meet the needs of those who are denied access to specialised facilities, for which they are eligible, because it is over-subscribed. The average length of stay in CADA accommodation rose by 50% in the four years from 1997-2001, from one year to 545 days. The main outcome of this log-jam in the CADA (and CPH) system is that, in practice, almost all available places are earmarked for families. This means that single people, although legally entitled to specialised accommodation, are consigned to the emergency provision or to sleeping rough. Second, emergency homeless accommodation is being used to meet the needs of territorial asylum seekers who have no rights of access to specialised CADA and CPH accommodation. In 2001 this affected 30,000 people, 80% of whom were from Algeria. Furthermore, almost two thirds of all convention asylum applications are in the Paris region where status determination times may average 9-10 months and hence this group are also forced to rely on emergency homeless accommodation or alternative informal housing arrangements. In addition, of course, asylum seekers whose applications have failed and undocumented immigrants also rely on the CHRS (centres d'hébergement et de réinsertion – accommodation and social re-integration centres) emergency homeless accommodation.

Hence, although there are no overall statistics to estimate the number of asylum seekers and undocumented immigrants using crisis services and accommodation, it is clear to all the voluntary and public agencies concerned that the system is near to breaking point. A survey by the Paris préfecture (county hall) found that nearly half of those present in emergency shelters and B&B hotels (in November 2001) were foreign nationals, two thirds of whom were asylum seekers (31%) or failed asylum seekers or undocumented migrants (35%). The implications of this crisis of provision and the effects of lengthy periods of stay in emergency accommodation are well described in a recent report by the Forum Réfugiés (2001):

> Up the line from accommodation centres, there is an ever-growing range of emergency provision which, as stays lengthen, quickly proves an unsuitable way of housing families. It is a non-evolving system which grows simply by layering one set of insecure provision on another, with reduced social and administrative support which further undermines those concerned and seriously prejudices the admissibility of their asylum applications. (p x)

Sweden has also experienced an increase in asylum applications in recent years (averaging 2,500 per month during 2002), which has meant that applicants have to wait, on average, 15 months for a determination on their case. Asylum applicants are allowed to make their own living arrangements on condition that they are registered with the Migration Board and report their address. In August 2002 34,600 people were registered awaiting residence permits while only 16,200 were living in their 'own' accommodation in this way (Sahlin, 2003). For the remainder, it is the Migration Board's duty to provide accommodation in refugee or asylum facilities. These consist of rented properties, hotel facilities or, occasionally, dispersed housing. However, most of this accommodation is shared, either shared rooms (in the case of single people) or shared apartments (in the case of families). The standard of accommodation is low. Furthermore, despite this tight control of accommodation arrangements, the available housing is insufficient and on several occasions in 2002 the Migration Board requested help from municipalities to release more housing. The rent allowance for those who make their own living arrangements is very low (55 euros for single people and 110 euros for families) and is not sufficient to rent a normal room on the open market. The housing problem and the low rent subsidy have thus led to a black housing market and, more importantly, to overcrowding among their relatives and fellow nationals with whom they are accommodated. Once an asylum application has been rejected the Migration Board has very tight controls for expulsion. Despite this, it is estimated that 5,400 refugees whose applications were rejected between 1999 and 2001 may be living clandestinely in the country.

Since the mid-1980s central government and municipalities have shared responsibility to house refugees who have been granted a residence permit. However, the National Board of Housing Building and Planning (NBHP) have indicated that about four fifths of municipalities (with agreements on refugee reception) find it difficult to acquire housing for refugees (Boverket, 2002, p 50). The dilemma is that those municipalities who can offer housing are mainly in areas with poor labour market opportunities. Hence, a secondary migration occurs when refugees move on to areas with better employment prospects. This creates particular problems for Stockholm whose Integration Department has lobbied to improve the prospects for settlement of refugees elsewhere. In practice Stockholm has been able to "offer help in obtaining housing only to families with children and refugees with severe physical or mental problems. Other refugees must solve their housing problems themselves. Many of these have unsatisfactory housing solutions and move around among friends and acquaintances" (Integration Department of Stockholm, 1999, p 3). This report points to the increased difficulties facing newly arrived immigrants, caused, in part, by the blockage in temporary refugee housing from those unable to move on to the open housing market. The report refers to "many examples of unsatisfactory housing solutions such as boutique premises, garages, tents and people being forced to sleep in night buses ... with the sharp increase in the number of refugees, homelessness among them has risen markedly" (pp 6-7).

The National Board of Health and Social Services (NBHW) has undertaken two national mapping exercises (in 1993 and 1999) using surveys of social work authorities, abuse treatment, penal institutions and voluntary organisations working with the homeless. The most recent survey indicated that 14% of the homeless, and 30% of homeless people aged under 25, were born outside Sweden or Finland. Since these are administrative statistics it is likely that there are appreciably larger numbers of newly arrived immigrants who are not known to social services agencies. Furthermore, refugee reception in the municipalities is separated from the social services and administers its own housing. This contributes to the fact that homeless refugees are not counted in social service statistics, nor are they charted by the NBHW.

The organisational structure for the reception of asylum seekers in Belgium has undergone radical change in recent years (De Decker, 2001). Until the mid-1980s the reception of asylum seekers was the responsibility of the local Public Social Welfare Centres (OCMW). Since then the government has created reception centres and a dispersal programme to local OCMW. Since 1996 asylum seekers who are at the beginning of their application (that is, the period in which their residential insecurity is greatest) are assigned to a reception centre organised and recognised by the state. If their application is ruled admissible they are then designated to an OCMW based on the rules of the dispersion plan and they can then take residence in that municipality. The number of applications in Belgium doubled from 10,892 in 1998 to 22,819 in 2000. The number of reception places increased to 6,846 by August 2001. In common with the situation in France and Sweden, the increase in asylum applications, the limitation on reception places and longer time-scale in processing applications meant that capacity at the reception centres shrank as asylum seekers tended to stay there longer. This scale of increase in applications put pressure on the cheapest segment of the housing market in the local OCMW areas to which applicants were referred. As a consequence in January 2001, the 1980 Aliens Act was amended to include an article to make rack-renting and multiple letting of the same premises punishable by imprisonment and/or fines.

Asylum seekers and refugees are clearly the most vulnerable to poor housing (if not outright homelessness) of all the streams of migrants currently entering the UK (Anderson, 2003). Although those who are granted refugee status are legally entitled to the same housing rights as UK citizens, they start from a disadvantaged position and need to negotiate the transition from asylum seeker to refugee. One evident response to the increase in asylum applications has been a degree of retrenchment in the UK law relating to asylum seekers that was amended in 1993, 1996, 1999 and 2002.

Reviewing the situation in the UK, Pearl and Zetter (2002, p 226) argue that "The reality for many asylum seekers is being homeless, stateless and status-less within a system that is far from welcoming" and "Housing is at the very corner stone of reception and resettlement". Controlling access to housing has been central to government asylum and immigration strategy. The 1996 Asylum and Immigration Act, which effectively excluded them from key welfare benefits, drove into destitution and homelessness thousands of mainly single asylum seekers who were deemed to fall outside of the homelessness legislation (Pearl and Zetter, 2002, p 230). Hence, the long-term impact of good or poor reception arrangements is significant.

There is a strong geographical concentration of asylum migration within a relatively small number of local housing authority areas which, for many years, shouldered the impact of high and increasing levels of demand (Anderson, 2003; Pearl and Zetter 2002). Asylum seekers and refugees tended to cluster in areas with established communities or near ports of entry or detention centres. The highest concentrations were very clearly in London and the South East of England, where social housing was already in short supply. Lett and Brangwyn (2000, p 47) concluded that asylum seekers and 'visitor switchers' (people entering the UK as short-term visitors but subsequently given an extension for a year or longer) accounted for 10% of in-migration to London. The current population of London was given as 7 million, including 1.8 million (24%) from black and minority ethnic groups, 250,000 to 350,000 of which were estimated to be from refugee communities. It was further estimated that London boroughs supported 51,000 destitute asylum seekers and that in the 12 months to September 1999 they accepted an additional 9,000 homeless asylum seekers (out of a total of 37,000 homeless households which they accommodated).

Given Home Office estimates of 60,000-70,000 asylum applications in 1999/2000 (6,000 per month), many authorities in London and the South East considered it would no longer be possible to provide temporary accommodation (for example, in hotels) for asylum seekers within the financial limits set by the level of government grant. Further, the numbers of destitute asylum seekers were expected to rise to about 41,500 in 2000/01, including 5,000 families, and 36,500 single people. They would be housed in local authority stock, by the private sector and in other forms of accommodation, but the majority were increasingly likely to be accommodated outside London and the South East for the six months while their applications are being considered (Lett and Brangwyn, 2000). The government dispersal programme implemented post-1999 was designed to alleviate these pressures.

Under the 1999 legislation, from April 2000, newly arriving asylum seekers have been the responsibility of the Home Office's National Asylum and Support System (NASS) and have been subject to a programme of dispersal to pre-allocated accommodation across the country. NASS pays all of the costs of housing and supporting asylum seekers under the contract agreements with local agencies (mainly local authorities). Once a final determination on status is made, households have only 14 days to vacate their accommodation, precipitating a potentially high risk of homelessness at that stage in the process. Advice on housing and benefits is only forthcoming once refugee status is determined. Pearl and Zetter (2002) have summarised some key features of the 1999 Immigration and Asylum Act. The system of dispersal across the UK on a no-choice basis aimed to minimise the incentive to economic migration, as well as to relieve the burden on London and the South East of England. The authorities hoped to avoid social exclusion and racial tension, by linking dispersal to existing settled immigrant communities. They also aimed to prevent asylum seekers moving back to London.

In practice, groups of asylum seekers (by country of origin) were dispersed in clusters to UK regions. Local authority participation in the scheme was voluntary and asylum seekers were generally relocated to areas with a pool of empty social housing (Pearl and Zetter, 2002, p 234). In general these were also areas of high unemployment and poverty (p 238). Hence the dispersal system relocated vulnerable asylum seekers to communities that were already marginalised. Glasgow was one of the UK cities which opted to assist NASS with the provision of accommodation for asylum seekers, resulting in a significant flow of new migrants to the city, almost all of whom were housed within the city council's own stock. A study conducted on behalf of housing NGO Shelter (Scotland) sought to evaluate the provision of housing and support to asylum seekers in Scotland (Buck, 2001). The study reported that 3,391 asylum seekers/households had been dispersed to Glasgow by June 2001 and that the number could rise to 15,000 by 2004.

Proposals to introduce an even more punitive regime for asylum seekers were presented to the UK Parliament in 2002 (Pearl and Zetter, 2002, p 242). The revised system involves housing all new asylum seekers in special purpose accommodation (detention) centres where they would live separately from local communities until their immigration status is decided. One outcome of this system would be to make the process of deportation of failed applicants much more straightforward.

Repatriates

Although repatriate immigrants have in the past enjoyed better access to housing, social protection and social support measures than other groups of immigrants, the reception arrangements for more recent repatriates has not been so beneficial. Furthermore, their integration into the host country has been managed in a manner that leaves a majority in a poor labour market situation or dependent on social protection and hence in a weak housing market situation. There is therefore a pattern of reliance on temporary accommodation for extended periods during the reception phase and a vulnerability to homelessness in later years. Evidence from Greece, Germany and Finland is cited here to illustrate these issues.

Pontic Greeks who came to Greece from the former Soviet Union are considered repatriates by the Greek authorities and are thus differentiated from the legal status of refugees. However, Pontic refugees are generally people who had never lived in Greece before. According to statistics from Greek embassies in countries from the former Soviet Union, which report the number of passport visas issued to Pontic Greeks, 79,083 arrivals of Pontic Greeks have been registered from 1987 to 1998 (Petropoulos, 1998). Recent data from a study by the Ministry of Macedonia-Thrace[1] shows that the population of repatriates from countries from the former Soviet Union amounts to about 160,000 people. In geographic terms, Pontic repatriates tend to settle mainly in the greater Athens area and in Northern Greece. More specifically, data from the study conducted by the Ministry of Macedonia-Thrace shows that about a fifth settled in Attica, Thrace and Macedonia with the highest concentration (about 51,000) in the prefecture of Thessalonica.

The Pontic repatriates are, in the main, younger working-age married people with a larger than average family size (Kasimati, 1992). However, their inclusion in the labour market has been difficult as a result of difficulties with the Greek language, lack of knowledge of the laws and bureaucracy, cultural differences, education, and their need for vocational training. Hence, unemployment is estimated at about 31% of the working population. Pontic Greeks who are employed work chiefly as construction workers, while most are engaged in alternative employment in the black economy (Vaïou and Hatzimihalis, 1997).

The government is trying to facilitate the integration of Pontic repatriates through various means, primarily through the National Institute for the Reception and Settlement of Pontic Greeks (known by the Greek acronym 'EIYAPOE') which was created by presidential decree in December 1990. The EIYAPOE is a Public Welfare Institute of Private Law under the auspices of the Minister of Foreign Affairs. The programme for the settlement of repatriates provides for the provision of services to repatriates based on a four-step plan:

a) On arrival, Pontic Greeks can be accommodated for 15-30 days in accommodation centres operated on the premises of the EIYAPOE, with a daily capacity of 240 people, or in temporary accommodation centres operated in hospitals or student dormitories. They are provided with initial accommodation, including room and board, medical care and Greek language lessons;

b) The next step is preparation for integration into society. The immigrants are accommodated in reception facilities, where they can stay for six months and undergo language and vocational training, while children are prepared for the education system. There are five such reception facilities in the prefectures of Trikala, Kavala, Xanthi, Rodopi and Evros, with a total capacity of 3,500 people.

c) The third stage entails accommodation for repatriates in rented housing units, as well as their occupational establishment. The Institute pays the rent until private housing can be obtained.

d) The last stage concerns their legal establishment.

To this end, the EIYAPOE is pursuing a housing programme in Thrace for all those who have taken part in its programme, by purchasing housing units, constructing facilities and pursuing a self-housing plan. However, the EIYAPOE, does not have many options to solve the problem of permanent housing for repatriates. During the first years of the Institute, Pontic Greeks tended to stay in reception centres eight to 10 months and in reception facilities two to four years. Such enormous delays led to passivity, marginalisation, institutionalisation and isolation of the people concerned. Furthermore, the lack of opportunities in areas where Pontic Greeks have settled hinders their daily lives and makes their integration difficult. As a result, Pontic Greeks prefer to move to the large urban centres where things are easier for them, especially in finding a job. Thus the proportion of Pontic repatriates settled by the EIYAPOE remains small. Of some 60,000 Pontic Greeks who settled permanently in Greece in the period from 1983 to 1998, the Institute involved only 15% in its programme (9,349 people or about 2,000 families) (Maureas, 1998).

Finland has traditionally been a country of emigration. Up to the end of the 1980s, most of the immigrants were migrants returning from Sweden. Finland began to receive a small number of quota refugees in the 1970s and 1980s. However, the immigration situation changed considerably during the 1990s, when ethnic Ingrian Finns and their families were offered returnee status. Ingrian Finns are Ingrians of Finnish descent who, together with members of their family from Russia, Estonia and other parts of the former Soviet Union, hold 'returnee' status in Finland. Altogether Finland has received about 25,000 Ingrian Finns. It has been estimated that, in 2002, a further 23,000 Ingrians or other persons of Finnish descent had registered on the return migration waiting list in Russia and Estonia. The main obstacle to families moving back is that they cannot find accommodation in Finland (Sorainen, 2002, pp 10-11).

According to the Ministry of Labour, most Ingrians who travel to Finland arrange housing by themselves, or with the help of relatives and friends, because it may take years before they would get a municipal dwelling. During the 1990s municipalities provided dwellings, but nowadays Ingrians are responsible for organising housing for themselves. Often this means that they first live with friends or relatives. Research shows that nearly all single Ingrians coming to Helsinki live first in a dormitory or boarding house and are homeless (Rastas, 2002, pp 54-5). Most move to municipal dwellings after temporary housing. The aim of the reception policy of Ingrians has been to direct returning Ingrians evenly to different parts of Finland (Reiman, 1999, p 5), but this has not been fully achieved. According to a report on the integration of Ingrians, their housing situation is difficult in the metropolitan region but not usually a problem in the small municipalities. In Helsinki Ingrians had to wait one-and-a-half to two years, on average, in temporary housing before getting a municipal dwelling. If Ingrians were located out of the centres of urban growth, their housing situation would be better (Ministry of Labour, 1998).

Homelessness among immigrants is generally considered to be a marginal but growing problem, although there are no previous figures for comparison since homelessness among immigrants was first included in a survey on homelessness in 2001. The proportion of immigrants in the various dormitories for homeless men and women in the Helsinki region has risen considerably in the past few years (Rastas, 2002). However, there is one dormitory for Ingrian women in Helsinki that is exclusively for immigrants. The proportion of immigrant applicants for municipal housing has also increased dramatically in recent years (14% in 2001). The biggest growth has been among immigrants other than refugees and Ingrian Finns because municipal housing is often the only solution for these immigrant groups (Korhonen, 2002, pp 36-7).

Until the late 1990s homeless immigrants were Ingrian Finns who had just arrived in the country and were in a state of transition in a new country. Now many homeless immigrants have been in the country for a long time and have arrived at homelessness by various paths. Some have moved from other parts of the country, some have got divorced and some are young people moving out of their parental home (Rastas, 2002, pp 23, 44-5). Many of the homeless families in the metropolitan region are Ingrian returnees in temporary apartments waiting for permanent housing or some other kind of accommodation. This is considered to be one reason for the increase in homeless families in the metropolitan region in general (Vesanen and Tiitinen, 1998).

Germany has the largest proportion of foreigners of any member state (7.3 million in 2000, of whom 5.8 million were born outside Germany). Apart from approximately 1 million additional immigrants who have been granted nationality in Germany, there is another group of much greater quantitative significance, namely repatriates – people of German origin coming from different Eastern European countries (predominantly the territory of the former Soviet Union). Repatriates have a legal claim to German citizenship. Their immigration to Germany was approved for political reasons until the late 1980s and supported and promoted through numerous forms of state financial assistance. However, their numbers increased sharply after the political changes in Eastern Europe and the former Soviet Union, reaching a peak in 1990. With almost 400,000 repatriates entering Germany each year, legal procedures were changed to allow a maximum of around 100,000 to 200,000 repatriates to enter Germany every year. In 2001, approximately 3.2 million repatriates were living in Germany.

Repatriates may be seen as one group of immigrants who were (at least until the mid-1990s) generally classified as a 'deserving' group by the German government and actively integrated by a range of positive measures including special financial and educational support, priority in the application of social housing and the provision of special housing programmes. The fact that the number of repatriates currently living in Germany is estimated at 3.2 million and that the number of repatriates who remained in temporary accommodation reserved exclusively for this group did not exceed an estimated 110,000 in 1999, demonstrates the success of the integration of this group into ordinary housing. A number of innovative projects and strategies have shown how integration of a large number of immigrants is possible. Problems remain in relation to significant cultural differences, language difficulties and a high unemployment rate especially among young family members and the discrimination of repatriates as 'foreigners' or 'the Russians'.

Undocumented immigrants

Homelessness among immigrants is often hidden, particularly among undocumented immigrants. Staying with friends or acquaintances, staying in employer-provided accommodation and moving from one area to another are common experiences among immigrants. Studies of female migration and its relationship to domestic service and to the sex industry also illustrate the hidden nature of homelessness among female migrants. There has been a rapid growth in the trafficking in women in the EU (Lim, 1997). A recent study of female migrants involved in prostitution in Athens (Psimmenos, 2000) describes a picture of shared and temporary accommodation that was changed frequently for security and for marketing reasons. The bleakness of their situation is tellingly described:

> ... the females that were not successful ... were mostly concentrated in crowded, downgraded third-class hotel accommodation. Homelessness, coupled with restrictive accommodation produced a spatial network of residence for women and children involved in prostitution. (Psimmenos, 2000, p 93)

The experience of immigrants living in inadequate or insecure housing was described in Chapter Four. While many immigrants tend to live in poorer housing and pay more for it compared with the local population, a proportion live in conditions that effectively constitute homelessness. This situation is typical throughout Europe. However, an Italian study provides some empirical evidence of the scale of the issue. This study suggests that one third of immigrants lived in extreme housing stress and that in the major cities the majority of immigrants lived in extreme housing poverty (Tosi, 2003, quoting Censis, 1993). Although the shanty towns of Lisbon and the bidonvilles of Paris are largely a thing of the past, the circumstances and living conditions for some groups of immigrants remain as precarious today as they ever were. A recent study of undocumented Albanian migrants in the Vathis and Omonia area of Athens, where almost half of the 3,000 Albanians were resident in 10 major third-class hotels, describes their life as:

> ... centred around day-to-day survival.... Up to 20 people were living together in most of the hotel rooms, in self-made wooden constructions, one on top of the other, whilst families usually had to negotiate with others to occupy one bedroom by themselves. (Psimmenos, 2000, p 92)

Homelessness among undocumented immigrants may be hidden because they are unable to access existing services for homeless people. In a number of countries it is difficult for service providers to make provision for undocumented immigrants. This occurs because, in many countries (for example, Austria, Greece, Netherlands, Denmark, Sweden) it is made illegal to provide shelter or work to undocumented immigrants. In other countries (for example, the Netherlands, Austria) service providers are only funded by the state to provide services to immigrants with a residence permit and may risk losing public sector funding altogether if they provide services for undocumented immigrants. In this situation, it is often only church and philanthropic bodies who are able to meet the needs of undocumented immigrants. Despite these restrictions, a recent survey undertaken by FEANTSA among its member organisations demonstrates:

- an increase both in the proportion and absolute number of immigrants among users of homeless services in recent years;
- that undocumented immigrants are now a large proportion, and often a majority, of the clients in low-threshold facilities;
- that homeless services focused on integration or resettlement and supported housing are not accessible to immigrants.

The situation in Italy and the Netherlands is described here to provide an illustration of the extent and nature of the problem of homelessness among undocumented immigrants.

The Italian Federation of Organisations for the Homeless (FIO.psd) undertook a survey among all public and voluntary organisations offering at least one of the following services to homeless people: night shelters, secondary reception/accommodation centres, day centres, street/mobile units, health centres and canteens. The survey was carried out in seven representative cities: Bari, Bergamo, Bolzano, Livorno, Milan, Rome and Turin. A key finding was that, although the proportion of immigrant users varies across the different services, 43% of services reported that more than half of their users were immigrants while 70% of the services questioned said they dealt with undocumented or irregular immigrants (especially night shelters and health centres). In Italy, immigration is a relatively recent phenomenon and the services for the homeless have themselves developed and expanded during the last 10 years. Nevertheless, two thirds of respondents reported an increase in foreign users of their services for the homeless. This is consistent across all types of services except for the more long-term secondary reception accommodation centres. Undocumented immigrants were reported as users, particularly among low-threshold services such as night shelters, canteens and health services. All the health centres receive foreign patients and, among those surveyed, immigrants made up the majority of users, while in 83% of cases the majority of immigrants are without legal residence (FIO.psd, 2002). Equally, the reception procedures of the night shelters are particularly suited to the needs of undocumented immigrants.

In Milan, research (Ismu e Province of Mantova, 2000) distinguishes between three types of immigrant: resident (having the greatest stability); non-resident documented or acquiring documents (semi-stable condition), undocumented with respect to stay permit (precarious). In 1999, 3.8% of 'resident' immigrants in the city of Milan and 11.3% of the 'residents' in the province were in precarious accommodation; among 'non-resident documented' immigrants the corresponding figures rose to 11.7% and 33.1%; while for undocumented immigrants the figure was 30% both for the city and the province. The difference confirms the relationship between legal status and housing accommodation, but the presence of documented immigrants in extreme forms of accommodation poses question marks over policies and invites a more careful consideration of the symptoms of hardship that arise in autonomous or rented accommodation.

During the 1990s homeless service providers in the Netherlands reported a very modest number of undocumented immigrants making use of their shelters (probably 3-6% of an annual number of 25,000 service users). The Federatie Opvang carried out a survey of its member organisations in March 2000 that indicated that three quarters of respondents received undocumented immigrants in their shelters in 1999, amounting to 1,600 adults. This excluded night shelters where clients are not required to register their legal status and hence the real figure is probably significantly higher than this (Federatie Opvang, 2000). A second survey in 2001 identified two distinct groups of undocumented immigrants making use of homeless services.

The first group consists of women and children who are escaping from situations of domestic violence making use of women's shelters. One third of undocumented immigrants in women's shelters had lost their residence status when they fled the perpetrator since their status depended on that of their husband. For a fifth of women it was unclear what caused the problem with their residence status, while the remainder were either women victims of trafficking or women whose asylum application had failed. In 2002 the Minister of Welfare declared that (under the UN 1979 Women's Treaty) women who are victims of domestic violence have a right to shelter and assistance regardless of their residence status. The second group consists mainly of single men without residence permits making use of night shelters and day centres. They accounted for 40% of the occupation in the night shelters. Approximately 45% of these came from the countries of the Russian Federation while a quarter came from Africa (Federatie Opvang, 2000).

In most countries there is very little information available in relation to undocumented immigrants who become homeless. In the UK, for example, it is clear that undocumented immigrants are likely to be at a high risk of homelessness, yet it does not appear that they make use of homeless services. Similarly in Denmark access to homeless services other than night shelters requires a legal right to stay. Despite this, services that can be accessed anonymously report very little use by undocumented immigrants. Undocumented immigrants involved in the black economy are engaged to work in industries such as agriculture or construction and presumably find (unsuitable) accommodation through the gangmaster who organises their work. Their housing circumstances are described in the previous chapter but it is clear that hidden homelessness is the best description of the situation for many undocumented immigrants.

Integration and homelessness

The framework for an EU immigration policy (COM(2000)757) stresses that action to integrate migrants should be a corollary of admission policies. This section considers whether immigrants are becoming assimilated into the housing market or whether vulnerability to precarious housing and homelessness persists. Several aspects of this issue are considered here. First, research from Italy is drawn on to consider the extent to which the housing careers of immigrants lead to an improvement in their housing situation and whether policies of integration assist in this process. This research generally suggests that vulnerability to precarious housing and homelessness persists for a significant proportion of immigrants and that the situation appears, across many areas of Italy, to be worsening (Tosi, 2003). Second, the section draws on research in the UK to examine whether second generation migrants are more susceptible to homelessness. This suggests that black minority ethnic groups are three times more likely to experience homelessness than white British households. While structure and agency factors are drawn on to explain this variation, the research suggests that there is an added dimension of racial prejudice and disadvantage at work to perpetuate vulnerability to homelessness among the children of immigrants (Anderson, 2003). Finally, the section considers the limited evidence of policies to prevent homelessness or to improve access to (rented) housing for immigrants and asylum seekers.

A typical housing career for immigrants in Italy, at least for those who came for employment and with long-term plans, would involve a move from a precarious housing situation to permanent secure housing; from visible or hidden homelessness or reception centres to secure housing (Bernardotti, 2001). A number of studies in Italy have documented the relationship between settlement and housing careers. The most significant data concerns the analysis of residential mobility and the relationship between housing conditions and period of immigration. The relationship between residential accommodation and the period of arrival or time spent in the country is clear. A recent study on immigration in Lombardy, for example, shows how the proportion living in owned or rented family accommodation increases over time while living with friends, in reception centres, hotels or extremely precarious accommodation diminishes. As far as housing mobility is concerned, the matrices that compare housing type at the time of arrival with current type of accommodation confirm the upward direction of mobility, a tendency towards less temporary and more satisfactory accommodation (Ismu e Province of Mantova, 2000).

Thus, improvements in the housing conditions of permanent immigrants over the last decade have been signalled in many areas in Italy, with increases in proper housing accommodation and 'autonomous' solutions and a certain reduction in (explicitly) precarious and assisted situations (Tosi, 2000; Observatorio Regionale, 2001). Nevertheless, the dynamics of the overall picture are not without problems and there are signs of things worsening. Almost all studies register a great variety of types of paths to housing according to the different ethnic/national groups. In the Milan area, a "tendency for housing conditions to worsen in the whole area and in Milan in particular" has been "made evident by the increase in overcrowding, precarious sharing and, not least, by the entrance into reception centres of foreigners who were capable, in the past, of finding alternative housing opportunities" (Ismu e Province of Milan, 2000). Precarious housing is now found for immigrant groups such as Asians who were not exposed to this problem in the past. Furthermore, housing is still signalled as the primary problem that immigrants have to face in a number of provinces and it is significant that this priority also concerns immigrants in rented accommodation and that it is reported independently of legal status (even if undocumented immigrants report it more often).

These recent developments are the result of the combined effects of ongoing changes in immigration and of changes that have occurred in housing markets. As far as immigration is concerned, different factors have contributed to the transformation of housing demand: the stabilisation of substantial proportions of the immigrant population, the growth in the number of families (family reunifications or the formation of new families), the different composition of new arrivals which includes immigrants with more modest financial and personal resources than those of previous phases (Zanfrini, 1998), or in very precarious conditions (for example, an increase of young undocumented immigrants; Palidda, 2000). Behind this phenomenon there lies an indisputable structural factor – the small size of the affordable rented market. On the supply side significant developments include the worsening of the situation in the rented market and a lack of innovation by the institutions in meeting this poor/marginal demand.

While the imbalance between demand and supply persists as far as social housing is concerned, opportunities on the (legal) privately rented market have declined. The supply of accommodation affordable by medium-to-low income groups has reduced and so has the marginal supply. This supply bottleneck makes it more difficult to pursue a housing career of the type pursued by many immigrants in the past. The situation on the rented and 'quasi-rented' market could worsen with a further expansion of the informal housing market. On the other hand, as many of the social welfare agencies involved in housing report, it has become more difficult to reproduce the successful models of intervention adopted by voluntary associations and municipalities in the 'emergency years', especially in areas where it was relatively easy for immigrants to find employment.

This situation poses significant obstacles to the integration of immigrants. For the most disadvantaged the alternative is to resort to welfare agencies and to accommodation in the informal housing sector with the risk of accelerating the drift into marginalisation. The consequences can, however, be serious even for immigrants with resources. The problem has been reported for some time in highly industrialised areas where the imbalance between immigrants in employment and housing opportunities is particularly evident:"there is a group in a visible unstable, or potentially unstable, equilibrium, whose prospects for permanent settlement are hindered by difficulties in finding satisfactory housing accommodation, as an effect of being discriminated against and of a difficult rented market" (Toniolo and Bragato, 1998, p 175). Hence there is a polarisation of housing accommodation in progress, at least in central and northern cities of Italy, reflected in an improvement for a proportion of immigrants who are permanently settled in society and a persistent precariousness or worsening situation for the weakest and those at the start of their migration path.

As with homelessness generally, the level of 'black homelessness' in the UK lacks accurate quantification. However, it is known to be highly significant. Anderson (2003) suggests that in the UK one of the main contributions to the analysis of homelessness among black minority ethnic groups sets out to provide a theoretical analysis of homelessness and 'race' and provides evidence of the scale of homelessness (Harrison, 1999). Evidence cited by Burrows (1997) demonstrated that 14% of UK households identifying as black had experienced homelessness at sometime in their housing careers, compared with 4.3% of the overall population. Hence, while most homeless people are white, the risk of homelessness is three times greater among black households. A recent analysis of dwellings let by housing associations to black minority ethnic households in England (Edgar and Doherty, 2003) shows that, while 40% of all supported accommodation was made to single homeless people, more than half of all houses let to young Black British Caribbean and African people were to single homeless people. In contrast, the proportion of Pakistani/Bangladeshi households who said they had been homeless was below the national average, although no clear explanation for this was put forward by either Burrows (1997) or Harrison (1999). Homelessness is also known to be particularly high among minority groups in London (which has a high concentration of black minority ethnic households), although it is recognised as a national phenomenon (Harrison, 1999, p 103).

Moving on to develop his theoretical analysis, Harrison draws on the established ideas of structure and agency (or choice versus constraint). Beyond this starting point, the analysis of homelessness among minority ethnic groups focuses on structural and demographic forces; racialised practices and events; and household strategies, preferences and constraints (Harrison, 1999). Harrison's broad analysis concurs with much of what has been written about 'race' and housing disadvantage more generally. Looking at structural factors, for example, labour market participation is seen as crucial to economic disadvantage and for black minority ethnic households this is still marked by negative discrimination, low pay and limited prospects. For example, youth unemployment is consistently higher among black minority ethnic groups than white groups (Modood, 1997). For these households, disadvantage in employment is matched by disadvantage in general housing conditions, although there are variations across ethnic groups/communities (Harrison, 1999, p 105). It is well established that black minority ethnic households are more likely to live in poor quality housing, face a shortage of appropriate dwellings, and experience inadequate amenities and overcrowding. All of these circumstances can link to eventual homelessness, although presentations to local housing authorities may only result after very long periods of tolerating serious overcrowding.

While acknowledging that homelessness is closely related to class and social position, Harrison argues that there is an added ethnic/racial dimension for black minority ethnic groups and that "racisms are interwoven into socio-economic and institutional arrangements in highly significant ways" (Harrison, 1999, p 106). Further, it is argued that racisms persistent over time (for example, long-lived adverse stereotypes) may have the equivalent effect of a structural factor. Racist ideologies may influence policies and practices, while direct prejudice in the form of racist intimidation, violence, and harassment restricts the choice of area or dwelling for such households and can also precipitate homelessness. Furthermore, negative experiences and perceptions of the social housing system may result in a disincentive to take up services, with subsequent under-recognition of the extent of black minority ethnic homelessness.

Harrison also examines the importance of the interaction between structural factors and experiential diversity in considering minority ethnic homelessness (1999, p 108). Black minority ethnic household strategies can include refusal to participate in 'white-led solutions' (such as homeless temporary accommodation) where cultural insensitivity and racist histories may reduce the value of provision for potential users.

A theme of Harrison's analysis is 'difference within difference' – that is to say, diversity within the black minority ethnic community that has implications for housing and homelessness. Examples are given of the problems which young people or women from Asian communities may experience if they reject a traditional family lifestyle. However, Harrison is also careful to point out that "it is very important not to substitute new behaviourist stereotypes for old ones based on crude black/white distinctions" (Harrison, 1999, p 112). Harrison concludes (as do many other analysts) that "economic resources and institutional structures remain the dominant long-term determinants of eventual housing outcomes" (p 112). The diversity of experience of homelessness among ethnic groups must be viewed as part of broader patterns of housing constraints and options. Some positive change can be identified, but "on the whole minority ethnic households do not seem to have found their opportunities and resources substantially improved in relative terms by the national economic and welfare strategies of the 1980s and 1990s" (1999, p 117).

The specific needs of black minority ethnic women in relation to housing and homelessness have been considered in detail by Gill (2002). Gill quotes evidence that while such groups are disadvantaged relative to the white population, there is also differentiation within the black minority ethnic population. The employment rate is lower for black women than white, and minority communities have been particularly affected by economic restructuring. The black minority ethnic community is over-represented among those experiencing homelessness with black minority ethnic women over-represented in B&B accommodation and at a high risk of racist, physical or sexual abuse. Older women and lone mothers are known to have the highest risks and the longest duration of poverty, and Caribbean women are more likely to live as lone-parent households. Moreover, African-Caribbean, Bangladeshi and Pakistani teenage women are all relatively over-represented among teenage pregnancies. Gill's overview of the available evidence concludes that black minority ethnic women are more likely to endure poor housing and homelessness than other social groups as a consequence of racial discrimination and their worse socioeconomic position (2002, p 162).

Gill (2002) contends that while there has been relatively little research on black minority ethnic women and homelessness, available evidence suggests it is increasing (p 167), although the true extent remains difficult to quantify as it is often hidden in nature. For example, it is argued that black minority ethnic women will rarely be found sleeping rough due to vulnerability to abuse. The need for more black minority ethnic specialist provision to support women fleeing domestic violence is acknowledged as another key problem (p 169).

Key findings on the collective experiences of homelessness of black minority ethnic women have been summarised by Gill (2002, pp 170-1) as follows:

- abuse is a principal cause of homelessness for black minority ethnic women;
- sleeping rough is not an option;
- many prefer to stay with friends;
- existing hostel provision does not cater adequately for their needs;
- single parents are particularly vulnerable to homelessness.

Generally across Europe it is hard to find policies targeted at the prevention of homelessness among recent or second generation immigrants. Chapter Four identified the importance of the rented housing sector for immigrants. The use of social housing in providing reception accommodation for asylum seekers in many countries was described earlier in this chapter. However, it is difficult to find policy measures that exist to improve access to rented housing for homeless immigrants. In all the member states, documented immigrants have the right to apply for public sector housing in the same way as national citizens (EU Directive 2000/43/EC). However, the reality is far from the fact of the legal intention, either because of the shortage of social housing or the process of allocation of such a scarce resource.

One limited example exists in Europe's largest social landlord – the City of Vienna (Schoibl, 2003). A segment of the municipal (social) housing market was opened in 2000, and a total of 1,000 small dwellings (of modest standard but at affordable rents) were made available for migrants in urgent need of housing. However, the prerequisite to access for these dwellings is proof of legal residence in Austria (for five years) or convention refugee status. All other foreign nationals are excluded from social housing. Given that some 257,000 people without Austrian nationality are living in Vienna, this initiative is clearly limited but nevertheless it is an important step towards the actual opening of access to municipal housing. Furthermore, an information campaign was launched as part of the activities of the 'Wiener Integrationsfonds', to support migrants in gaining access to social housing. The Vienna Integration fund provides financial support for adult foreign nationals. This should increase the number of migrant households that apply for subsidised rent housing beyond that achieved in recent years.

In Italy, Law 40 established the right of documented immigrants "to gain access to public sector housing under the same conditions as Italian citizens" (this right had already been granted for some time by most regional governments). New legislation in 2002 has made it more difficult to enter or remain in the country and makes access to rights in general more difficult (Tosi, 2003, p 9). Access to public housing is still possible, but the conditions are harder, and regions that have responsibility for public housing may define criteria for access (such as length of residence in the region) that may penalise immigrants. Here too there was considerable variation from region to region in the criteria adopted and generally formal recognition failed to translate into concrete facts on any significant scale. This was basically due to the lack of public sector housing in the country. Problems also resulted from the different allocation criteria employed. The variety of local situations prevents any generalisation being made over immigrant access to public housing. The weakness of general social housing policies has, on different scales, constituted the main reason for the housing problems of immigrants. Two areas have been particularly critical: the extremely limited supply of affordable rented accommodation and the insufficient attention to the processes in which housing poverty becomes bound up with risks or marginalisation and social exclusion.

Under recent legislation in the UK, from April 2000, newly arriving asylum seekers have been the responsibility of the Home Office's National Asylum Support Service (NASS) and have been subject to a programme of dispersal to social rented accommodation across the country. NASS pays all of the costs of housing and supporting asylum seekers under the contract agreements with local agencies (mainly local authorities). Local authority participation in the scheme was voluntary and asylum seekers were generally relocated to areas with a pool of empty social housing (Pearl and Zetter, 2002, p 234). In general these were also areas of high unemployment and poverty (Pearl and Zetter, 2002, p 238). Hence the dispersal system relocated vulnerable asylum seekers to communities that were already marginalised.

Once a final determination on status is made, households have only 14 days to vacate their accommodation, precipitating a potentially high risk of homelessness at that stage in the process. Advice on housing and benefits is only forthcoming once refugee status is determined (Pearl and Zetter, 2002). Pearl and Zetter also pointed out that refugee community organisations could have been more effectively empowered to self-help in the reception and resettlement of asylum seekers.

The weakness of this approach to asylum reception in terms of prevention of homelessness or the eventual integration of immigrants into the housing market is shown by a study conducted on behalf of housing NGO Shelter (Scotland), which sought to evaluate the provision of housing and support to asylum seekers in Scotland (Buck, 2001). A sample of 40 asylum seekers, housed by Glasgow City Council, under the dispersal scheme, took part in the study. Participants reported a lack of choice in coming to live in Scotland (Buck, 2001) and a lack of choice of accommodation within the City of Glasgow. Furthermore, support services were not meeting their needs in terms of settling into local communities. Most participants quickly began to feel isolated. Asylum seekers quickly realised they were largely housed in areas characterised by poverty and social problems. The study heard reports of people's fears for their security and the widespread experience of harassment and abuse. The study also highlighted problems at the point of transition to refugee status. NASS support ends after two weeks and households must apply for other benefits and accommodation during that very short time. It was found that policy regarding the possible transfer to other accommodation had been slow to develop and implement. The majority of participants appeared to have been left in the same accommodation by default.

In most countries access to housing for immigrants is made more difficult by the direct or indirect discrimination by landlords. This is an issue in all rented sectors but is a particular problem in countries that do not have a well-developed social rented sector. In this respect recent EU policy may become important. In 2000 the EU adopted the directive on Race Equality (2000/43, June 2000), concerning discrimination in different fields including employment and access to the housing market. It is evident from the review of the implementation of the directive that direct and indirect discrimination continues to exist in regard to access to housing (see http://europa.eu.int/comm/employment_social/fundamental_rights/index_en.htm). However, very few examples exist of policy measures taken to act against exploitation or discrimination of immigrants in the housing market. One such example is described in Belgium (De Decker,

2001). The Aliens Act (in Flanders) was amended in 2001 to fight against rack-renting. Under this amendment, a rack-renter can henceforth be prosecuted under the human trade act if he "directly or through an intermediary abuses the vulnerable position of a foreign national, owing to the latter's undocumented or precarious administrative situation, by selling letting or making available rooms or any other housing with a view to abnormal gain". Thus rack-renting is defined as exploitation of the weak bargaining position of immigrants by charging rents that are excessive under normal market conditions. Foreigners who are victims of rack-renting, and who are prepared to cooperate in the criminal investigation of exploitation practices, may request residence documents and possibly obtain a regularisation of their status. The Department of Immigration, after consultation with the Office of the Public Prosecutor, decides on whether to issue the temporary residence documents. What the attitude of the Department of Immigration and the Office of the Public Prosecutor will be is still uncertain since the legislation is relatively new and no prosecutions have yet been completed.

Conclusions

This overview of immigration and homelessness in Europe has described a situation in which there is a hierarchy of vulnerability to homelessness among immigrants. Furthermore, in recent years an increasing proportion of all immigrants have personal characteristics (young, single and so on) and an immigrant status (undetermined or undocumented) that makes them vulnerable to housing exclusion and homelessness. This pattern has resulted in an increase in the number of immigrants among users of homeless services in many countries. In particular, undocumented immigrants are now a large proportion, and often a majority, of the clients of low-threshold homeless services. In a number of countries homeless services have provided refuge for asylum seekers left homeless by inadequate asylum facilities and procedures. In addition, there is an evident increase in 'hidden' homelessness both among undocumented immigrants and among young second generation immigrants. In the face of this apparent increase in the level of homelessness reported in many countries, there is a lack of policies to prevent housing exclusion and to facilitate integration of immigrants into the housing market. This suggests that the importance of the role of homeless services in meeting the needs of an increasing number of homeless immigrants will persist and hence the next chapter considers the implications of this situation for the provision, adaptation and development of those services.

Note

[1] This study was carried out in different periods (1997, 1998, 1998 and up to the end of 2000), and the main aim was to 'map' with the greatest accuracy possible, the number, age, social and employment situation of repatriates from the former Soviet Union.

SIX

Homeless services and immigration

Introduction

Although the majority of legal immigrants manage to find suitable housing, there is a sizeable and growing proportion who face difficulties in accessing affordable decent housing and who experience actual or hidden homelessness as a result. Structural changes in the housing markets in Europe have resulted in a retrenchment of state investment in provision that has led to a lack of affordable rented housing in many areas. In most countries this combination of public expenditure restraint and economic growth has led to an overheating of metropolitan and capital city housing markets, resulting in severe difficulties for all low-income households. Against a background of increasing immigration in most countries in Europe since the 1990s, this has created particular problems for immigrants (and minority ethnic or second generation immigrant households) who tend to concentrate in the major cities. This housing situation means that legal immigrants, even those with skills or a good education, struggle to find decent affordable housing in the areas where jobs are abundant. Evidence suggests that policies for dealing with asylum seekers – whether using reception centres or dispersal programmes – fail to provide support to find suitable housing for those whose applications are accepted. The increase in immigrants among service users reported by homeless service providers, described in the previous chapter, illustrates in particular the increasing precariousness of asylum seekers whose applications are rejected and of those who are regarded as undocumented immigrants.

It is relatively easy to describe the precarious housing circumstances of increasing proportions of immigrants in all countries in Europe; it is more difficult to describe what is happening to prevent homelessness among immigrants and to support their integration into the housing market. Our research evidence suggests that there are different problems to be addressed. First, there is a need for a coordinated integration strategy for asylum seekers to provide support or supported accommodation while immigrant families find employment and adjust to their new life situation. This may often involve homeless service providers working in partnership with other agencies including those representing refugees and immigrant groups. Our evidence suggests that part of the reason for the increase in immigrants in traditional homeless hostels is due to the blockages caused by a lack of adequate asylum accommodation. The implications of this situation for homeless services providers need to be recognised. Second, there are numerous examples, in different countries, of projects that have emerged to meet the special needs of vulnerable immigrants. These include projects for women immigrants fleeing violent partners; projects for immigrants with mental health problems associated with the cause of their displacement; and projects for young unaccompanied immigrants. Third, there are problems related to the needs of immigrants (including undocumented immigrants) using homeless services. The legal barriers that homeless NGOs face in providing services to immigrants, some of whom may be or may become undocumented, needs to be confronted. The management issues arising from the increase in immigrant service users include the need for appropriate funding to enable service providers to train staff and provide services related to the needs of immigrants as well as indigenous homeless populations. There is a need to consider the role of homeless NGOs, beyond alleviation and emergency provision, in facilitating the integration of immigrants into appropriate transitional or permanent housing.

This chapter examines the nature of services available to immigrants to either prevent them from becoming homeless or to meet their needs if they are homeless. A key focus of the chapter is to examine the role played by homeless service providers. In this context it is important to consider the nature and appropriateness of the services they provide and the constraints that may exist to influence their role in meeting the needs of homeless immigrants. We examine the nature of vulnerability of particular groups of immigrants and the emergence of specialist services. In this context we examine the understanding and discourse of the needs of homeless immigrants and, conversely, how the increase in immigrants among service users is affecting the provision and development of services.

We have described the search for a common EU strategy for immigration in Chapter Two. A key aspect of this emerging strategy (European Commission, 2000) is to emphasise the need for member states to have clear integration strategies as part of their admission and reception policies. Previous chapters have indicated the effects of the lack of such integration strategies and the impact of the underprovision of reception centres for refugees and asylum seekers on homeless services. In effect, homeless services have become the last safety net for immigrants who are excluded from the housing market or from facilities provided for repatriates, asylum seekers or refugees. In this context it is arguable that homeless services should be included in the development of integration strategies for immigrants and that they have an important role to play in developing services and managing specialist accommodation and support facilities. The chapter concludes by considering this argument.

The profile of homeless immigrants

It is difficult to find reliable information on the characteristics of homeless immigrants. Such information is generally gleaned from data held by service providers and thus does not cover the full range of homeless immigrants. However, a number of features can be summarised in relation to the ethnicity or country of origin of homeless immigrants and their changing sociodemographic composition and family status. Among homeless service users, there is, historically, a pattern of immigrants from neighbouring countries – for example, the Irish in London, the Finns in Stockholm, the Portuguese in Madrid. Apart from this phenomenon there is a pattern of dominance of particular ethnic groups among the homeless compared with the composition of all immigrants, suggesting an increased vulnerability to homelessness for these groups. Although the origin of these groups varies between member states, North Africans, sub-Saharan Africans and, more recently, Eastern European groups tend to predominate. There is also evidence of changes in the demographic composition of homeless immigrants characterised mainly by an increase in younger people and a feminisation of the population. However, in some countries there is also a contrary trend of an ageing of longer-term immigrants in workers' hostels. These features are illustrated here by reference to Spain and France.

A recent survey by Caritas, among the network of centres caring for the homeless in Spain (Cabrera, 2000), shows that there was an obvious predominance of people from North Africa or Sub-Saharan Africa. The nationalities most frequently identified were Moroccans, Algerians and Portuguese. A survey of 139 homeless agencies throughout Spain conducted for the European Observatory on Homelessness (Cabrera and Malgesini, 2003) confirms the significance of North African immigrants. Almost one third of homeless people came from North Africa, a quarter from Latin America, a quarter from Eastern Europe, one tenth from the EU and the remainder from Sub-Saharan Africa or elsewhere. This survey also suggests that these foreign homeless people are younger, and include a larger number of women who in many cases are accompanied by young children; as a result, the entire population of homeless immigrants is getting younger and more feminised (see Table 6.1).

However, a centre opened in 2001 to cater for immigrants found sleeping rough in Madrid shows a different population among its clientele. After a year of operating virtually at full occupancy, it had served 481 adult immigrants

Table 6.1: 'What is the family situation of foreign users of the centre?' (%)

	Women	Men
Single, no children	19	51
Living together, no children	9	5
Married, no children	6	3
Divorced, no children	1	2
Single, with children	16	3
Living together, with children	13	6
Married, with children	43	33
Divorced, without children	6	10
Total (N)	100 (79)	100 (111)

Note: Multiple answers.
Source: Cabrera and Malgesini (2003)

(without children) who had previously been sleeping in the streets. Of these literally homeless immigrants, 55% came from Eastern Europe (Bulgaria, Ukraine, Rumania), and 25% from Latin America (Colombia, Ecuador, Peru) (Cabrera and Malgesini, 2003). In this respect, the extreme residential precariousness hit harder those who lack the elements that facilitate their integration, such as language or historical and cultural affinities with the host population, which could explain why Eastern Europeans are over-represented compared with Latin Americans who are the most populous colony in Madrid.

Evidence from NGOs working with the homeless in France also suggests significant changes in the family structure of immigrants. They report a steady rise in inflows of families with children over the past 10 years, creating new and far more pressing requirements as regards essential accommodation and housing provision. One third of men and 40% of women are married or in a partnership, although this conjugal status data does not necessarily signify an arrival by both members of the couple. The number of accompanying children is also very hard to estimate as OFPRA (the French Office for the Protection of Refugees and Stateless Persons) did not count children before June 2001. This makes it hard to get a clear statistical picture of family arrivals, but the numbers of women and children are high and likely to be rising given the reliable first-hand knowledge of the reporting voluntary agencies. To illustrate this issue there was an observed 20% increase in family arrivals in Greater Paris between 2000 and 2001. Of these families, 44% were lone-parent families and 20% are 'large' families (3+ children) (Maurel, 2003).

For a certain number of families, particularly larger families, squatting constitutes a solution to their extreme housing need. Such families do not appear in the statistics of homeless service providers but are nevertheless enduring real homelessness. Thus the Senior Committee for the Housing of Disadvantaged Populations (Haut Comité pour le Logement des Populations Défavorisées) raised this problem, which particularly affects larger African families, in its eighth report (2002). The Committee referred to a confidential report delivered to the Minister of Housing where it was noted that nearly 2,000 apartments were occupied illegally, principally in Paris and Seine-Saint-Denis (a district adjacent to Paris). The occupants of these apartments were essentially immigrants from Sub-Saharan Africa, half of whom were large families who had to pay organised traffickers to stay in the squat.

Contrary to widely held opinion, the occupants of squats are not only people in an irregular residential status, or with insufficient resources, but a good number of them have a reasonable level of resources and are legal residents. They were forced into this solution by the absence of housing. Set up for a large number of big families, their difficulties are linked to the lack of large accommodation in Ile-de-France in particular, but also to "the rejection by public housing landlords and elected officials who fear having to manage large families, considered as potential sources of nuisance and housing degradation" (Haut Comité pour le Logement des Populations Défavorisées, 2002, p 37).

Thus, a study carried out by the GIP (Groupement d'intérêt public habitat et interventions sociales pour les mal loges et les sans-abri) (Home and Social Interventions) on three squats in the Ile-de-France region (the conurbation around Paris) showed that two thirds of heads of household had lived in France for more than 10 years and their arrival in the squat was the result of a laborious housing journey: 46% declared that they had been housed in their parents' or friends' houses before their arrival in the squat, 30% said they had been tenants of private landlords, generally living in housing that was too small or insalubrious, and only 3% had been public housing tenants. It is most often an increase in the size of the family that led them to squat in order to have a better quality of life.

It is important to add that the strongest concentration of African families is in the Ile-de-France region, the region where the housing market is particularly tight, which increases the hurdles limiting access to decent housing for these families. In fact, although those of Sub-Saharan African origin only represent 0.4% of the population of mainland France, they are essentially concentrated in Ile-de-France and above all in Seine-Saint-Denis, where 2.4% of the population is of this origin. They are also established, but on a smaller scale, in certain large conurbations such as Marseilles, Lyons, Bordeaux and Toulouse (Desplanques, 1996).

In addition to this increase in the proportion of families, there is also evidence from France of the ageing of immigrants who live in workers' hostels, often for many years. INSEE surveyed 150,988 people living in hostels in 1999 (all nationalities included). A total of 130,164 were men and 20,824 were women; this compared to the 1990 figures of a total population of 176,232 (151,722 men and 24,460 women). There are six principal characteristics of the resident hostel population (see Table 6.2):

- the majority are male foreign nationals, North Africans and Sub-Saharan Africans made up 90% of this group in 1999;
- their ageing is obvious. The number of male residents over 60 years old has increased from 10,156 in 1990 to 21,018 in 1999. Therefore the number in this older category has almost doubled between the two censuses, representing 10.7% in 1990 and 28.6% in 1999;

Table 6.2: Ageing of hostel residents between the two censuses, by nationality, men over 60 years

Nationality	Number 1990	%	Number 1999	%	Change 1990/99
Algerians	7,008	7.4	13,524	18.4	93.0
Moroccans	1,232	1.3	3,002	4.1	143.7
Tunisians	880	1.0	1,627	2.2	84.9
North Africa	**9,120**	**9.7**	**18,153**	**24.7**	**321.6**
Other Africans	424	0.4	1,692	2.3	299.1
Other nationalities	612	0.6	1,173	1.6	91.7
Total 60+	10,156	10.7	21,018	28.6	107.0

Source: INSEE (1999)

Table 6.3: Age groups of immigrants in workers' hostels in France

307 FTM	<25 yrs	25-54 yrs	55-69 yrs	>70yrs	Total
Residents	3,240	27,173	15,230	1,853	47,496
%	6.8	57.2	32.1	3.9	100

Note: FTM = migrant workers' hostels.
Source: FASILD

- this ageing principally affects those of North African origin (Algerians, Moroccans, and Tunisians). In 1990, 9,120 residents of 60 years or more were Algerians, Moroccans and Tunisians, being 89.8% of the total male residents. In 1999, this group numbered 18,153 residents, being 86.4% of those men over 60 years;
- it is the Algerians who have the highest percentage of ageing people in hostels. In 1999, Algerians represented 40% of total residents, but represented 64.3% of men over 60 years of age;
- the other peculiarity of this population (Thave, 1999) is that three quarters of the older immigrants living in hostels are married, their family having stayed in their country of origin.

The FASILD inquiry (Fonds d'action et de Soutien pour l'intégration et la Lutte contre les Diserminations [Social Action and Support Fund for Integration in the Fight against Discrimination] carried out in 307 immigrant workers' hostels in France provided some precise data on age ranges and confirms this trend (Bas–Theron and Michel, 2002). A total of 47,596 residents were surveyed, of whom 17,083, or 36%, were over 55 years old (see Table 6.3).

SONACOTRA (Société Nationale de Construction de Logement pour Les Travailleurs), the most important manager of migrant hostels, has also noted this massive evolution in the ageing of its residents. Among a reasonably constant total number of residents, those of 61 years and over have increased successively, from 7% in 1990 to 27.7% in 2001. The number of residents of 70 years and above has increased to 4,000 in 2001. This ageing has particularly affected those of North African origin, notably those of Algeria. Thus in 2001, among 17,810 residents over 61 years old, 85% were from North Africa. This phenomenon of the ageing of hostel residents, according to the prospective studies of SONACOTRA (2002), is going to continue through 2010-20. Thus, if the over-55s represent 42.8% of the resident population of SONACOTRA in 2001, they will represent more than 55% in 2011.

These diverse and changing characteristics of homeless immigrants, illustrated here by reference to Spain and France, can be expected to affect both their use of homeless services and the requirements placed on service providers to meet their needs. This provides the context for the following sections that examine the nature of homeless services and their response to the needs of immigrants.

Exclusion from homeless services

In order to obtain support, immigrants must first know about the services available to them and be able to access those services. This can be difficult for a variety of reasons, including legal constraints, lack of services or lack of information (due to resource constraints on NGOs), lack of cooperation between the public sector and the NGOs, and simply the lack of services in areas where immigrants are located (especially in rural areas).

Legal constraints

In a number of countries access to homeless services is denied to non-citizens and to undocumented immigrants. This arises either through the legal basis for social welfare claims by foreign nationals or by the nature of the funding for homeless services. For example, the institutions that provide support to the homeless in Austria are essentially subject to provincial social welfare laws and are financed as 'social services' by social welfare funds. For years social welfare services have essentially been geared to native citizens because, under the previous legal structural conditions, foreign recipients of social welfare benefits had to have legal residence status. As a result of recent reforms and amendments of the legal requirements for residence, these pitfalls have now been largely removed and yet, according to data from institutions financed by social welfare agencies that deal with homelessness, specific assistance for migrants is still the exception rather than the rule. Specialised institutions have in the best of cases concluded exception regulations and agreements with social welfare agencies, under which foreign nationals are 'allowed' access to their institutions under specific conditions. This can be a prior application for admission or an exemption granted to the institution to resort to what is known as over-capacity, which is not financed by the social welfare agencies, however. Assistance to immigrants in extreme housing need consequently relies on services provided by the institutions for which they receive no public funding. The sole systematic empirical survey of the situation of homelessness and support for housing in Austria to date (Eitel and Schoibl, 1999) has revealed a spectrum pretty much devoid of assistance for foreigners.

In Germany, the legal basis for social welfare claims by foreign nationals (Section 120 of the 1962 Federal Social Welfare Act) essentially excludes asylum seekers and undocumented immigrants from assistance. These social welfare legislation hurdles either completely exclude the use and financing of assistance (Section 72 of the 1962 Federal Social Welfare Act) for certain groups of immigrants, or leave it to the discretion of the social welfare authorities. One implication of this is that there is only a very small proportion of non-EU nationals and refugees in (stationary and semi-stationary) institutions of organisations working with the homeless, and survey results demonstrate that refugees and asylum seekers often get no help from these institutions (Busch–Geertsema, 2003).

Furthermore, Section 92 of the 1991 Aliens Act determines that those who provide repeated help to foreigners without legal residence status are liable to prosecution, with imprisonment of up to five years. Migrants who are in the federal territory without a residence permit or valid personal documents risk imprisonment of up to one year, a fine or deportation. People without legal residence status will turn to the anonymity afforded by homeless institutions if they are confronted with a problem that they can no longer solve on their own, for instance, health problems or lack of means because of loss of the source of income.

Similar situations of exclusion of certain categories of immigrant are repeated in other member states and, in particular, the right to assistance is denied to undocumented immigrants. In the Netherlands, for example, the national government introduced a law in 1998 wherein social benefits and health care for undocumented immigrants were explicitly forbidden. Since then, it has been difficult for care providers to provide care to migrants who have no legal residence status, because municipalities are no longer inclined to pick up the costs. Until the *Koppelingswet* [1998 Linking Act] came into force, shelters provided normal care to victims of domestic violence who had become undocumented immigrants as a result of fleeing the abuser. This has now become much more difficult.

Resource constraints

The lack of services is another key factor hindering access to support for immigrants. This is a feature of countries (for example, in Southern Europe) where only in recent years a history of net emigration has been replaced by immigration. In this situation services have been relatively slow to develop and have had to rely on precarious, inadequate or voluntary sources of funding.

Since the early 1990s, the massive rise in immigration has resulted in radical changes in Greek society, characterised by the presence of immigrants – either economic or political refugees and asylum seekers – as distinct social groups facing acute social, economic and housing problems. The presence of these groups has generated a need for new kinds of services to address their urgent housing and social needs. According to reliable sources, immigrants, mainly undocumented immigrants and refugees, account for a high percentage of all the homeless in Greece (Ligdopoulou and Arapoglou, 2002). Indeed, most of the infrastructure services for the homeless are geared chiefly to immigrants and to refugees.

Initiatives to meet the accommodation or housing needs of immigrants are thus very recent in origin and their capacity in relation to the number of those in need of housing is restricted. The facilities tend to be concentrated in the big cities, where there is also the largest concentration of immigrants. For example, the Social Work Foundation, a well-established voluntary agency operating since 1967, has recently launched the operation of supported housing projects for refugees and asylum seekers, combining provision of accommodation in shared flats for up to six months, along with provision of social work assistance, networking with employment, health and social services with a view to promoting their overall social integration. The aim is to provide accommodation and support until the legal status of the asylum seeker is clarified or until they are granted a temporary permit to stay in the country that, in theory, renders them capable of securing independent rented accommodation for themselves. These projects have only been in operation since 2002 in two areas of Athens (Glyfada and Menidi).

This Social Work Foundation project, like most voluntary sector services, is affected decisively by the lack of regular sources of funding and, as a consequence, they face chronic insecurity in relation to their operation. Some services receive grants from the Ministry of Health and Welfare or other sources such as the UNHCR. However, the majority of homeless services run by NGOs in Greece, such as the Social Work Foundation project, operate mainly on EU funding. Their operation is under constant threat as they continuously rely on time-limited grants or particular time-limited programmes, and they are constantly in a process of having to apply for their renewal. Furthermore, the very future of the services is uncertain as there is no commitment by the Greek government or any other body as to the continuation of the funding of these services after EU funding stops.

In Italy two traits of government action can be discerned (Tosi, 2003). The first is the historical development of the *centri di accoglienza* (reception centres) in the early 1990s (underlying Law 39), although later legislation has provided for a wider range of housing opportunities. The other, interrelated with the first, is the tendency to delegate responsibility to local authorities and to NGOs. In the case of housing the local adaptive model has predominated. This has meant, on the one hand, a considerable capacity for innovation and relatively effective action where local conditions were favourable. On the other hand, all the limitations of the model are manifest, including great disparity between different local situations and initiatives remaining dependent on local willingness to act; a certain tendency for action to be residual and relegated to the voluntary domain; and an overlap of responsibilities in the absence of both horizontal and vertical coordination, with the result that policies lost their power to make an impact. In addition, the high cost of housing intervention is also an expression of the political difficulty in implementing genuine housing action for immigrants. Hence the predominant type of housing action has been the emergency and reception centre type (Synergia, 1998, 2001).

As far as reception centres are concerned, provision was delegated to regions, and there is great variation according to geographical area. Direct public sector commitment occurred in only a few regions and municipalities (mainly in central northern Italy). On the other hand, neither of the two laws made the setting up of centres by municipalities compulsory. Even in a region such as Tuscany, one of the most committed regions in this field, less than 10% of local authorities have used the funds available to them (under Law 39), and in any case the supply was insufficient to satisfy the demand. Voluntary and third sector organisations have often stood in when the public sector has been unable to take action rapidly on an emerging problem, and a myriad of independent non-profit social welfare providers, usually on a small scale, has developed alongside the public sector.

On the whole, the success of reception centres has been limited and not just because of the small size of the supply. The lack of success is partly due to the implementation policies, but the main problems are to be found at the roots of the project, in the initial concept of reception centres. Under Law 39 these centres were supposed to provide temporary lodging and social support in the initial settlement phase (supervision, cultural counselling, advice) for immigrants who had just arrived. As a consequence the centres were not able to satisfy the real needs of immigrants, nor did they take account of the limits of the general housing system. The reception centre philosophy did not recognise that, for most immigrants, the problem was housing and not social work support; nor did it recognise that the problem of immigrants reflects and multiplies the effects of general failings in the housing system (Tosi, 2003). In the absence of adequate social/affordable housing supply, and therefore of housing chains that allow a passage from one form of housing to another, the centres were destined to be transformed into improper surrogates for ordinary housing arrangements.

Lack of cooperation or interagency working

Access to services often relies on cooperation between the public sector and NGO organisations or other forms of partnership working. However, such approaches are relatively rare in the evidence available from our research. Two illustrative examples are to be found in Finland and Portugal.

The Unit for Immigrant Services of the City of Helsinki offers social services for refugees and Ingrian Finns[1] who move to Helsinki (most other cities in Finland have similar units). It offers rent for temporary housing from the Y-Foundation (the biggest NGO in Finland, providing a fifth of its housing stock for refugees) for immigrants and provides help to find a permanent dwelling. The Helsinki Unit has about 300 immigrant clients and 50 temporary dwellings. Most of its clients are immigrants who have moved in from other municipalities. The Unit also provides housing advice and guidance. The initial reception and housing guidance is part of their work and they give practical advice, solve intercultural problems, distribute information to immigrants and co-partners and develop cooperation. Workers visit dwellings when there are new residents to discuss the equipment, environment and provide general information about life in Finland.

In Portugal, Chambers for the Support of Immigrants have been created at the initiative of local autonomous authorities throughout the country where the presence of immigrants had, up to that time, not been part of a social reality but is now characterised by a process of settlement by immigrants from Eastern Europe. Some of these initiatives have been specifically geared to supporting those segments of the immigrant population that are more vulnerable, and in particular those who, in increasing numbers, are turning to services for the homeless:

- *Saudável Night Project:* provides social and health services to immigrants and homeless people who are in a precarious situation in the Lisbon area, raising the awareness of the population to prevent illness and to promote health, and elucidating the rights and obligations of citizens as regards access to healthcare. This project, an initiative of the Doctors of the World, provides basic healthcare services and guidance for users from a mobile unit that moves about in the city of Lisbon. The great majority of users are Eastern Europeans, so the project team includes a Russian/Portuguese translator.
- *Viana without Borders Project:* faced with an increasing number of immigrants from Eastern Europe with an obvious social vulnerability, the Family Planning Bureau (known by the Portuguese acronym GAF, located in Viana do Castelo, northern Portugal) is running a project that has two main strands of action. First, it aims to profile its client population and evaluate the service intervention, raise awareness of the project's objectives, establish local partnerships and promote cooperation between public and private entities at local level (in particular, the Foreigners and Frontiers Service), and advise volunteers to develop informal support networks for Eastern European immigrants. Second, it provides specific services for Eastern European immigrants including psychosocial support, personalised advice and guidance in the process for integration into employment and sociocultural and interpersonal cohabitation.

Lack of services in rural areas

Although immigrants often tend to congregate in the major metropolitan urban centres, there is a significant trend of rural migration in some countries. A feature of such immigration is often associated with seasonal employment and immigrants are vulnerable both because of the temporary nature of such employment and because of the lack of services for homeless people in rural areas.

Recent research in Spain demonstrates that in rural areas accommodation near the work areas far from the urban centres enhances the dependence on employers and makes social integration difficult, while promoting isolation and segregation (Leal, 1996, p 136). The situation in which many of these immigrants live – in housing that is either free or in exchange for rent paid or deducted from the salary – simply increases the subjugation of the workers to the rural employers. In a study conducted among Moroccans in Murcia, only 1% shared a flat with Spaniards while the majority (58%) were in accommodation assigned by the owner (Izquierdo Escribano, 1996). According to Izquierdo Escribano, in rural areas subject to high seasonal fluctuations of employment there is bound to be a high turnover of workers in line with the cycle of the harvests, which inevitably leads to a certain nomadic pattern among some foreign workers. In these circumstances immigrants cannot achieve a stable housing situation. Izquierdo Escribano (1996) suggests that the housing ambitions of immigrants will depend on whether they want to save money in order to return to their country, or to settle in Spain, and whether they want to save in order to build a home in their country of origin or to bring their family here. According to his evidence a large proportion of the first waves of immigrants opted for family reunion and settlement in Spain, so that return home acquires more of a mythical dimension than a real alternative.

An example of the situation of immigrants in rural areas is described in a recent study of the Rioja region (Cabrera and Reyes, 2002). Between 1995 and 1999, the number of immigrants living in the Rioja wine region tripled and increased to 9,324 people at the end of 2003. This figure refers only to documented immigrants, but it is important to take into account the group of undocumented immigrants, because it is one of the social profiles that has become more prominent among the homeless (Cabrera and Reyes, 2002). However, as Cabrera demonstrates, the significance of this increase in immigration lies not in its scale but rather in the impact it has on small settlements. More than half of the foreigners were in one municipality (Logroño). At the same time, foreigners formed a high percentage of the population of small municipalities (like Padrejon and Autol in La Rioja Baja). This pattern is significant in understanding exclusion processes that have occurred in areas like housing.

Data from social services and voluntary associations show that people of foreign extraction have increasingly occupied spaces intended for the homeless in the provincial capital (Logroño), while elsewhere in the region day labourers have to survive under highly precarious housing conditions. This means that in Rioja, two situations are evident with respect to homelessness:

- a rapid and significant increase in immigrants who are concentrated in the larger cities, saturating the (scarce) social accommodation services (shelters) intended for the homeless;
- a significant increase of immigrants in villages with a small population and low levels of rented housing, and insufficient provision of accommodation by rural employers (who are only required to provide accommodation to workers under legal contract).

Services for homeless immigrants

This section examines a range of issues related to the role of homeless services in meeting the needs of immigrants. Chapter Five described how the vulnerability of immigrants to housing exclusion and homelessness is, in part at least, the result of their legal status. Hence the role of services for the homeless will be different for the various groups of immigrants – documented immigrants, asylum seekers, refugees, repatriates and undocumented immigrants. For example, separate structures exist in many countries to accommodate asylum seekers and hence the role of homeless services is more limited for this group. Furthermore, it is evident that undocumented immigrants tend to have to rely on low-threshold services rather than gain access to supported accommodation or stationary facilities. Equally we can find evidence to suggest that young immigrants, the children of immigrants and female immigrants may avoid traditional homeless accommodation services. Finally, the increase in the number of immigrants using homeless services requires a response from service providers in relation to specialist staffing, coping with conflict and racism within the services and providing culturally sensitive services. We illustrate these issues by reference to particular countries, but the issues are evident across Europe.

Separate structures

Separate structures have been introduced in many countries to accommodate asylum seekers while their status is determined. The practice in accommodating asylum seekers varies across Europe and within countries policy has changed during the late 1990s. The organisational structure for the reception of asylum seekers has changed in recent years in response to the number of new applications and the duration of the process. A comparative study (Greek Council for Refugees, 2002) reveals two types of reception system in use. In Southern European countries the reception and care of asylum seekers is entrusted to existing social services that are also responsible for the indigenous population. The other organisational model, common elsewhere in Europe, provides a separate structure for the reception of asylum seekers. In January 2003 the European Community adopted a directive laying down minimum standards on the reception of asylum applicants in member states (Directive 2003/9/EC). The directive deals with the issues of accommodation, information, documentation, freedom of movement, healthcare, schooling of minors, access to the labour market and to vocational training.

In 1999, under the aegis of the Department of Justice, Equality and Law Reform, the Irish government established the Directorate for Asylum Support Services (DASS), which merged with the Refugee Agency in 2001 to form the Reception and Integration Agency (RIA) (O'Sullivan, 2003). The role of the RIA is to coordinate "the provision of services to both asylum seekers and refugees; coordinate the implementation policy for all refugees and persons who, although not refugees, are granted leave to remain; and responding to crisis situations which result in relatively large numbers of refugees arriving in Ireland within a relatively short period of time, for example, the Kosovar nationals who were invited ... in 1999" (RIA, 2002, p 1). Prior to April 2000, asylum seekers were placed in B&B-type accommodation, primarily in Dublin, or else sought accommodation in the privately rented sector, where they were entitled to a rent supplement. To deal with the increasing number of asylum seekers entering the country the government, via the RIA, adopted a policy of dispersed and direct accommodation provision (in 2000). This is possibly the most contentious issue in relation to the housing of migrants in Ireland (O'Sullivan, 2003).

By mid-2002, the RIA had established a number of main reception centres in Dublin where asylum seekers are accommodated for up to two weeks prior to their dispersal to provincial centres, and over 80 accommodation centres throughout the country. These accommodation centres, usually hotels or other B&B-type accommodation, provide full board and accommodation while the social welfare system provides a 'comfort' payment (see Faughnan et al, 2002, for further details). As of June 2002, approximately 5,000 asylum seekers were in direct provision accommodation. Only in exceptional circumstances are asylum seekers given permission to leave direct provision accommodation.

The decision to provide dispersed and direct accommodation was criticised by a number of NGOs, particularly in light of the views advanced in the report of the Interdepartmental Working Group on the Integration of Refugees in Ireland, which in its review of how best to promote the integration of asylum seekers, refugees and other non-nationals, argued that "this requires us to look at how we do things and how we respond to people from different backgrounds and cultures. We must continuously monitor how we respond to changes in society." (Interdepartmental Working Group on the Integration of Refugees in Ireland, 2000, p 3). Comhlamh, for example, argued that while the system facilitated short-term needs,

> being confined to designated accommodation centres and dependent on hostel staff has a clear impact on the self-sufficiency of asylum seekers and their ability to regain their independence and autonomy. The lack of personal space and privacy tends to become a source of friction and contribute to stress and frustration. Financially impeded from accessing suitable private accommodation many asylum seekers have no control over many fundamental aspects of their private life. (Comhlamh, 2001, p 8)

They concluded that "present policy is militating against the social inclusion of asylum-seekers and refugees into their new communities" (p 11).

Access to homeless services

It is evident that in many countries immigrants access emergency and low-threshold homeless services, such as day centres, soup kitchens and direct access hostels, for example. Their use of transitional, stationary and supported accommodation is limited. This is mainly, but not entirely, affected by their legal status. This is well documented in Germany and France, for example, but also applies in many other member states.

The most recent available data in Germany (EBIS, 2001) on the clientele of independent organisations working with the homeless nationwide show relatively close similarities in the breakdown of foreigners from EU or non-EU countries among the clients of these organisations, compared with the

Figure 6.1: Proportion of foreigners in homeless services compared with the population overall (2001)

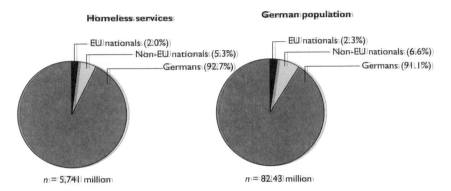

Homeless services

- EU nationals (2.0%)
- Non-EU nationals (5.3%)
- Germans (92.7%)

n = 5,741 million

German population

- EU nationals (2.3%)
- Non-EU nationals (6.6%)
- Germans (91.1%)

n = 82.43 million

Source: Statisches Bundesamt (2002, Table 1.3)

overall German population. However, several ad hoc polls among selected institutions run by organisations working with the homeless, clearly show that foreigners tend to be under-represented in stationary institutions, and more frequently found in ambulant or low-threshold institutions.

One survey conducted among around a hundred member institutions of the Catholic Federation of Organisations Working with the Homeless showed that in more than half of the institutions, which gave usable answers to this question, the proportion of migrants (including repatriates) among the clients was stable in 1997–99, at 11–12%. The largest proportion of immigrants in these institutions were non-EU nationals and were, to a considerable extent (over one third) without legal residence status. "The groups are to be found above all in low-threshold institutions and overnight-stay accommodations. The open structure and working methods of these institutions enable these people to seek help without fearing about legal consequences" (Kunz, 2001, pp 101–2). In an earlier survey conducted among selected institutions of organisations working with the homeless, one expert came to the conclusion that, "the proportion of foreigners in stationary aid structures pursuant to Section 72 of the [1962] Social Welfare Act (Bundessozialhilfegestz) is clearly lower than in ambulant consulting services for the homeless and is in no respect as minimal as in therapeutic housing" (Hammel, 2000, p 40). Finally, a recent paper at a conference of a Berlin agency stressed the anonymity aspect of the low-threshold assistance for the homeless, whereby people without legal status can avail themselves of such assistance. For instance, 22% of those using the emergency overnight accommodation facilities of the Berlin Municipal Mission in 2000 were foreign residents: "People come to us because they know that here they will receive assistance without bureaucratic red tape, without being asked for their passport or about their residence status" (Kretzschmar, 2002, p 77).

Immigrants' experiences of homeless services

We have already made reference to the fact that, for cultural and religious reasons, female immigrants will often not use mixed gender hostels for the homeless and that other aspects of the service provision in mainstream homeless services do not cater for their needs. However, perceptions as well as experiences can lead to some immigrants avoiding the use of hostels and other homeless services. This is apparent from a recent review of research in the UK (Harrison and Phillips, 2003).

While most homeless people in the UK are white, the risk of homelessness is three times greater among black households (Burrows, 1997). While acknowledging that homelessness is closely related to class and social position, Harrison argues that there is an added ethnic/racial dimension for minority ethnic groups and that "racisms are interwoven into socio-economic and institutional arrangements in highly significant ways" (Harrison, 1999, p 106). Further, it is argued that racisms persistent over time (for example, long-lived adverse stereotypes) may have the equivalent effect of a structural factor. Racist ideologies may influence policies and practices, while direct prejudice in the form of racist intimidation, violence, and harassment restricts the choice of area or dwelling for minority ethnic households and can also precipitate homelessness. Furthermore, negative experiences and perceptions of the social housing system may result in a disincentive to take up services, with subsequent under-recognition of the extent of minority ethnic homelessness. Harrison also examines the importance of the interaction between structural factors and experiential diversity in considering minority ethnic homelessness (1999, p 108). Minority ethnic household strategies can include refusal to participate in 'white-led solutions' (such as temporary accommodation), where cultural insensitivity and racist histories may reduce the value of provision for potential users.

Drawing on research in Nottingham and Oxford, Steele (2002) considered the experience of homelessness among young black people. Again, evidence is cited to indicate that young black households are at greater risk of homelessness than their white counterparts. Steele argues that the causes of homelessness among black youth are similar to white youth (for example, family breakdown, domestic violence, threat of violence), but that their experience of homelessness is slightly different. A key issue raised is the lack of awareness of need and cultural sensitivity in service provision, raising the question of whether solutions to minority ethnic youth homelessness lie in developing specialist provision or in improved mainstream services. In accordance with other analyses, Steele (2002) notes that minority groups are over-represented as homeless but are much less likely to sleep rough than white youth. It is considered that they are more likely to stay temporarily with various friends/family. It is also argued that a lack of knowledge of housing options in the face of homelessness means that minority ethnic youth rely on informal networks for survival (p 181). Further, as with minority ethnic women, minority ethnic youth often considered that formal services for homeless people were not sensitive to their needs. Rather they were seen as monocultural and dominated by white staff. Ethnicity of staff, in particular, was seen as very important in services being 'welcoming' to minority ethnic young homeless people. In Steele's Nottingham study, one fifth of young homeless people had not approached any agency for help (Steele, 2002, p 182). Hostel accommodation was often considered inappropriate, dominated by white males, and consequently disliked because minority ethnic youth did not feel comfortable in the environment. For cultural or religious reasons, some minority ethnic women will not use mixed hostels. Other areas where provision for cultural needs was lacking included provision of appropriate food and space to practise religious worship.

Management issues

The recent and rapid rise in the number of immigrants using services for the homeless, documented in many member states, has created a number of management issues for service providers. These include organisational as well as operational issues and increasingly, to remain effective or to adapt to the needs of immigrants, this will also include strategic planning issues (for example, funding, development of specialist services, staff training). Cabrera (2003) carried out a survey of the homeless agencies in Spain, in connection with this research, to ascertain their role in dealing with immigrants.

Cabrera estimated that the response to the survey equalled a quarter of the homeless services available, and provided a usable sample of 139 completed questionnaires from service providers throughout the country. This survey provides a good illustration of the management issues facing providers of homeless services in dealing with a relatively new and growing client group of immigrants. There is a very clear perception that the basic problem faced by immigrant service users lies in the lack of employment and their legal situation. Other difficulties that obstruct their possible integration include difficulties with the language, administrative and bureaucratic red tape, rejection and racism – all of which make it doubly difficult to find housing – and the lack of family support. In this way recent immigrants are perceived by service managers to be different from their traditional clients, and that homeless immigrants make a transitional and opportunistic use of their services while getting established in the country: "Immigrants are transients, they do not share the characteristics of this [native] group. They [tend to be better educated] and come looking for work. They use this service until they manage to get settled" (Cabrera, 2003, p 48). This finding is reflected by a similar study in Italy conducted on behalf of FIO.psd (Federazione Italiana degli Organismi per le persone senza dimora) (see Chapter Five; Tosi, 2003).

The respondents to the survey provided the normal range of services available in homeless services. However, what immigrants expected to receive from the network of such centres are shelter and information (a service available in 86% of the centres that replied), clothing (66%) and food (62%), as well as assistance solving their problems with red tape and seeing to administrative formalities (53%), transitional accommodation (44%) and assistance with legal immigration advice (31%).

In the end, the centres for the homeless have to deal with a situation with very different characteristics from those they have had to face to date. This entails new difficulties and challenges for professionals and volunteers who staff these services, the first of which is obviously the language. Problems of communication with everything this entails top the list of difficulties professionals have to overcome to do their work. Cabrera suggests that, in a country where the knowledge of other languages is not widespread, the presence of immigrant workers is conducive to meeting this need.

Apart from the 30% of respondents who said they did not encounter any specific difficulty in caring for immigrant homeless people, the second major difficulty encountered is dealing with the confrontations between immigrants and Spanish users of the services. As Cabrera (2003) comments, "for those who move within the same boundaries of subsistence, the fact of having to compete for what are certainly scarce resources, must not be an easy experience [and] calls for tolerance and understanding" (p 53). This is reflected in the response to one questionnaire which indicated how "on occasion, the services for the homeless are absorbed by the large number of immigrants, which limits or cancels the offer of places and services for (native) homeless persons" (Cabrera, 2003, p 53). The rapid increase in immigrants among the users of shelters and canteens for the homeless in Spain has considerably exacerbated conflicts between the users of these facilities. The importance of introducing training and awareness-raising programmes for intercultural understanding is therefore clearly required. Consequently, it is not uncommon to hear arguments for the separation of the care for immigrants from centres for the homeless.

Finally, the feeling of being overwhelmed by the increase of homeless immigrants is reflected in the response that the major achievements of the centres with respect to foreign users was in 'redirecting immigrants to appropriate services' (64%). This can be interpreted as indicating that service providers do

Table 6.4: 'What are the two major difficulties that your centre faces in caring for foreign users?' (%)

Communication problems (language, etc)	72
No particular difficulties	30
Confrontations with native citizens	20
Lack of respect for the rules of the centre	10
Ignorance of minimum cohabitation standards	10
Other	10
Aggressiveness	9
Confrontations among users	6
Insubordination to authorities or technicians	6
Poor maintenance of the centre's infrastructure	2
Theft	1
Threats	1
Total responses	125

not consider centres for the homeless as being the most appropriate to tend to the needs of immigrants. This also reflects the conviction that homeless immigrants do not have the prominent characteristics of social exclusion and alienation that other groups of homeless marginal people exhibit. However, this response may also reflect the view that "the intervention methodology requires appropriate strategies to prevent the immigrant population from becoming chronically stuck in its social situation" (Cabrera, 2003, quoting respondents to the questionnaire) because, it is argued, "we are beginning to see the emergence of immigrants with more similar profile to that of Spanish homeless people" (p 54). For the same reason, there are those who advocate separating the institutional resources intended for the two groups: "the problems of foreign users and those of other homeless people are very different, so in our view, there is a need for social welfare resources (accommodation, subsistence and other basic needs) to be independent" (response to questionnaire, in Cabrera, 2003, p 55).

Nevertheless, it is obvious that there is neither the preparation nor the resources needed to be able to do this type of more in-depth work with the more excluded immigrants so, during their stay there, these centres can scarcely do more than redirect them to appropriate services or provide moral and psychological support (46%) that will enable them to recover emotionally, acquire valid references to look for and to find a job (33%), and improve their language and social skills (31%). Although limited, this is no mean achievement, taking into account the situation in which immigrants arrive in this last network of social protection, which was not initially designed to care for them, but has adapted to their needs, to a limited degree, because there is nothing better on offer at the moment.

Services for vulnerable immigrants

Some immigrants are more vulnerable than others as a result of their gender, age or mental state (resulting from the trauma of asylum or torture). This has implications for the management of homeless services (for example, understanding these specific needs, cultural context of needs, translation issues, conflict with traditional client groups) and for the need for specialist services (for example, services targeted at specific groups). Evidence in the national reports suggests that services have emerged to meet the needs of three specific groups: women, young people and those immigrants suffering from mental health problems as a result of their displacement. This raises a number of questions regarding existing services: are they being skewed by such specialist needs?; are they managing to adapt to such needs?; is there a need for specialist services?

Women

Evidence from a number of countries (including Belgium, Denmark, Germany, the Netherlands, and the UK) indicates that the proportion of immigrants (or women from minority ethnic communities) in shelters for women fleeing domestic abuse has been increasing in recent years. Research in Denmark describes the issues arising for these crisis centres, while in Germany and the UK one response has been the establishment of specialist refuges.

A recent survey in Denmark showed that the share of women from minority ethnic groups at crisis centres is continuing to rise (RICSW, 2000). The survey, covering the period from 1 July 1997 to 31 December 1998, gathered information from 2,634 women, 855 of whom were of non-Danish origins. Women from minority ethnic groups comprised 35% of all resident women during the period in which the survey took place. It can also be seen that the distribution of the number of women from minority ethnic groups varies, as the Municipality of Copenhagen and the County of Copenhagen have the highest numbers of refugees.

Compared with the population as a whole, more women from minority ethnic groups live in a legal marriage prior to moving into a crisis centre due to the fact that, for most of these women, marriage is the legal ground for their residence permits in Denmark. Because of this, more women from minority ethnic groups return to their husbands than is the case for Danish women. The survey suggests that these women are poorly integrated in Danish society and as a result they had little insight with regard to their own rights and opportunities (and moreover had a very fragile or non-existing social network). Most of the women interviewed found it difficult to utilise the information they received. For some of the women, it was a considerable problem that they were unable to talk with crisis centre personnel and get the necessary information due to their poor command of Danish. This is especially significant during the first part of a stay, and statistics also show that a large number of women from minority ethnic groups move back to their husbands within 14 days. For the women who do not speak Danish, the possibility for support from crisis centre personnel is quite limited. Almost half of the women relate that it was not possible to speak with anyone during the first part of their stay at the crisis centre.

The women are generally satisfied with their stay at the crisis centre, and this extends to their relationships with the other residents. However, there are also conflicts when people live in close proximity to each other, as the women must at the crisis centres. Most often these are problems concerning practical everyday things, as well as varying views on child rearing among the various cultures. Here, language problems can increase conflicts and keep problems from being solved easily among the women themselves. Bicultural (or multilingual) personnel at the crisis centres would not solve all of the problems, but the conclusion is that this could be especially appropriate for offering support to women from minority ethnic groups and contributing to them getting the information they need at the right time.

The social workers interviewed in the survey indicated that discrimination is taking place. Discrimination is seen as being an expression of the fact that the crisis centres have reached a threshold level for how much and how many they can accommodate with their current resources. More than a third of the municipal caseworkers relate that they have experienced that women from minority ethnic groups are discriminated in the distribution of housing. It is mainly the municipal caseworkers in the greater Copenhagen area who have described their experience in dealing with this form of discrimination. This also serves to strengthen the statistical picture that shows that women at crisis centres in the greater Copenhagen area have longer stays.

A number of barriers and dilemmas are identified that ought to be addressed if the support for these women and children is to be effective. In summary, the many issues in connection with women from minority ethnic groups staying at crisis centres require higher prioritisation of these groups in municipal welfare departments, including more target-oriented and need-determined counselling. The study concludes that increased cooperation between the crisis centres and municipal departments is required, as well as thinking in other than traditional individual social work patterns. Finally, the report points to the need for bicultural personnel and specialist training.

The Dutch umbrella organisation for the homeless, Federatie Opvang, conducted a survey of its member organisations in 2001 and concluded that there are two groups of immigrants without a residence permit making use of the homeless services in the Netherlands. The first group consists of women and children who are experiencing domestic violence from their partner or father. Their residence permit depends on the residence permit of the partner/father. They have no independent rights to housing or social security. Once they flee their homes they often end up in women's shelters or crisis centres. These clients are called *clients with uncertain resident status*. The second group consists of mainly single men without residence permits (undocumented aliens) who make use of the services of night shelters and day centres.

Immigrants from the former colonies (Surinam and the Antilles) usually have Dutch nationality. Very often women from Morocco and Turkey migrate to the Netherlands by way of marriage. If the marriage fails within three years the wife has no right to an independent resident status. Even in the case of domestic violence a woman has, at the time of writing, no rights other than those connected to the marriage and the resident status of her husband. The survey found therefore that women using shelters were mainly of Moroccan or Turkish origin, with one third coming from Eastern Europe, South America or Asia.

The reason for the high proportion of women who seek refuge in women's shelters, despite the fact that they become 'undocumented', can be found in both the culture from which these women originate as well as in the Dutch immigration laws. Most of these women have grown up in their native country and were married to a countryman in the Netherlands. They lead isolated lives, do not speak the language and sometimes have had no schooling. It is usually not accepted for a wife to divorce or to return to her family when there are marriage problems. In most cases the social network of these women is very limited. All these factors combined with the legal rule that a person can get no independent residence permit within the first three years of the marriage cause women to seek refuge outside of their families and cultural network.

In the 2001 survey it was found that women with uncertain resident status stay on average 181 nights in a shelter; clients with no legal problems concerning their residency stay on average 47 nights. The reason for the difference in average stay is that it takes a lot of time to deal with the legalities of the situation. There are legal procedures that have to be initiated on behalf of the client that can lead to granting a resident permit on humanitarian grounds. After this permit has been granted housing, social security and health insurance can be arranged. For some clients there is no such solution; they have to return to their native country or seek refuge with churches or charities. In 2002 the Minister of Welfare declared that women who are victims of domestic violence should have a right to shelter and help (according to the 1979 UN Women's Treaty) regardless of their resident status. It is unclear however, if this statement can be implemented in the sense that those victims have a right to social assistance and housing.

In Scotland, specialist women's refuges have been established in the main cities of Glasgow (since 1982) and Edinburgh (since 1988) in response to the needs of women from minority ethnic communities. However, in recent years these refuges also report increasing numbers of immigrant women among their clientele. These include asylum seekers and women whose residence status is dependent on their husband. According to present immigration rules women who enter the UK to join a husband may be granted a one-year probationary period, at the end of which they can apply for the right to settle (referred to as the one-year rule). This application can only be made by the resident spouse on behalf of the woman. A snapshot analysis of the reception figures in 2001 indicated that 15% of women in the Glasgow shelter were immigrants in this category.

In Germany, statistics from the women's housing coordination authority show that some 50-80% of the occupants in women's shelters in large cities such as Berlin, Hamburg and Munich are migrants (Busch-Geertsema, 2003). Women of immigrant background are also over-represented in accommodation provided by organisations working with the homeless. The National Federation of Organisations Working with the Homeless echoes the Dutch experience, suggesting that the role of gender in migration history may be of consequence here: "female migrants in institutions of organisations working with the homeless are perhaps women and young girls who have fled from their family of origin living in Germany, or a marriage with migrants or with German men because of violence, and have no right of abode of their own. Like the female clientele of organisations working with the homeless, these women fleeing violence are trying to find safe women's institutions or accommodation" (Rosenke, 2002, p 7). Women migrants in particular often have no other alternative than a women's shelter if they want or if they have to get out of a violent family relationship. The absence of bureaucratic red tape and anonymity of women's shelters further distinguishes such institutions from other social support services, where foreign nationality and residence status is often a barrier to admission.

The first intercultural women's shelter in Germany – the Interkulturelle Initiative – was established in Berlin in 2001 (Lehmann, 2002). The initiative provides a range of services, in addition to emergency shelter and transitional sheltered accommodation, including:

- advice for victims of domestic violence and their children;
- accompanying social support and translation support;
- free legal advice;
- follow-up advice and advice for family members;
- advice from experts;
- information days;
- telephone hotline.

Experience has shown that immigrant women's longer stay in shelters might be due to their insecure immigration status and its impact on the women's living conditions. Women leaving the emergency shelter often feel pressure to find a new home and make decisions about their future life. This might contribute to returning to abusive situations. Transitional housing can be an option for them, because it provides a safe home where they can get back on their feet without being confronted by the emergency shelter's permanent fluctuation and the individual crises of newly arriving women. The apartment units of the Initiative's sheltered housing project provide medium or long-term accommodation for 25 women.

The Interkulturelle Iniative employs 13 staff (including nursery school teachers, social workers, house management workers and project administration workers) who are of multicultural background, multilingual and who have a broad intercultural knowledge.

Young immigrants

There is evidence that the number of young immigrants and especially unaccompanied minors (under 18 years of age) has been increasing at the same time as the number of immigrants has increased. Additionally, there is evidence that the children of immigrants (the second generation immigrants) are more vulnerable to housing exclusion and homelessness than native-born citizens. Due to intergenerational and cultural conflicts, integration problems and other reasons, many young immigrants are trapped between two cultures. Some of them leave or are forced to leave home. Approaches to meeting the needs of these young people and the role of homeless services in this situation vary between countries.

In Finland, supported accommodation has been provided as a result of close cooperation between public agencies and the main homeless NGOs. However, according to research and the personnel working with young immigrants, there is a shortage of supported housing for this group in the metropolitan region. In 1999, there were over 80 immigrant youngsters in a need of supported housing. With the help of supported housing they can be encouraged to carry on with their studies, to look for jobs and to take control of their lives (Reiman, 1999, p 13). *Ehjä ry* is an NGO offering supported housing alternatives in communes and apartments for young adults aged 17-22 in need of special supervision to prepare them for more independent living. The Finnish Slot Machine Association and municipalities finance these supported flats. Although most of the young people living in Ehjä-supported flats have been refugees, they come from a variety of backgrounds. Some come from a childcare institution, their biological family, foster care or from the street. Others have lived with relatives and have run into problems with them. Some have come to Finland without their parents and have been in Finnish institutional care until they reach the age of 18. Some refugees come straight from reception centres. Young immigrants living in supported flats need considerable support. For many of them, being provided with a dwelling is not enough, because without support they would soon lose the dwelling. They need substantial support in their everyday lives to develop the skills needed for independent living. However, for the most part, local volunteer workers provide this support rather than full-time paid employees.

In France, the Committee for Refugees defines lone or unaccompanied children as 'children under 18 who have left their country of origin and have been separated from both their parents or their legal guardian'. Although figures are unreliable and incomplete there is a discernible rise in the numbers arriving in France over the past three years and, while the figures are low compared with other European countries, voluntary agencies estimate the numbers at between 3,000 and 10,000. These children cannot legally be removed but they can be kept in a holding area for several days, while the validity of their applications is checked, after which they must be reported to the Youth Protection and Prosecution Office who will refer them to the Children's Court. From that time they come under the ordinary law governing the protection of children at risk in France, and may be placed in département-based institutions. This procedure where child welfare takes precedence over immigration control is flawed in many ways (Maurel, 2003). Hence, many children remain unprotected for a variety of reasons: because they are not referred to the Youth Protection and Prosecution Office, because départements (county councils) are unwilling to pick up the problem which they argue is a matter for national solidarity, and the high attrition rate of child runaways rejoining families or being press-ganged by crime networks. In addition to this approach two specialised reception centres have been opened (in 1998 and 2002), and a trial mobile outreach accommodation and care scheme has been handed to five voluntary groups. But the growing numbers of street children in big towns and cities have reached disturbing proportions.

There is also concern regarding the increase in homelessness among the children of immigrants. Busch–Geertsema suggests that, in Germany, the dismantling of the positive integration procedures for repatriates during the 1990s has impacted on the vulnerability and housing exclusion of the children of those immigrants (2003, pp 38-9). The freedom of domicile of repatriates, who were allocated transfer benefits, was already limited to three years by the early 1990s by a law that provided for the allocation of temporary housing to incoming repatriates by the authorities. Overall, the integration chances of newly arrived repatriates worsened decisively in the 1990s, especially as more and more of the repatriates and their families who came to Germany during that time were relatively unfamiliar with German culture, language and customs and thus required more integration measures. Young repatriates in particular, who came to Germany as family members with their parents and grandparents, were often confronted with exclusion and disillusionment. Whereas they were stigmatised as 'the Germans' in their country of origin, once they resettled in Germany they were designated as 'the Russians' and were more prone to tensions with the locals and with other groups of migrants who had lived longer in Germany. However, there is no indication of any specific initiatives designed to meet the needs of these excluded and alienated repatriate youths.

Mental health and disability

It is known that asylum seekers may have mental health needs associated with persecution and torture in the countries from which they have fled. There are examples of a number of projects that have emerged to meet this need. Perhaps one of the oldest is to be found in the Netherlands, where a project for asylum seekers and refugees who require intensive care and therefore cannot stay in the traditional asylum centres (ABRI) was opened in 1989. The project caters for individual asylum seekers or families who are unable to live independently in a reception centre (COA) because they have problematic and anti-social behaviour. Generally the cause of the bad behaviour is known in the reception centre or through mental health organisations (CGZ). Most of their problems are behavioural problems, double diagnoses, personality disorders, (possible) domestic abuse or neglect, mental health problems (psychiatric illnesses) combined with behavioural problems.

The first aim of this project is to provide safe, supported accommodation. ABRI then tries to develop and implement an individual or family reintegration trajectory by providing support in relation to:

* medical/psychiatric area (accepting problems, stabilisation of the person, prepare and support for treatment);
* behaviour (regulation of aggression, social skills, education, and so on);
* accommodation ('teach how to live', prepare for next accommodation);
* day programme (day activities, day structure);
* practical matters (management of benefits, finances).

Multiagency working is essential to achieve these aims and ABRI concentrates on supported housing and activation while other care and support are provided by other external organisations. ABRI has structured cooperation with the mental health organisation (CGZ) of Amsterdam for the purpose of diagnosis and psychiatric support and treatment. A general practitioner is part of the multidisciplinary team. The organisation providing care at home in Amsterdam (*Thuiszorg*) provides additional support. There are also contacts with the organisation working with refugees in Amsterdam (*Vluchtelingenwerk*) and interpreters.

In addition to mental health issues associated with the causes of migration, Anderson (2003) points to a study in Scotland that has also revealed very significant mental health problems directly associated with housing provided on arrival. Interviewees reported being rehoused in communities where they felt afraid of racial harassment and attack, as well as high levels of crimes within the community generally (Ferguson and Barclay, 2002). Some families felt afraid to leave their dwellings and in extreme cases felt their environment was worse than that from which they had fled.

There appears to be very little literature relating to the needs of immigrants or asylum seekers with disabilities. Anderson (2003) refers to one study in the UK relating to the position of asylum seekers with disabilities (Roberts and Harris, 2002). No official data is collected on disability among asylum seekers but a survey of 44 community groups/organisations identified more than 5,000 asylum seekers known to have a disability, and in-depth interviews were conducted with a small sample of these. Common issues raised included a lack of suitable housing and of aids and equipment, as well as unmet personal care needs. People often lacked sufficient knowledge of available support and how to obtain this (for example, Community Care Assessments). Service providers also lacked appropriate knowledge as to entitlement. Under the 1999 legislation, refugees and people with exceptional leave to remain have the same entitlements to disability-related benefits and services as other disabled people. Asylum seekers cannot claim disability benefits but they can request a Community Care Assessment. It is then for the local authority to determine eligibility for services, what can be provided and whether a charge will be made. A clear need for better liaison between NASS and local authority social services was identified in order to better meet the needs of asylum seekers with disabilities.

Comparative analysis

Existing comparative frameworks, such as the Esping-Andersen welfare typology (Esping-Andersen, 1990), do not provide good predictive models by which to explain the differences in migration experience and in policy response to homelessness among immigrants. The detail of the level, increase and form of immigration in the member states is described in Chapter Two and policy responses to that immigration is discussed in Chapter Three. However, it is apparent that there are differences as well as common experiences across Europe, not only in the nature of immigration that is experienced but also in the nature of homelessness and in the response of the public and voluntary sector to that homelessness and housing exclusion. In this section we endeavour to provide a tentative categorisation of the member states in order to highlight some of the reasons for the specific responses perceived in the role of the homelessness services.

For this purpose we suggest four broad groupings of countries. First, there are countries where immigration is relatively recent in origin; these include the Mediterranean countries, Ireland and Finland. Second, there are countries where, until very recently, immigration was influenced by the country's colonial history; these include France, the Netherlands and the UK. Third, there are countries where service response to immigration has been heavily influenced by government policy; these include Austria and Germany. Fourth, there are countries where the impact of immigration on the homeless sector has been very limited; these include Belgium, Denmark, Luxembourg and Sweden.

Emigration countries

These are countries that have traditionally been net exporters of people and where net immigration is a relatively recent phenomenon. These include Portugal, Spain, Greece, Italy, Ireland and Finland.

The experience of the Mediterranean countries has been that of a recent and rapid rise in immigration, mainly (although not entirely) affecting the larger cities. A key characteristic of this recent increase is that it has been fuelled by undocumented immigration. The homeless sector in these countries is, in itself, relatively recent in origin and operates in a weak social welfare regime (Edgar et al, 1999; Edgar and Doherty, 2003) so that it is heavily dependent on charitable and uncertain funding. The increase in (undocumented) immigrants among service users has affected the emergency/crisis or low-threshold services. The lack of services overall and especially in rural areas (see the Spanish case study, p 135) has, on the other hand, meant that the needs of immigrants for even these basic level services are often not met. Differences exist between the Mediterranean countries. Italy, for example, developed reception centres for immigrants during the early 1990s, but these have been strongly developed in only a few regions and with a concentration of service provision in the north of the country. Portugal experienced a growth of shanty town developments around Lisbon that has largely been dealt with under EU-funded urban regeneration projects and hence the impact of immigration on homeless services was minimised by this experience. Greece has made specific provision for repatriate Pontiac Greeks. Although a number of large reception centres have been provided, response to the recent influx of asylum seekers is uncoordinated and almost entirely dependent on voluntary sector effort. In addition, and as a result of this landscape of limited provision, undocumented immigrants (especially those from Albania) survive without recourse to formal services, for example, in the cheap hotels of Omonia district in central Athens.

Although immigration in Finland and Ireland is also relatively recent in origin in the history of those countries, the impact on homeless services and their response to it is very different. In both countries the level of immigration remains relatively low compared with the Mediterranean member states, and the nature of immigration tends to be legal, refugee or asylum immigrants rather than undocumented migrants. In Ireland, the main increase in immigration has been in asylum applicants and the government provision of direct accommodation has meant that this has had only marginal impact on homeless services. In Finland specific provision has been made for returning Ingrians of Finnish origin and refugees are accommodated under normal conventions. In addition, coordinated action between government and the national homeless agency (the Y-Foundation) has provided supported accommodation for specific groups. This, together with the universal system of welfare rights, has lessened the impact of immigrants on the homeless sector. The movement of immigrants back to the capital region and the effects of an overheated Helsinki housing market have led to this being the main reason for homelessness among immigrants.

Countries with colonial migration

The pattern of immigration in these countries, since the 1950s, has meant that the pressure on homeless services may come both from second generation immigrants as well as from recently arrived immigrants and asylum seekers. It also tends to mean that the nature of homelessness takes the form of insecure and inadequate housing and hidden homelessness, as well as recourse to direct homeless services. Policy response and tight immigration restrictions have different impacts on homeless services in the four countries. In the UK, the recent rapid increase in asylum applicants led to the creation of a specific agency (NASS) and a dispersal programme using social housing in regional cities. This has lessened the impact of that section of immigration on the homeless service sector. Second generation (black) immigrants are more likely to be homeless but are less likely to use traditional homeless hostels. In France, a more complex picture emerges. However, this is a picture of strong central concentration in the Paris region and a spillover from the CPH/CADA (Centres d'Accueil pour Demandeurs d'Asile/Centre Provisoire d'hébergement) (asylum accommodation) provision, resulting in the homeless sector acting as a last refuge for an increasing number of immigrants, mopping up the failures of the asylum system. In the Netherlands, high proportions of service users in women's centres (60%), crisis centres (33%) and shelters for the homeless (25%) were Dutch nationals of non-Dutch origin. Asylum seekers are usually housed in special reception centres. Immigrant women who have left their husbands have limited rights and an uncertain resident status. Women's shelters house an increasing proportion of such women. Shelter organisations reported increasing numbers of undocumented immigrants towards the end of the 1990s. Recent legislation prevents people without resident status making use of services. Hence, some shelters and crisis centres do not accept people without resident status any more since they do not receive any subsidy for these people. Undocumented aliens therefore sleep rough or turn to day centres and night shelters that are able to receive people without having to ask for identification.

Countries with strong policy influence

Germany and Austria have specific immigration problems resulting from their geographical position and history; in the case of Germany, of guest workers from Turkey and Aussiedler repatriates. However, separate systems of provision for repatriates in Germany and asylum applicants in both countries affects the situation regarding service provision for homeless people. In addition, welfare legislation excludes certain categories of immigrants and non-citizens from access to homeless services.

Only very few homeless people who do not have Austrian nationality are looked after by institutions dealing with homelessness and support for housing. This state of affairs is in particular attributable to specific legal and administrative structural conditions, whereby non-EU nationals seeking assistance risk entanglements with immigration enforcement officials if they formally apply for (social) welfare benefit, and thus tend to avoid such welfare assistance institutions as much as possible. Hence the number of (at least) 7,000 homeless migrants throughout Austria referred to in previous chapters in this report is only a rough estimate (Eitel and Schoibl, 1999, p 35).

In Germany there are also separate accommodation systems geared exclusively to migrants and homeless immigrants, in the form of communal accommodation for refugees and repatriates. Residence and social welfare legislation hurdles either completely exclude the use and financing of assistance for certain groups of immigrants, or leaves it completely to the discretion of the social welfare authorities. Immigrant women fleeing domestic abuse are catered for in women's shelters that are also separately administered from the homeless sector.

Countries with low service impact

Stringent regulations in some countries (Belgium, Denmark, Luxembourg and Sweden) regarding undocumented immigration, together with a separate (and adequate) system of reception accommodation for asylum seekers, means that the impact of immigrants on traditional homeless services is minimal. However, this implies street homelessness and hidden homelessness for those denied access to services. In Denmark and Sweden issues for immigrants also revolve around the inadequate housing and segregation. These fit into FEANTSA's definition of housing exclusion rather than visible homelessness.

In Belgium, the availability of relatively cheap poor quality housing allows immigrants access to the housing market and the government is attempting to control rack-renting in these situations. The enormous influx of asylum seekers required the creation of separate structures. The most recent trend is that reception is increasingly developing as a separate sector in which the OCMWs (Public Social Welfare Centres) no longer have the main responsibility for the reception. A variety of methods are now used to receive asylum seekers, including federal centres and Red Cross centres and places created through agreements with umbrella organisations for refugees (OCIV and CIRE) (Overlegcentre voor Integratie van Vluchtelingen and Coordination et Initiative pour réfugiés et étrangers). Hence traditional homeless service providers are not affected to the same degree as in other countries.

Denmark, for example, has a separate asylum system and undocumented immigrants are excluded from homeless services. The proportion of immigrants in homeless services (Article 94, 1998 Social Services Act) is the same as in the population overall. However, the majority of these appear to be immigrant women fleeing domestic abuse. In Luxembourg, the records of the country's only night shelter and main day centre for the homeless reveal no direct immigration effect on the make-up of the homeless community. However, stringent regulations mean that immigrants unable to prove prior residence in the country have no access to homeless services. Reception centres are available only to asylum seekers. Undocumented immigrants are effectively homeless and denied all rights to any form of assistance or support. Sweden also has reception housing for asylum seekers and excludes undocumented immigrants from homeless services. Immigrants with residence status suffer from poor housing quality, overcrowding and segregation but do not appear in the official social services statistics on homelessness. Consequently, homelessness among immigrants is not quantifiable in statistics and is hardly even perceptible in the homeless shelters.

Conclusions: the future role of homeless services in the integration of immigrants

It is evident from our analysis that homeless services are responding to different needs in relation to providing accommodation and services to immigrants. They have a role to play in responding to the needs of both recently arrived immigrants and second generation immigrants. In particular they meet the needs of undocumented immigrants in low-threshold services, they respond to the needs of immigrant women fleeing domestic abuse and they, in part, meet the needs of second generation immigrants who are vulnerable in the housing market. In addition, they act as a safety net for asylum seekers in countries where asylum reception facilities are blocked and cannot respond to the recent rapid increase in demand. This latter situation may be a transitional role while governments adjust their asylum reception and processing procedures and facilities. However, experience suggests it is likely to be a more enduring situation.

Many of the national reports produced as part of this research indicate that the needs of (recently arrived) immigrants are different from the needs of native users of homeless services. The main characteristic, it is suggested, of immigrant users of homeless services is that their stay is transitional and one-off and their main needs relate to their residence status and their need for accommodation. In contrast, the needs of native homeless service users are characterised as being related more to relationship and personal problems and social exclusion and to be more enduring in nature, requiring both housing and support to resolve. However, there is some indication that, over time, the needs of immigrant users of homeless services and, it is implied, of foreign-born users who are citizens, are changing to be more similar to the 'native' homeless population. In addition, some more vulnerable immigrants require more specialised services or services separate from mainstream homeless provision to provide for their specific needs (especially women and young people). Equally, mainstream services have often had to adapt to respond to the cultural, religious and language needs of immigrants. Although the argument in favour of immigrant-led or black-led separate services requires detailed discussion, it is clear that mixing immigrants (who are often younger) with native homeless people (who tend to be older and have different needs) in mainstream services can lead to conflict that has to be appropriately managed. This requires appropriate staffing and management regulations and will be more difficult to achieve in hostels that are inadequately designed (for example, communal or shared dormitories, no facilities for self-catering or private washing).

This summary of the existing situation regarding the role of homeless services and the needs of immigrants suggests that, in some countries at least and in some situations, the existing situation is inadequate. At the present time, homeless services mainly tend to provide emergency and crisis services to immigrants. There is an argument for a wider range of services including supported and transitional accommodation linked to resettlement or integration support. There is also an argument, if not for immigrant-only homeless services, at least for appropriate staffing with specialist training and language skills. The high proportion of immigrant and foreign-born women in women's shelters suggests the need for specialist refuges for women fleeing domestic abuse on the model provided, for some time, in Scotland and, more recently, in Berlin.

The prevention of homelessness among immigrants requires strategic planning and coordination. Our analysis suggests two aspects to this approach. First, where homeless services are filling the gap left by the inadequate provision of asylum accommodation this needs to be recognised and addressed. Second, immigration policies should incorporate appropriate integration strategies that include strategies to facilitate integration into the housing market as well as into the labour market. Homeless services have a role to play, in cooperation with other agencies, in ensuring that adequate information and advice is available to immigrants on housing matters.

Our analysis indicates that the recent (and rapid) rise in some forms of immigration, and in the 'new wave' immigration (asylum seekers and Eastern European immigration), has created new problems to which service providers have adapted and responded. However, this is probably not a transitional phenomenon. Therefore it will be increasingly necessary to ensure that there is appropriate planning and management of services in the medium to long term. This will be necessary to enable those immigrants who require it to access stationary homeless services and supported housing as well low-threshold emergency services. The role of homeless services in the integration of immigrants and asylum seekers given residence status should be explained in the local and national context and the role (if any) planned in coordination between the public sector and NGOs. This would probably also be improved by joint working between the homeless sector and immigrant NGOs. This strategic planning needs to be informed by appropriate (national or local) research on existing needs and experiences of immigrants and the resultant gaps in provision.

It has been argued (Cabrera, 2003) that all these circumstances lead many to conclude that welfare services for immigrants should be institutionally separated from those for homeless excluded people, but the fact is, that given the absence of residential alternatives at this time, the network for the homeless is absorbing a large part of the problem of the residential exclusion affecting the poorer immigrants without social networks. There are no prospects of the trend changing in the short term; on the contrary, it is expected to continue to gain momentum. However, the need for specialist services and for specialist staffing and training within existing services probably requires local research to determine the benefits and the nature of the need.

Note

[1] Ingrians are people of Finnish descent living in areas annexed from Finland in the past.

SEVEN

Conclusions

Introduction

This book aimed to provide a comparative European perspective on the relationship between immigration, housing exclusion and homelessness. The evidence on which this analysis is based has been drawn in large part from the 15 national reports of the researchers of the European Observatory on Homelessness (accessible at www.feantsa.org).

Migrants make up a considerable component of European society, and immigration will continue to remain a significant feature of European population change as member states adjust to predicted shifts in their demographic composition, particularly those resulting from an ageing of their populations. There is an increasing recognition by the European Commission and a number of the member states of the need for immigration to be maintained as a replacement skilled and unskilled labour supply[1].

We have argued in the preceding chapters that among many of the immigrants arriving in the late 20th and early 21st centuries, there has been an increasing vulnerability to housing exclusion and homelessness. We suggest that a 'hierarchy of vulnerability' (Chapter Two) can be identified, with the position of immigrants in the hierarchy determined in large part by their legal status (itself a reflection of the tightening of immigration controls and the increasing rigour of asylum procedures), but also associated with the characteristics of immigrants themselves (their skill levels, their relative wealth, their gender, age and so forth). The vulnerability of immigrants to housing exclusion and homelessness is, however, also clearly linked to the changing structures of national and regional housing markets and is perpetuated by the lack of compensatory alleviating or preventive policies (reflecting in large measure the changing role of welfare in all member states). This book has explored the nature of immigrant vulnerability to housing exclusion and homelessness through an examination of the nature and scale of the problem in each member state, through an exploration of the factors explaining the perpetuation of the problem, by identifying who is affected and what (albeit limited) responses have emerged to cope with the situation.

In this concluding chapter we summarise our key findings in order to the address their implications for policy and practice; implications which relate to the role of the European Commission, the member states as well as NGOs working with immigrants and the homeless. The aim is not to be prescriptive in relation to policy recommendations (indeed the research on which the book is based is not detailed enough to allow prescription); rather we are concerned with identifying the most urgent areas of policy development and policy implementation.

Increasing vulnerability of immigrants to housing exclusion

High levels of immigration, of all types, have placed increasing pressure on most member states in recent years. This has been true both of countries for whom immigration is a relatively recent phenomenon and for those whose experience of immigration has been more long-lasting. One reaction to this increasing pressure has been a tightening of immigration policies and of restrictions on welfare support for foreigners and non-citizens. This tightening of EU and national immigration policies and border controls has effectively reserved the right of residence (mostly on a temporary, time-limited basis) to those with perceived skills needed by national economies – this includes service and agricultural workers as well as business executives and professionals. Those immigrants who do not fit these categories (and that includes those seeking family reunion as well as asylum seekers) are increasingly exposed to rigorous checks and barriers to entry, forcing many into the ranks of the irregular, undocumented migrants whose precarious position is exacerbated by the constant threat of exposure and deportation. As we have observed previously, undocumented or unauthorised migrants comprise an estimated 10-15% of the total number of migrants in Europe and make up 20-30% of incoming flows. All the evidence suggests that undocumented immigration will continue and even increase as immigration controls tighten. The vulnerability of migrants, especially those who occupy the lower ranks of the hierarchy of vulnerability (temporary, especially unskilled, workers, asylum seekers with unresolved status and undocumented immigrants) is compounded by their exposure to the hostility emanating from xenophobic and racist sections of the host populations and by the decreasing ability (willingness) of welfare states to provide even safety-net services in the form of benefits and care. The changing structures of the housing market in all EU countries – reflecting the impact of commodification and contraction in the provision of affordable social housing – further contributes to the vulnerabilities of some immigrants by exposing them to the threat of housing exclusion and possible homelessness. The continuation of present immigration trends will increase the pressure on those segments of the housing market on which the poorer and more vulnerable migrants and asylum seekers depend. Housing policies and homeless services cannot ignore this situation.

It is increasingly recognised that effective immigration policy requires appropriate and effective integration strategies. This holds whether the policy is directed towards opening (see Coleman, 2000; Hayter, 2000; Harris, 2003) or bolting the door to further immigration – although as the tenor of this book suggests, such integration programmes will be more difficult to implement in the context of a 'Fortress Europe' policy than in the context of a less restrictive policy. Effective integration strategies need to include procedures to facilitate access to adequate and affordable housing. Evidence available to us during the compilation of this book suggests that such strategies are not in place at this time (in relation to access to housing) and that this 'policy blindness', linked to the vulnerability of an increasing proportion of immigrants, leads to discrimination and exploitation. However, integration strategies need to be adequately resourced and to be capable of implementation. It is questionable if there is the institutional/administrative capacity to do this in some countries. This understanding points to a need for action at EU level as well as at national level. Within the context of the EU Race Equality Directive, anti-discrimination directives need to be effectively implemented and robustly enforced. Within the context of the EU Strategy to Combat Poverty and Social Exclusion, the National Action Plans should be required to identify policies and procedures to address these issues.

We argue that national policies have, to date, had more to do with immigration control and tightening procedures for asylum applications rather than dealing with integration policies focused on the housing outcomes for migrants. While EU directives have emerged in recent years on race equality, anti-discrimination and immigration policies, national policies should also focus on integration into the housing market since this is a national level competence.

It is perhaps axiomatic to suggest, as we have done, that it has been the weakest social groups who have been most affected by changes in European housing markets. However, it remains an evident truth and one which identifies recent immigrants and younger second generation immigrants as vulnerable to housing exclusion and homelessness. Evidence presented in the previous chapters indicates that immigrants are more likely to occupy the worst housing and to pay a disproportionate share of their income to acquire it. Evidence has also been presented to indicate that, in most countries (at least in the metropolitan cities of those countries), homeless service providers are reporting a significant increase in immigrants and foreign-born citizens among their clients. Hence many immigrants are 'doubly' at risk of social exclusion, both as a result of their residence status as immigrants and as a result of their risk of housing exclusion arising from their relative poverty and the risk of discrimination.

The lack of access to decent and affordable housing is a key factor in preventing the assimilation or integration of immigrants. There is evidence that segregation is persisting and that while there may be positive effects arising from clustering of cultural groups, more generally, the effects are negative on the life chances of immigrants. Attempts to achieve social balance within neighbourhoods or housing blocks can also be exclusionary, as well as leading to the intended effect of improving social cohesion. Since, in most countries, immigrants tend to cluster in the metropolitan conurbations, or in the 'job-rich' regions, this tends to exacerbate the problems immigrants face in accessing decent and affordable housing.

The importance of the role of social housing in providing access to the housing market is stressed in our discussion in Chapter Four. However, access to social housing is increasingly difficult as a result of the decline in provision in recent years and the lack of supply (or availability), especially in metropolitan (and rural) areas where immigrants are concentrated. There is some indication that allocation rules discriminate, directly or indirectly, against immigrants and foreign-born citizens. In countries with low levels of social housing the general absence of policies (to facilitate access to affordable rented housing) provides the basis for discrimination and exploitation of which poor housing circumstances or homelessness are the end result.

The persistence of housing exclusion and homelessness, evident from this analysis, again emphasises the importance of effective implementation and enforcement of existing EU directives. However, housing exclusion and homelessness among immigrants also requires explicit approaches developed within the context of the National Action Plans on social exclusion and in the context of national and local housing policies and strategies. This is not to ignore the fact that local responses by some metropolitan authorities, referred to as the integration pacts (see Chapter Three), have emerged and are worthy of evaluation and wider dissemination.

Homelessness among immigrants

Within a broader definition of homelessness it appears that the more vulnerable immigrants often resort to inadequate and insecure housing and to the informal housing sector, and thus are not counted among the street homeless or among users of homeless services. The nature of such coping strategies was described in Chapter Four. Our review of the literature has also suggested that, despite the lack of detailed empirical research in many countries, hidden homelessness among immigrants is evident and this may be more prevalent among some social and cultural groups (for example, women, young people and people from particular religious or cultural traditions).

Despite this, the scale of recorded homelessness among immigrants and foreign-born citizens in homeless services has been increasing in many (if not all) countries. The lack of reception facilities combined with lengthy determination periods for asylum seekers has meant that, in some countries, homeless services have been left to 'mop up' for the failure of immigration policies by accommodating an increasing proportion of immigrants among their clientele. This has often led to the exclusion of other homeless immigrants, who are not going through the asylum process, from these services. However in some countries, where asylum reception procedures are tightly enforced and legislation and funding restrictions (officially) exclude undocumented immigrants from homeless services, the proportion of immigrants among homeless service users has been low and shows only a modest increase. In such countries the use made of homeless services by second generation immigrants and foreign-born citizens is also relatively low, leading to the suspicion that the scale of hidden homelessness, which is neither recorded nor researched, is high.

The profile of homeless immigrants reflects a hierarchy of vulnerability. The risk of vulnerability is created both by the legal status acquired by the putative immigrant and by the economic situation (education and employment status) at the time of migration. Their ethnic origin, relative to the ethnic composition of the host country, will also affect their ability to find support and avoid discrimination in the workplace or in the housing market. However, vulnerability is also affected by the stage in the lifecourse at which migration occurs, and hence it is also influenced by factors related to gender and age. Probably the greatest risk of vulnerability lies in the increase in undocumented migrants arising from a tightening of immigration controls and increasing rejection of asylum applications. It is therefore no surprise to see an increase in this group among the users of low-threshold services, and among the street homeless and the hidden homeless. The dominance of particular ethnic groups among the homeless indicates an increase in the proportion of people coming from countries where their economic position at the time of migration is weak and their ability to compete in the labour market in the host country is also weak. Such groups, facing discrimination, exploitation or lack of social support, are thus at greater risk of homelessness. There is also evidence of changes in the demographic composition of homeless immigrants, characterised mainly by an increase in younger people and a feminisation of the population. However, there is also a contrary trend of the ageing of longer-term immigrants in workers' hostels in some countries.

Although in the past we may have expected that immigrants, arriving through labour recruitment or family reunion, would eventually assimilate into the host community by their own efforts and with social support, it is arguable that the increased vulnerability of more recent arrivals requires more formal support to facilitate integration. Furthermore, although in many countries the increase in immigrants among homeless service users is a relatively recent phenomenon, the indications suggest that this is not a transitional situation. This situation will persist and even increase if policies are not directed to recognise the issue and deal with it. This has significant implications for the providers of homeless services.

Impact of immigration on homeless services

There has been little research undertaken about the needs of homeless immigrants and how these may differ between different groups or how they may change over time. However, throughout this book we have identified a number of important issues which can be summarised in the following four main observations. First, the needs of more recent immigrants relate mainly to their difficulties in gaining access to decent housing and dealing with their immigrant status. Second, there are some, more vulnerable, immigrants (for example, women, people with mental health problems) who do require specific, or longer-term, support in order to gain access to housing or to live independently in their new country. Third, the needs of second generation immigrants (or the children of repatriates) are more complex than solely housing needs. Fourth, the needs of immigrants in homeless services are generally very different from those of traditional client groups whose needs are well understood by service providers.

In a number of countries, legislation or the nature of funding regimes deny access to homeless services to non-citizens and to undocumented immigrants. Hence service providers are at risk of prosecution or withdrawal of funding if they assist such groups, or they can choose do so without state funding. One implication of this is that immigrants are mainly restricted to using low-threshold emergency services — integration support and supported accommodation services are not normally available to them. The exception to this occurs where specialist services have been established (examples given in this book include asylum seekers with mental health problems and immigrant women fleeing domestic abuse). Over many years homeless services have been developing beyond provision of emergency services to the provision of reintegration support for homeless people. Denial of this level of service and expertise to homeless immigrants can only serve to make it more difficult to assimilate such immigrants into the host community.

There is clear evidence that, in some countries, second generation immigrants are at greater risk of homelessness than the indigenous population. However, their lack of visibility in official statistics indicates that they do not use homeless services. The precise reasons for this require more detailed research but probably relate to the negative perception of services and to the fact that services are not geared to meeting the specific needs of this group. This indicates a need both for improved information and advice appropriately targeted, and for service providers to examine their staffing, their accommodation and their operational procedures.

The challenge of meeting the needs of homeless immigrants creates a number of management issues for service providers including resource issues, organisational issues (including operational procedures, staffing and training) and, increasingly, planning issues. The nature and complexity of these issues, described in Chapter Six, point to the need for multiagency working. However, during the course of the preparation of this book we have found only limited evidence of multiagency working. These challenges imply action is needed by the state as well as by NGOs. The state (at national and local level) needs to re-examine the restriction of access to homeless services for certain categories of immigrants, to recognise its role in meeting the shortfall in asylum and immigration procedures and to recognise the inadequate levels of funding available to meet this emerging need. Homeless service providers need to address the planning of services and related management issues, to learn from existing practice and to develop more effective partnership roles with immigrant organisations.

Specialist services for vulnerable immigrants have emerged and have been described in Chapter Six. The complexity of need, and of challenging behaviour encountered in existing reception facilities and homeless services, has led to the creation of specialist support services. These services appear to have been reactive rather than proactive. Women's shelters have responded to the increasing proportion of immigrant women in their services by establishing specialist shelters. Apart from the women's shelters, the existence of immigrant-led or ethnic-led organisations have been noticeable by their absence. The appropriateness of specialist services or immigrant-led services is an issue requiring local evaluation and decision but should be based on an assessment of need and appropriate planning.

In the context of the prevention of homelessness, the ageing of immigrants, many of whom have lived in member states for some years already and who lack family or social support, is a specific issue that may emerge as an increasing problem in a number of countries. Issues of the mental health needs and of the ageing of immigrants in migrant workers' hostels require direct intervention to deal with and merit further detailed research to inform practice.

Our attempt to present a comparative analysis of the impact of immigration on homeless services across Europe (see Chapter Six) indicates a broad grouping of countries with diverse experiences and issues and points to the need for action at European, national and local level. Countries which have recently experienced high levels of immigration are also, for the most part, countries where homeless services are of recent origin and of limited capacity and where the state welfare regime is also weak. This situation points to a role for the EU in the context both of the social exclusion strategy and the search for a common immigration strategy. It would also merit the provision of resources to make good the existing deficit in institutional capacity in these countries. This already occurs to a limited extent in Greece. In countries which have a longer history of immigration and more developed homeless services the issues revolve more around the management of existing services, the development of specialist services and interagency working. It is clear that in some countries few immigrants are catered for in homeless services. This situation arises both as a result of legal (and funding) constraints, particularly in relation to undocumented immigrants and as a result of the organisation of social services for the homeless. While the level of homelessness among immigrants may well be lower in these countries, the policy landscape in which homeless services operate should be adjusted to reflect the reality of the needs of immigrants. This implies legislative action as well as policy prescription. In all countries, the failure to recognise the extent and nature of the problem of homelessness among immigrants can only create difficulties of integration into the housing market both in the short term (in the immediate post-determination stage) and in the long term.

Implications for policy and practice: the way forward

Policy measures designed to improve access to housing for immigrants (including second generation immigrants) require action at the EU level, national and local level as well as at the level of the NGO.

Effective implementation of EU directives on race equality and anti-discrimination and the programme to combat racism would make a significant difference. To some extent this is a matter of timing – the recent nature of these directives allows that new legislation is emerging in many member states.

However, it is also dependent on political will to enforce the legislation and to provide adequate resources, including in relation to issues such as housing exclusion and homelessness. This involves action at the national level.

Access to housing for immigrants needs to be an integral part of national integration policies and strategies. Furthermore, since there are no prospects of change in short term (either in the level of immigration or in the provision of reception facilities), the role of homeless services in the residential inclusion of vulnerable immigrants (without social networks) needs to be acknowledged by government and appropriately funded and regulated. This implies action, not only in relation to immigration policies but also with regard to housing (and homelessness) strategies, which should be reflected in the National Action Plans on social inclusion.

We have identified a range of management issues arising for homeless service providers as a result of the increase in immigrants among service users. Taken together, these issues suggest the need to think strategically about the services provided to immigrants to prevent homelessness, to deal with their needs while they are homeless and to facilitate their integration into adequate housing. Strategic thinking will also be necessary to allow decisions to be made on the adaptation of existing services and the need for development of additional or specialist services. Such considerations, however, are likely to raise issues of accommodation provision and management, staffing and staff training and operational procedures, all of which have resource implications. If this is not to be to the detriment of existing homeless services, then a dialogue with public sector funding bodies will be needed. Since there is little existing research on the needs of immigrants and since it cannot be assumed that attitudes of service providers will not be influenced by stereotypical perceptions, it is important that immigrant communities and organisations are consulted in the decision making involved in adapting and developing such services. It has been argued elsewhere in the book that interagency working will be an important feature of the improvement and development of services for homeless immigrants. This is unlikely to occur without local commitment, coordination and guidance, and suggests an important role for local authorities and funding agencies.

Improved information and advice can, we assume, help prevent homelessness and exploitation in the housing market. While there are some examples of good practice in this regard, it is probable that real change will only occur if local strategies are developed and funded that recognise the importance of this approach. Some of the local initiatives that have been described in this book provide examples of innovation in approach that illustrate the benefits to be gained from improved exchange of experience in this new and changing field. We have also pointed to the need for further research. Fruitful areas may include the consideration of the need for specialist services, the nature and extent of hidden homelessness, and the nature of housing careers of immigrants.

Note

[1] The impact of the enlargement of the EU to, initially, 25 member states is as yet unclear and it has been beyond the scope of this book to consider these issues; but given the very different housing histories of the accession states and their variable demographic composition it is likely that they will add a new dimension to the issues associated with access to decent and affordable housing for immigrants and minority ethnic groups.

References

Abu-Lughod, J. (1978) 'Recent migrations in the Arab world', in W. McNeill and R. Adams (eds) *Human migration: Pattern and policies*, Bloomington, IA: Indiana University Press.

Ackers, L. (1998) *Shifting spaces: Women, citizenship and migration within the European Union*, Bristol: The Policy Press.

Agnew, J. (2003) *A world that knows no boundaries? The geopolitics of globalization and the myth of a borderless world*, CIBR Working Papers in Border Studies CIBR/WP03-2 and in D. Conway and N. Heyman (eds) *Globalization's dimensions*, Lanham, MD: Rowman and Littlefield, pp 7-13.

Alt, J. (1999) *Illegal in Deutschland: Forschungsprojekt zur lebenssituation "illegaler" migranten in Leipzig*, Karlsruhe: von Loeper Literaturverlag.

Anderson, I. (2000) 'Housing and social exclusion – the changing debate', in I. Anderson and D. Sim (eds) *Social exclusion and housing: Contexts and challenges*, Coventry: Chartered Institute of Housing.

Anderson, I. (2003) *Migration and homelessness in the UK*, Report for the European Observatory on Homelessness, Brussels: FEANTSA.

Anderson, J. (2004: forthcoming) 'Only sustain...: the environment, "anti-globalisation" and the runaway bicycle', in J. Johnston, M. Gismondi and J. Goodman (eds) *Reclaiming sustainability*, London: Zed Books.

Anthias, F. (2000) 'Metaphors of home: gendering new migrations in southern Europe', in F. Anthias and G. Lazaridis (eds) *Gender and migration in Southern Europe*, Oxford: Berg.

Anthias, F. and Lazaridis, G. (eds) (1999) *Into the margins: Migration and social exclusion in Southern Europe*, Aldershot: Ashgate.

Anthias, F. and Lazaridis, G. (2000) *Gender and migration in southern Europe*, Oxford: Berg.

Appadurai, A. (1997) *Modernity at large*, Minneapolis, MN: University of Minnesota Press.

Ares 2000 (2001) *Il colore delle case: Primo rapporto sulla condizione abitativa degli immigrati in Italia*, Rome: Ares.

Baldwin-Edwards, M. (2002) 'Immigration and the welfare state: a European challenge to American mythology', Mediterranean Migration Observatory, Working Paper No 4 (www.mmo.gr/pdf/publications/mmo_working_papers/MMO_WP4.pdf).

Ball, M. (2002) *RICS European housing review 2002*, London: Royal Institute for Chartered Surveyors.

Ball, M. and Harloe, M. (1998) 'Uncertainty in European housing markets', in M. Kleinman, W. Matznetter and M. Stephens (eds) *European integration and housing policy*, London: Routledge.

Barrett, A. and O'Connell, P. (2001) 'Is there a wage premium for returning Irish migrants?', *Economic and Social Review*, vol 32, no 1, pp 1-21.

Bartelheimer, P. (1998) 'Durchmischen oder stabilisieren? Plädoyer für eine Wohnungspolitik diesseits der "sozialen Durchmischung"', in Widersprüche, Heft 70, Dezember, pp 45-67.

Basch, L., Glick Schiller, N. and Blanc, C.S. (1994) *Nations unbound: Transnational projects, postcolonial predicaments and deterritorialised nation-states*, London: Gordon and Breach.

Bas-Theron, F. and Michel, M. (2002) 'Rapport sur les immigrés vieillissants', Rapport No 2002, 126, Paris: FASILD.

Bauman, Z. (1998a) *Globalization: The human consequences*, Cambridge: Polity Press.

Bauman, Z. (1998b) 'Europe of strangers', Transnational Communities Programme, Working Paper No 3, available at www.transcomm.ox.ac.uk

Becker, R. (1988) 'Notwendigkeit und Bedingungen des sozialen Wohnungsbaus als Bestandteil einer sozial orientierten Wohnungspolitik', in T. Specht, M. Schaub and G. Schuler-Wallner (eds) *Wohnungsnot in der Bundesrepublik – Perspektiven der Wohnungspolitik und – versorgung für benachteiligte Gruppen am Wohnungsmarkt*, Berlin: Dokumentation einer Fachtagung zum Internationalen Jahr für Menschen, pp 166-79.

Becker, R. (1997) 'Im Labyrinth der Wohnungspolitik. Anmerkungen zu Mieten, Belastungen, Förderungsmodellen und Subventionsformen – Ist der soziale Wohnungsbau obsolet geworden?', in V. Roscher und P. Stamm (eds) *Wohnen in der Stadt – Wohnen in Hamburg. Leitbild – Stand – Tendenzen*, Hamburg, pp 80-97.

Behrendt, U., Eichener, V., Höbel, R. and Schüwer, U. (1996) 'Vermittlungschancen verschiedener Gruppen von Wohnungssuchenden. Eine empirische Untersuchung über Wohnungssuchende in Dortmund', *Wis-Bericht*, no 19, Bochum: University of Konstanz.

Bell, N. (2002) 'Contribution', Borders and Migration Conference, Vienna, Austrian League for Human Rights, European Civic Forum (www.social.coe.int).

Bellaviti, P., Granata, E., Novak, C. and Tosi, A. (2001) *Le condizioni abitative e l'inserimento territoriale degli immigrati in Lombardia*, Osservatorio Regionale per l'integrazione e la multietnicità, Milan: Osservatorio.

Bernardotti, M.A. (2001) *Con la valigia accanto al letto. Immigrati e casa a Bologna*, Milan: FrancoAngeli.

Betton, R. (2001) *Access to housing for vulnerable groups: The French national report 2000*, Brussels: FEANTSA.

Boal, F. (2000) 'Exclusion and inclusion: segregation and deprivation in Belfast', in S. Musterd, and W. Ostendorf (eds) *Urban segregation and the welfare state: Inequality and exclusion in western Europe*, London: Routledge, pp 94-109.

Böcker, A. and Havinga, T. (1997) *Asylum migration to the European Union: Patterns of origin and destination*, Luxembourg: European Commission.

Body-Gendrot, S. (1996) *Réagir dans les Quartiers en Crise: La Politique des Empowerment Zones*, Paris: La Documentation francaise.

Body-Gendrot, S. and Martiniello, M. (2000) *Minorities in European cities: The dynamics of social integration and social exclusion at the neighbourhood level*, Houndsmill: Macmillan Press.

Boëldieu, J. and Thave, S. (1996) *Le logement des immigrés en 1996*, Paris: INSEE.

Boeri, T., Hanson, G. and McCormick, B. (eds) (2002) *Immigration policy and the welfare system*, Oxford: Oxford University Press.

Bolt, G. and Van Kempen, R. (2002) 'Moving up or moving down? Housing careers of Turks and Moroccans in Utrecht, the Netherlands', *Housing Studies*, vol 17, no 3, pp 401-22.

Boverket (2002) *Bostadsmarknadsläge och förväntat bostadsbyggande år 2002-2003*, Karlskrona: Boverket.

Bowes, A. and Sim, D. (2002) 'Patterns of residential settlement among black and minority ethnic groups', in P. Somerville and A. Steele (eds) *Race, housing and social exclusion*, London: Jessica Kingsley, pp 40-60.

Bruto da Costa, A. and Baptista, I. (2001) *Access to housing for vulnerable groups: The Portuguese National Report 2000*, Brussels: FEANTSA.

Buck, B. (2001) *Dispersed? Housing and supporting asylum seekers and refugees in Scotland*, Edinburgh: Shelter (Scotland).

Burda, M.C., Haerdle, W., Mueller, M. and Werwatz, A. (1998) 'Semiparametric analysis of German East-West migration intentions: facts and theory', *Journal of Applied Econometrics*, vol 13, no 5, pp 525-41.

Burrows, R. (1997) 'The social distribution of the experience of homelessness', in R. Burrows, N. Pleace and D. Quilgars (eds) *Homelessness and social policy*, London: Routledge, pp 50-68.

Busch-Geertsema, V. (2003) *Immigration and homelessness in Germany*, Report for the European Observatory on Homelessness, Brussels: FEANTSA.

Cabrera, P.J. (2000) *La acción social con personas sin hogar en España*, Madrid: Foessa-Cáritas.

Cabrera, P.J. (2001) *Access to housing for vulnerable groups: The Spanish National Report 2000*, Brussels: FEANTSA.

Cabrera, P.J. and Malgesini, G. (2003) *Immigration and homelessness in Spain*, Report for the European Observatory on Homelessness, Brussels: FEANTSA.

Carbrera, P.J. and Reyes, C. (2001) 'Immigration in the Rioja region of Spain', Paper presented to the European Observatory on Homelessness, Madrid, October 2002.

Cardoso, A. and Perista, H. (1994) 'A cidade esquecida – pobreza em bairros degradados de Lisbon', *Sociologia, Problemas e Práticas*, vol 15, pp 5-30.

Castells, M. (2000) *The rise of the network society*, Oxford: Blackwell.

Castles, S. and Kosack, G. (1973) *Immigrant workers and class structure in western Europe*, London: Oxford University Press.

Censis (1993) *Indagine sulla condizione abitativa in Italia. Analisi della domanda marginale, Rapporto finale per conto del CER*, Rome: CER.

Centrum voor Gelijkheid van Kansen en voor Racismebestrijding (2003) *Op stap naar diversiteit. Jaarverslag 2002*, Brussels: Centrum.

Cesari, J. (2000) 'Islam in European cities', in S. Body-Gendrot and M. Martiniello (eds) *Minorities in European cities: The dynamics of social integration and social exclusion at the neighbourhood level*, Houndsmill: Macmillan Press, pp 88-99.

Chambers, I. (1994) *Migrancy, culture and identity*, London: Routledge.

Clann Housing Association (1999a) *From Bosnia to Ireland's rented private sector: A study of Bosnian housing needs in Ireland*, Dublin: Clann Housing Association.

Clann Housing Association (1999b) *A study of labour market progression of refugees, with emphasis on related housing issues: A case study of refugee participants in pre-vocational training in FÁS Training Centre, Baldoyle*, Dublin: Clann Housing Association.

Cohen, R. (1996) *The sociology of migration*, Cheltenham: Elgar.

Coleman, D. (2000) 'Why Europe does not need a "European" migration policy', House of Lords, Select Committee on the European Union, Sub-Committee F (Social Affairs, Education and Home Affairs), evidence submitted to the Inquiry on the Collinson, S. (1993) *Europe and international migration*, London: Pinter.

Collinson, S. (1993) *Europe and international migration*, London: Pinter.

Comhlamh (2001) *Refugee lives: The failure of direct provision as a social response to the needs of asylum seekers in Ireland*, Dublin: Comhlamh.

Comitato Oltre il razzismo (2000) *Casa, lavoro, istruzione: azioni per l'uguaglianza*, Turin: Associazione Nazionale Oltre le Frontiere.

Council of Europe (2003a) *Foreigners' integration and participation in European cities*, Strasbourg: Council of Europe.

Council of Europe (2003b) *Policies for the integration of immigrants in Council of Europe member states*, Strasbourg: Council for Europe Doc 9888.

Criacp Veneto – Irsev (1992) *La domanda abitativa espressa dagli immigrati extracomunitari: prima ricognizione*, Venice: Osservatorio Regionale Immigrazione Veneto, Agenzia per l'impiego del Veneto.

Crisp, J. (1999) 'Policy challenges of the new diasporas: migrant networks and their impact on asylum flows and regimes', Geneva: Policy Research Unit, UNHCR WPTC-99-05.

Da Costa, B. and Baptista, I. (2003) *Immigration and homelessness in Portugal*, Report for the European Observatory on Homelessness, Brussels: FEANTSA.

Daly, G. (1996) 'Migrants and gatekeepers: the links between immigration and homelessness in Western Europe', *Cities*, vol 13, no 1, pp 11-23.

Daly, M. (1999) 'Regimes of social policy in Europe and the patterning of homelessness', in D. Avromov (ed) *Coping with homelessness: Issues to be tackled and best practices in Europe*, Aldershot: Ashgate, pp 309-30.

De Decker, P. (2001) *Access to housing for vulnerable groups: The Belgian National Report 2000*, Brussels: FEANTSA.

De Decker, P. and Kesteloot, C. (2003) *Migration, housing and homelessness*, Report for the European Observatory on Homelessness, Brussels: FEANTSA.

De Feijter, H. (2003) *Immigration and homelessness in the Netherlands*, Report for the European Observatory on Homelessness, Brussels: FEANTSA.

De Feyter, H. (2003) *Access to housing for vulnerable groups: The Dutch National Report 2000*, Brussels: FEANTSA.

Defensor del Pueblo (2001) *Informe del Defensor del Pueblo 2000*, Madrid: Cortes generales.

Desplanques, G. (1996) 'La répartition des populations d'origine étrangère en France. Espace', *Population et Sociétés*, vol 313.

Donzelot, J. and Jaillet, M.C. (1997) *Deprived urban areas: Summary report of the pilot study*, Report No 215, Geneva: NATO.

Dörr, S. and Faist, T. (1997) 'Institutional conditions for the integration of immigrants in welfare states: a comparison of the literature on Germany, France, Great Britain and the Netherlands', *European Journal of Political Research*, vol 31, pp 401-26.

Drever, A. and Clark, W. (2002) 'Gaining access to housing in Germany: the foreign-minority experience', *Urban Studies*, vol 39, no 13, pp 2439-53.

EC (European Council) (1999) 'Presidency conclusion', EC meeting at Tampere, Finland (http://www.europarl.eu.int/summits/tam_en.htm).

Edgar, W. and Doherty, J. (2003) *Ethnicity and housing: The contribution of housing associations*, CORE Analysis Paper No 5, London: The Housing Corporation.

Edgar, W., Doherty, J. and Meert, H. (2002) *Access to housing: Homelessness and vulnerability in Europe*, Bristol: The Policy Press.

Edgar, W., Doherty, J. and Mina-Coull, A. (1999) *Services for homeless people: Innovation and change in the European Union*, Bristol: The Policy Press.

Eichener, V. (1998a) *Ausländer im Wohnbereich. Theoretische Modelle, empirische Analysen und politisch-praktische Maßnahmevorschläge zur Eingliederung einer gesellschaftlichen Außenseitergruppe*, Regensburg: Universität Köln.

Eichener, V. (1998b) 'Zur Entwicklung von Sozialstruktur und räumlicher Segregation – Ist das Ende einer sozial ausgleichenden Wohnungspolitik gekommen?', in H. Brühl and C.P. Echter (eds) *Entmischung im Bestand an Sozialwohnungen. Dokumentation eines Seminars*, Berlin: Deutsches Institut für Urbanistik, pp 19-48.

Eitel, G. and Schoibl, H. (1999) *Grundlagenerhebung zur Wohnungslosensituation in Austria*, Vienna: BAWO.

Ellwood, W. (2001) *The non-nonsense guide to globalisation*, London, Verso.

Esping-Andersen, G. (1990) *The three worlds of welfare capitalism*, Cambridge: Polity Press.

Esping-Andersen, G. (ed) (1996) *Welfare states in transition: National adaptations in global economies*, London: Sage Publications.

EU (2000) 'Race directive: implementing the principle of equal treatment between persons irrespective of racial or ethnic origin', *Official Journal of the European Communities*, Directive 2000/43/EC: 29 December, Brussels (http://europa.eu.int/eur-lex/en/oj/).

Eubusiness (2003) 'Pensions in the European Union' (www.eubusiness.com/guides/pensions).

European Commission (2000) Communication from the Commission to the Council and the European Parliament on a Community immigration policy, COM(2000) 757 final, Brussels: European Commission.

European Network (2004) 'European manifesto: towards a convergence, a coming together of the struggles of sans-papiers, refugees and migrants in Europe', European Network of Migrants, Refugees and Sans-papier, available at www.pgaconference.org/-postconference-/an_network_nopapers.htm

Eurostat (2001) 'European population trends in 2001' (http://europa.eu.int/comm/eurostat/).

Eurostat (2003) *A statistical eye on Europe 1991-2001*, European Commission, Luxembourg: Eurostat.

Fainstein, S.S., Gordon, I. and Harloe, M. (1992) *Divided cities: New York and London in the contemporary world*, Oxford: Blackwell.

Faist, T. and Häubermann, H. (1996) 'Immigration, social citizenship and housing in Germany', *International Journal of Urban and Regional Research*, vol 20, no 1, pp 83-98.

Faughnan, P., Humphries, N. and Whelan, S. (2002) *Patching up the system: The community welfare system and asylum seekers*, Dublin: UCD Social Science Research Centre.

Federatie Opvang (2000) *Dilemma's in de Maatschappelijke Opvang. Inventarisatie van illegalen en ex-asielzoekers in de Maatschappelijke Opvang*, Utrecht: Federatie Opvang.

Ferguson, I. and Barclay, A. (2002) *Seeking peace of mind: The mental health needs of asylum seekers in Glasgow*, Stirling: University of Stirling.

FIO.psd (2002) *Immigrazione e persone senza dimora*, Bergamo: FIO.psd.

Ford Foundation (2002) 'Our mission' (www.fordfound.org/).

Forum Réfugiés (2001) *Rapport 2001*, Paris: Forum Réfugiés.

France Terre d'Asile (2001) *Favoriser l'accès des réfugiés au logement*, Paris: France Terre d'Asile.

Freudenthaler, E., Gschwandtner, U. and Pichler, W. (1994) *Zur Wohnsituation von ArbeitsimmigrantInnen im Bahnhofsviertel/Elisabethvorstadt*, Salzburg.

Fukuyama, H. (1992) *The end of history and the last man*, Harmondsworth: Penguin.

Gibney, M.J. (2001) *Outside the protection of the law: The situation of irregular migrants in Europe*, Oxford: Refugee Studies Centre, University of Oxford.

Giddens, A. (1990) *The consequences of modernity*, Cambridge: Polity Press.

Gill, F. (2002) 'The diverse experiences of black and minority ethnic women in relation to housing and social exclusion', in P. Somerville and A. Steele (eds) *Race, housing and social exclusion*, London: Jessica Kingsley, pp 159-77.

Glick Shiller, N., Basch, L. and Sanzon Blanc, C.S. (1992) *Towards a transnational perspective on migration: Race, class, ethnicity and nationalism reconsidered*, New York, NY: Academy of Science.

Goodhart, D. (2004) 'Discomfort of strangers', *The Guardian*, 24 February.

Granovetter, M. (1973) 'The strength of weak ties', *American Journal of Sociology*, vol 78, no 6, pp 1360-80.

Gray, J. (2000) 'Transnational migration in the modern world: implications for citizenship issues', available at www.carleton.ca/ces/papers/may01/JuliaGray.pdf

Greek Council for Refugees (2002) *Reception facilities for asylum seekers in the EU member states*, Athens: Greek Council for Refugees.

Gruttadauria, D. (1994) *La domanda marginale nel sistema residenziale di Palermo*, Palermo: Municipality of Palermo, Planning Department – Ripartizione Urbanistica.

Gubbay, J. (1999) 'The European Union role in the formation, legitimation and implementation of migration policy', in G. Dale and M. Cole, *The European Union and migrant labour*, Oxford: Berg, pp 43-67.

Hall, B. (2000) *Immigration in the European Union: Problem or solution?*, Geneva: OECD Observer.

Hall, S. (1978) 'Racism and reaction', in Commission for Racial Equality (ed) *Five views of multi-racial Britain*, London: CRE, pp 23-35.

Hammar, T. (1985) *European immigration policy*, Cambridge: Cambridge University Press.

Hammel, M. (2000) *Zur Stellung der allein stehenden Wohnungslosen ausländischer Nationalität im Hilfesystem des BSHG* (Reihe Materialien zur Wohnungslosenhilfe, Heft 42), Bielefeld: Verlag Soziale Hilfe.

Harding, J. (2000) *The uninvited: Refugees at the rich man's gate*, London: Profile.

Harris, N. (2003) 'Open borders: a future for Europe, migrants, and world economy', available at www.opendemocracy.net

Harrison, M. (1999) 'Theorising homelessness and "race"', in P. Kennet and A. Marsh (eds) *Homelessness: Exploring the new terrain*, Bristol: The Policy Press, pp 101-22.

Harrison, M. and Phillips, D. (2003) *Housing and black and minority ethnic groups: Review of the evidence base*, London: ODPM.

Harvey, D. (1989) *The condition of postmodernity*, Oxford: Blackwells.

Häußermann, H. and Siebel, W. (2001) *Soziale Integration und ethnische Schichtung – Zusammenhänge zwischen räumlicher und sozialer Integration*, Berlin/Oldenburg: Gutachten im Auftrag der Unabhängigen Kommission "Zuwanderung".

Haut Comité pour le Logement des Populations Défavorisées (2002) *Vers un droit au logement opposable*, Paris: Haut Comité, October.

Haynes, M. (1999) 'Setting the limits to Europe as an "Imagined Community"', in G. Dale and M. Cole (eds) *The European Union and migrant labour*, Oxford: Berg, pp 17-42.

Hayter, T. (2000) *Open borders: The case against immigration controls*, London: Pluto Press.

Hemat Gryffe (2001) *Annual Report 2001*, Edinburgh: Hemat Gryffe.

Henderson, J. and Karn, V. (1987) *Race, class and state housing: Inequality and the allocation of public housing in Britain*, Aldershot: Gower.

Hirst, P. and Thompson, G. (1996) *Globalisation in question: The international economy and possibilities*, Cambridge: Polity Press.

Hogan, D. (2004) *Fortress Europe: Increased integration of EU asylum and immigration policy*, Dublin: Workers Solidarity Movement.

Hudson, R. and Lewis, J.R. (1985) *Uneven development in southern Europe: Studies of accumulation, class, migration and the state*, London: Methuen.

INE (Instituto Nacional de Estatística) (2001) *Destaque do INE*, 21 de Outubro de 2001, Lisbon.

INSEE (1999) *National Institute of Statistics and Economics Information: The census of the population*, Paris: INSEE.

Inslegers, G., De Decker, P., Hermans, H., Philippeth, K., Vanden Eynde, M., Van Leuven, E., Lingier, J., Loobuyck, F., Raus, H., Vaernewyck, P., Janssen, P., Meert, H., Fret, L., Martens, A., Goossens, L. and Pataer, P. (2004) 'Pak de armoede aan in plaats van de armen', *De Standaard* (daily), 14 May.

Integration Department of Stockholm (1999) *Alarmerande hemlöshet bland nyanlända flyktingar. Lägesbeskrivning av bostadssituationen*, Tjänsteutlåtande, Dnr 99-610/891, Stockholm: Integration Department.

Interdepartmental Working Group on the Integration of Refugees in Ireland (2000) *Integration: A two-way process*, Report to the Minister of Justice, Equality and Law Reform, Dublin.

Ismu e Province of Mantova (2000) *L'immigrazione straniera nella provincia di Mantova, 2000*, Mantova: Rapporto statistico dell'Osservatorio Fondazione Cariplo, University of Milan.

Ismu e Province of Milan (1997) *L'immigrazione straniera nell'area milanese*, Milan: ISMU.

Ismu e Province of Milan-Bicocca (2001) *Rilevazione campionaria per l'Osservatorio Regionale per l'integrazione e la multietnicità*, Milan: ISMU.

Izquierdo Escribano, A. (1996) 'La inmigración en las zonas rurales de España: aspectos de la integración social en el caso de los marroquíes que trabajan en la Región de Murcia', in J. Leal and C. Mayeur (eds) *Vivienda e integración social de los inmigrantes. Seminario europeo*, Madrid: Ministerio de Trabajo y Asuntos Sociales.

Jennings, M. (2002) 'Trade unions and the immigrant worker', *Cornerstone: The Magazine of the Homeless Agency*, no 13, p 18.

Jessop, B. (2002) *The future of the capitalist state*, London: Blackwell.

Kärkkäinen, S.-L. and Mikkonen, A. (2002) *Immigration and homelessness in Finland*, Report for the European Observatory on Homelessness, Brussels: FEANTSA.

Kasimati, K. (1992) 'Immigrants from Pontos, ex Soviet Union: their social and economic inclusion', Athens: General Secretariat for Greeks Abroad (in Greek).

Kesteloot, C. (1998) 'Over de beperkingen van sociale mix als beleidsstrategie', *Planologisch Nieuws*, vol 18, no 3, pp 143-7.

Kesteloot, C. (2003) 'Verstedelijking in Vlaanderen: problemen, kanen en uitdagingen voor het beleid in de 21ste eeuw', in L. Schets (ed) *De eeuw van de stad, over stadsrepublieken en rastersteden, Voorstudies*, Brussels: Ministerie van de Vlaamse Gemeenschap, pp 15-39.

Kesteloot, C. (2003) 'Verstedelijking in Vlaanderen: problemen, kanen en uitdagingen voor het beleid in de 21ste eeuw', in L. Schets (ed) *De eeuw van de stad, over stadsrepublieken en rastersteden*, Voorstudies, pp 15-39.

Kesteloot, C. and Meert, H. (1999) 'Informal spaces: the socio-economic functions and spatial location of urban informal economic activities', *International Journal of Urban and Regional Research*, vol 23, no 2, pp 233-52.

Kesteloot, C. and Meert, H. (2000) 'Segregation and economic integration of immigrants in Brussels', in S. Body-Gendrot and M. Martiniello (eds) *Minorities in European cities: The dynamics of social integration and social exclusion at the neighbourhood level*, London: Macmillan Press, pp 54-72.

Kesteloot, C. and Van der Haegen, H. (1997) 'Foreigners in Brussels 1981-1991: spatial continuity and social change', *TESG Tijdschrift voor Sociale en Economische Geografie*, vol 88, no 2, pp 105-19.

Kesteloot, C., De Decker, P. and Manço, A. (1997) 'Turks and housing in Belgium, with special reference to Brussels, Ghent and Visé', in S. Ozüekren and R. Van Kempen (eds) *Turks in European cities: Housing and segregation*, Rotterdam: Eromer, pp 67-97.

King, R. (1998) 'From guestworkers to immigrants: labour migration from the Mediterranean periphery', in D. Pinder (ed) *The new Europe: Economy, society and environment*, Chichester: Wiley, pp 263-80.

King, R., Lazaridis, G. and Tsardanidis, C. (2000) *Eldorado or Fortress Europe? Migration in southern Europe*, London: Macmillan Press.

Klein, N. (2003) 'The US and Europe are both creating multi-tiered regional strongholds', *The Guardian*, 16 January

Koch-Nielsen, I. (2003) *Immigration and homelessness in Denmark*, Report for the European Observatory on Homelessness, Brussels: FEANTSA.

Korhonen, E. (2002) *Asunnottomuus Helsingissä: Helsingen kaupungin tietokeskus*, Research Series no 4, Urban Facts, Helsinki.

Kortteinen, M. and Vaattovaara, M. (2000) 'Onko osa Helsingistä alikehityksen kierteessä?', *Yhteiskuntapolitiikka*, vol 65, no 2, pp 13-24.

Koser, K. and Lutz, H. (1998) *New migration in Europe*, London: Macmillan Press.

Kreibich, V. (2000) 'Self-help planning of immigrants in Rome and Madrid', *Habitat International*, vol 24, no 2, pp 201-11.

Kretzschmar, S. (2002) 'Hilfemöglichkeiten und Hilfeansprüche ausländischer Wohnungsloser', in M. Berthold (ed) *Wohnungslosenhilfe: Verbindlich verbunden! Kooperationen – Verbundsysteme – Bündnisse* (Reihe Materialien zur Wohnungslosenhilfe, Heft 51), Bielefeld: Verlag Soziale Hilfe, pp 69-87.

Kunz, S. (2001) 'Arbeit der Einrichtungen nach Section 72 BSHG mit wohnungslosen Migranten und Migrantinnen. Eine Umfrage im Auftrag der Katholischen Arbeitsgemeinschaft Wohnungslosenhilfe (KAG-W) unter den Mitgliedseinrichtungen', *Wohnungslos*, vol 3, pp 100-4.

Lawrence, F. (2004a) *Not on the label: What really goes into the food on your plate*, London: Penguin.

Lawrence, F. (2004b) 'Victims of the sands and the snakeheads', *The Guardian*, 7 February.

Lawrence, F. (2004c) 'Wanted: workers who are flexible, cheap and expendable', *The Guardian*, 9 February.

Le Voy, M., Verbruggen, N. and Wets, J. (eds) (2003) *Undocumented migrant workers in Europe*, Brussels: PICUM.

Leal, J. (1996) 'Condiciones residenciales e integración de los inmigrantes: problemas residenciales de los inmigrantes y definición de las políticas de actuación pública', in J. Leal and C. Mayeur (eds) *Vivienda e integración social de los inmigrantes. Seminario europeo*, Madrid: Ministerio de Trabajo y Asuntos Sociales, pp 127-40.

Lehmann, N. (2002) *Migrantinnen im Frauenhaus = Interkulturelles Frauenhaus?*, Münster: Vortragsmanuskript.

Leitner, H. (1997) 'Reconfiguring the spatiality of power: the construction of a supranational migration framework for the European Union', *Political Geography*, vol 16, no 2, pp 123-43.

Lesthaeghe, R. (1995) 'The second demographic transition in western countries: an interpretation', in K. Oppenheim-Mason and A.M. Jensen (eds) *Gender and family change in industrialising countries*, Oxford: Oxford University Press, pp 17-62.

Lett, J. and Brangwyn, M. (2000) 'The London dimension', in R. Bate, R. Best and A. Holmans (eds) *On the move: The housing consequences of migration*, York: Joseph Rowntree Foundation, pp 41-8.

Ligdopoulou, T. and Arapoglou, V. (2002) *Homeless immigrants and refugees in Greece*, Report submitted for FEANTSA, ARSIS – Voluntary Work: Athens.

Lim, L. (1997) *Flexible labour markets in a globalising world: The implications of international female migrants*, International Labour Office Report, Geneva: ILO.

Loescher, G. (2003) 'Asylum crisis in the UK and Europe', Open Democracy, available at www.opendemocracy.net

London Borough of Camden (2001) *Unemployment in Camden 1983-2000*, London: Environment Department, LBC.

Malpass, P. and Murie, A. (1997) *Housing policy and practice*, Basingstoke: Macmillan Press.

Martínez Veiga, U. (1996) 'Alojamiento de los inmigrantes en España', in J. Leal and C. Mayeur (eds) *Vivienda e integración social de los inmigrantes. Seminario europeo*, Madrid: Ministerio de Trabajo y Asuntos Sociales.

Maureas, M., (1998) 'Dimensions of social exclusion: refugees from Pontos and Southern Albania in Greece', *Greek Review of Social Research*, vol 96-97, pp 36-42 (in Greek).

Maurel, E. (2003) *Immigration and homelessness in France*, Report for the European Observatory on Homelessness, Brussels: FEANTSA.

Meert, H., De Rijck, T. and Bourgeois, M. (2002) *Omvang en ruimtelijk-economische dimensie van het grijze wooncircuit in Vlaanderen: een experimenteel onderzoek naar methodiekbepaling*, research commissioned by the Vlaamse Gemeenschap (Flemish Community), Brussels.

Meert, H., Mistiaen, P. and Kesteloot, C. (1997) 'The geography of survival: household strategies in urban settings', *Tijdschrift voor Sociale en Economische Geografie*, vol 88, no 2, pp 169–81.

Mikkonen, A. and Kärkkäinen, S. (2003) *Homeless immigrants in Finland: The Finnish National Report*, Brussels: FEANTSA.

Ministry of Labour (1998) *Turvapaikanhakijoiden vastaanotto ja sen kehittäminen*, Maahanmuutto-osaston monisteita, nro 3, Helsinki: Työministeriö.

Mitchell, K. (2003) 'Cultural geographies of transnationality', in K. Anderson, M. Domosh, S. Pile and N. Thrift (eds) *Handbook of cultural geography*, London: Sage Publications, pp 74-87.

Mitchell, M. and Russell, D. (1998) 'Immigration, citizenship and social exclusion in the new Europe', in R. Sykes and P. Alcock (eds) *Developments in European social policy: Convergence and diversity*, Bristol: The Policy Press, pp 75-94.

Modood, T. (1997) 'Employment', in T. Modood, R. Berthoud, J. Lakey, J. Nazroo, P. Smith, S. Virdee and S. Beishon (eds) *Ethnic minorities in Britain: Diversity and disadvantage*, London: Policy Studies Institute, pp 83-149.

Murie, A. (1998) 'Segregation, exclusion and housing in the divided city', in S. Musterd and W. Ostendorf (eds) *Urban segregation and the welfare state: Inequality and exclusion in western cities*, London: Routledge, pp 110-25.

Musterd, S. and Murie, A. (2002) *The spatial dimensions of urban social exclusion and integration: Final report*, Amsterdam: AME.

Musterd, S. and Ostendorf, W. (1998) *Urban segregation and the welfare state: Inequality and exclusion in western cities*, London: Routledge.

Muus, P. (2001) 'International migration and the European Union: trends and consequences', *European Journal on Criminal Policy and Research*, vol 9, no 1, pp 31-49.

O'Sullivan, E. (2003) *Immigration and homelessness in Ireland*, Report for the European Observatory on Homelessness, Brussels: FEANTSA.

Observatorio Regionale per l'integrazione e la multietnicità (2001) *Rapporto 2001/Report on migrations in Lombardy 2001*, Milan: Region of Lombardy e Ismu.

Olabuénaga Ruiz, J.I., Ruiz Vieytez, E.J. and Vicente Torrado, T.L. (1999) *Los inmigrantes irregulares en España: La vida por un sueño*, Serie Derechos Humanos, vol 4, no 2, Bilbao: Universidad de Deusto.

Open Democracy (2004) 'People flow: migration in Europe', debate at www.opendemocracy.net

ORIV (Osservatorio Regionale Immigrazione Veneto) (1998) *Primo rapporto sull'immigrazione in Veneto*, Venice: ORIV.

Oxley, M. and Smith, J. (1996) *Housing policy and rented housing in Europe*, London: E&FN Spon.

Özüekren, S. and Magnnusson, L. (1997) 'Housing conditions of Turks in Sweden', in S. Özüekren and R. van Kempen (eds) *Turks in European cities: Housing and urban segregation*, Utrecht: ERCOMER, pp 191-222.

Palidda, S. (ed) (2000) *Socialità e inserimento degli immigrati a Milano*, Milan: Municipality of Milan and FrancoAngeli.

Papastergiadis, N. (2000) *The turbulence of migration: Globalisation, deterritorialization and hybridity*, Cambridge: Polity Press.

Pärtty-Äyräväinen, K. (2001) *Tunteita ja tuoksuja kerrostalossa: Selvitys maahanmuuttajien asumisongelmista ja asumisen tukimuodoista ja niiden tarpeista Helsingissä*, Helsinki: Helsingin kaupunki, sosiaalivirasto/yhteispalveluosasto, maahanmuuttoyksikkö.

Pearl, M. and Zetter, R. (2002) 'From refuge to exclusion: housing as an instrument of social exclusion for refugees and asylum seekers', in P. Somerville and A. Steele (eds) *Race, housing and social exclusion*, London: Jessica Kingsley, pp 226-44.

Peck, J. and Tickell, A. (2002) 'Neoliberalising space', *Antipode*, vol 34, no 3, pp 380-404.

Pels, M. and Borsenberger, M. (2003) *Immigration and homelessness in Luxembourg*, Report for the European Observatory on Homelessness, Brussels: FEANTSA.

Perrone, L. (1994) *Quali politiche per l'immigrazione? Stranieri nel Salento*, Lecce: Milella Universita degli Studi di Lecce.

Petropoulos, N. (1998) *SOPEMI Report on Greece*, Paris: OECD.

Phillips, D. (1986) *What price equality? A report on the allocation of GLC housing in Tower Hamlets*, GLC Housing and Research Policy Report No 9, London: GLC.

Phizaclea, A. (ed) (1983) *One way ticket: Migration and female labour*, London: Routledge.

Pieke, F. (2002) *At the margins of the Chinese world system: The Fuzhou diaspora in Europe*, Oxford: Oxford University Press.

Piore, M. (1979) *Birds of passage: Migrant labour and industrial societies*, Cambridge: Cambridge University Press.

Piracha, M. and Vickerman, R. (2002) 'Immigration, labour mobility and EU enlargement', available at www.kent.ac.uk/economics/research/1europe/reports.html

Polanyi, K. (1944) *The great transformation*, Boston, MA: Beacon Press.

Popoola, M. (1998) 'Det sociala spelet om Romano Platso', *Dissertations in Sociology*, vol 22, Lund: Department of Sociology, University of Lund.

Portes, A. and Rumbaut, R. (1996) *Immigrant America: A portrait* (2nd edn), Berkeley, CA: University of California Press.

Psimmenos, I. (2000) 'The making of periphractic spaces: the case of Albanian undocumented female migrants in the sex industry of Athens', in F. Anthias and G. Lazaridis (eds) *Gender and migration in Southern Europe*, Oxford: Berg.

Rastas, M. (2002) *Maahanmuuttajien asunnottomuus Helsingissä*, Suomen ympäristö 582, Helsinki: Ympäristöministeriö.

Reception and Integration Agency (2002) Annual report, Dublin.

Rees, P., Stillwell, J., Convey, A. and Kupiszewsk, M. (eds) (1996) *Population migration in the European Union*, Chichester: Wiley & Sons, pp 13-90.

Reiman, T. (1999) Seudullisen monikulttuurisuuden kehittämishankkeen loppuraportti. Uudenmaan työvoima- ja elinkeinokeskus. Työvoimatoimiston julkaisuja 2/1999.

Rex, J. and Moore, R. (1967) *Race, community and conflict: A study of Sparkbrook*, Oxford: Oxford University Press.

RICSW (Research and Information Centre for Social Work) (2000) *Women from ethnic minorities at crisis centres in Denmark*, Esbjerg: RICSW.

Roberts, K. and Harris, J. (2002) 'Disabled people in refugee and asylum seeking communities in Britain', *Findings*, York: Joseph Rowntree Foundation.

Roque, M.-À. (2000) 'Mujer y migración, una doble Miranda en el Mediterràeo occidental', in G. Aubarell and M.-À. Roque (eds) *Mujer y migración, una doble Miranda en el Mediterràeo occidental: Tradiciones culturales y cicdadania*, Barcelona: Icaria.

Rosenke, W. (2002) *Migration und Wohnungslosigkeit. Ein Bericht zur Situation in Deutschland*, Bielefeld: Bundesarbeitsgemeinschaft Wohnungslosenhilfe/ FEANTSA.

Saey, P. and Van Nuffel, N. (2003) 'Nevels of Christaller. Regionalisering van de woonmarkt als structurerend ruimtelijk principe', *Ruimte en Planning*, vol 23, no 3, pp 156-76.

Sahlin, I. (2003) *Immigration and homelessness in Sweden*, Report for the European Observatory on Homelessness, Brussels: FEANTSA.

Salt, J. (1997) *Current trends in international migration in Europe*, Strassbourg: Council of Europe.

Salt, J. (2001) 'Current trends in international migration in Europe', Geneva: Council of Europe, CDMG (2001) 33.

Sapounakis, A. (2003) *Immigration and homelessness in Greece*, Report for the European Observatory on Homelessness, Brussels: FEANTSA.

Sarkassian, W. (1976) 'The idea of social mix in town planning: a historical review', *Urban Studies*, vol 13, no 3, pp 231-46.

Sassen, S. (1999) *Guests and aliens*, New York, NY: The New Press.

SCB (2002) *Befolkningens boende. Bakgrundsfakta till befolknings- och välfärdsstatistik 2002:4*, Statistika Centralbyrån, avd för Befolknings- och Välfärdsstatistik.

Schill, M.H., Friedman, S. and Rosenbaum, E. (2001) 'The housing conditions of immigrants in New York City', *Journal of Housing Research*, vol 9, no 2, pp 201-36.

Schoibl, H. (2003) *Immigration and homelessness in Austria*, Report for the European Observatory on Homelessness, Brussels: FEANTSA.

Schubert, H. (1999) 'Soziale Segregation in der Stadt – Signale zur Jagd auf einen Mythos derSozialplanung', *Landeshauptstadt München*, pp 7-23.

Sim, D. (2000) 'Housing inequalities and minority ethnic groups', in I. Anderson and D. Sim (eds) *Social exclusion and housing: Contexts and challenges*, Coventry: Chartered Institute of Housing, pp 93-107.

Simon, P. (1999) 'Les discriminations raciales et ethniques dans l'accès au logement social', *Note de synthèse no 3 du GIP*, Paris: GELD (Groupe d'étude et de lutte contre les discriminations).

SONACOTRA (2002) 'The bulletin of documentation of the SONACOTRA', *11ᵗʰ Avenue*, no 41, Winter 2001/02, Paris: SONACOTRA.

SOPEMI (2003) *Trends in international migration*, Paris: OECD.

Sorainen, O. (2002) 'Finland, the Ministry of Labour, Helsinki', available at www.mol.fi

Stalker, P. (1994) *The work of strangers*, Geneva: ILO.

Stalker, P. (2000) *Workers without frontiers*, Geneva: ILO.

Stalker, P. (2001) *International migration*, London: Verso.

Statistisches Bundesamt (2000) *50 Jahre Wohnen in Deutschland*, Wiesbaden: Stabu.

Statistisches Bundesamt (2002) *Sozialleistungen: Leistungen an Asylbewerber 2000, Fachserie 13/Reihe 7*, Wiesbaden: Stabu.

Steele, A. (2002) 'Black youth homelessness', in P. Somerville and A. Steele (eds) *Race, housing and social exclusion*, London: Jessica Kingsley, pp 178-91.

Sunia Ancab – LegaCoop (2000) *Condizioni abitative degli immigrati in Italia*, Rome.

Synergia (1998) *Gli interventi di politica abitativa per gli immigratti in Provincia di Milano*, Milan: Provincia di Milan.

Synergia (2001) *Gli interventi di politica abitativa per gli immigratti relle Provincia di Milano* (ed D. Cologna), Milan: Il Rapporto.

Thave, S. (1999) 'Les immigrés de 60 ans ou plus', *Gérontologie et Société*, no 91, December, pp 21-33.

Toniolo, M. and Bragato, S. (1998) 'Birds of passage o cittadini? La casa come principale ostacolo all'inserimento degli immigrati nel Veneto', *Politiche del lavoro*, no 24, pp 159-76.

Tosi, A. (2001a) 'L'abitazione', in G. Zincone (ed) *Commissione per le politiche di integrazione degli immigrati. Secondo rapporto sull'integrazione degli immigrati in Italia*, Bologna: Il Mulino, pp 193-214.

Tosi, A. (2001b) 'Rom e Sinti: un'integrazione possibile', in G. Zincone (ed) *Commissione per le politiche di integrazione degli immigrati. Secondo rapporto sull'integrazione degli immigrati in Italia*, Bologna: Il Mulino, pp 685-744.

Tosi, A. (2003) *Immigration and homelessness in Italy*, Report for the European Observatory on Homelessness, Brussels: FEANTSA.

UN (United Nations) (2002) *International Migration Report 2002*, New York, NY: UN.

Vaattovaara, M. (2002) 'Future developments of residential differentiation in the Helsinki Metropolitan Area: are we following the European model?', *Yearbook of Population Research in Finland*, Helsinki: Population Research Institute, Family Federation of Finland, pp 107-23.

Vaïou, N. and Hatzimihalis, K. (1997) *With the sewing machine in the kitchen and the Poles in the fields: Cities, regions and informal employment*, Athens: Exantas (in Greek).

Van der Heijden, H. (2002) 'Social rented housing in Western Europe: developments and expectations', *Urban Studies*, vol 39, no 2, pp 327-40.

Veenkamp, T., Bentley, T. and Alessandra B. (2003) *People flow: Managing people in a new European Commonwealth*, London: Demos.

Vesanen, P. and Tiitinen, V. (1998) Ongelmia asunnottomuuden vähentämisessä. Toimenpide-ehdotuksia tilanteen parantamiseksi. Suomen ympäristö 210, Helsinki: Ympäristöministeriö.

Walter, A. and Grübl, J. (1999) 'Junge Aussiedler im Jugendstrafvollzug', in K.J. Bade and J. Oltmer (eds) *Aussiedler: Deutsche Einwanderer aus Osteuropa*, Osnabrück: University of Osnabrück, pp 177-89.

Watt, P. (2003) 'Urban marginality and labour market restructuring: local authority tenants and employment in an inner London borough', *Urban Studies*, vol 40, no 9, pp 1769-89.

White, P. (1993) 'The social geography of immigrants in European cities: the geography of arrival', in R. King (ed) *The new geography of European migrations*, London: Belhaven, pp 41-59.

White, P. (1999) 'Ethnicity, racialisation and citizenship as divisive elements in Europe', in R. Hudson and A.M. Williams (eds) *Divided Europe: Society and territory*, London: Sage Publications, pp 210-30.

White, P. and Hurdley, L. (2003) 'International migration and the housing market: Japanese corporate movers in London', *Urban Studies*, vol 40, no 4, pp 687-706.

Widgren, J. (1994) 'The need for a new multilateral order to prevent mass movements from becoming a security threat in Europe', Paper prepared for the Conference on the Security Dimensions of International Migration in Europe, Centre for Strategic and International Studies, Washington, April.

Wiener Integrationsfonds (2002) MigrantInnen in Vienna 2001 and Report 2001, Vienna: Integration Fund.

Winter, H. (1999) 'Wohnsituation der Haushalte 1998. Ergebnisse der Mikrozensuserhebung. Teil 2: Haushalte und ihre Mieten', *Wirtschaft und Statistik*, no 11, pp 858-64.

Wren, K. and Boyle, P. (2002) *Migration and work-related health in Europe: A pilot study*, Stockholm: Saltsa – Joint Programme for Working Life Research in Europe.

WTO (World Trade Organization) (2001) *International trade statistics*, Geneva: WTO.

Wusten, H. van der and Musterd, S. (1998) 'Welfare state effects on inequality and segregation: concluding remarks', in S. Musterd and W. Ostendorf (eds) *Urban segregation and the welfare state: Inequality and exclusion in western cities*, London: Routledge, pp 328-47.

Zanfrini, L. (1998) *Leggere le migrazioni*, Milan: Ismu e Franco Angeli.

Index

Numbers in italics are page numbers of figures